The Prophets

A LIBERATION-CRITICAL READING OF THE OLD TESTAMENT
Alice L. Laffey, Series Editor

The Pentateuch
Alice L. Laffey

Israel's Wisdom Literature
Dianne Bergant

The Prophets
Carol J. Dempsey

The Prophets

A Liberation-Critical Reading

Carol J. Dempsey

Fortress Press
Minneapolis

THE PROPHETS
A Liberation-Critical Reading

Cover and book design: Joseph Bonyata
Cover art: Sandra Bowden. Used by permission.

Library of Congress Cataloging-in-Publication Data

Dempsey, Carol J.
    The Prophets : a liberation-critical reading / Carol J. Dempsey.
        p. cm. — (A liberation-critical reading of the Old Testament)
    Includes bibilographical references (p.).
    ISBN 0-8006-3116-1 (alk. paper)
        1. Bible. O.T. Prophets—Criticism, interpretation, etc. 2. Liberation theology. 3. Feminist criticism. I. Title. II. Series.

BS1505.2 .D46 2000
224'.06—dc21   99-058914

Manufactured in the U.S.A.   AF 1-3116
05   04   03   02   01   00   1   2   3   4   5   6   7   8   9   10

Contents

Editor's Foreword vii
Preface ix
Abbreviations xiii

INTRODUCTION 1

PART 1
POWER AND DOMINATION 5

1. Amos: "You Have Turned Justice into Poison" 7
2. Micah: "You Tear the Skin off My People" 23
3. Jeremiah: "You Have Polluted the Land" 35
4. Baruch and Lamentations: "Women Are Raped in Zion" 55
5. Habakkuk and Zephaniah: "You Have Devised Shame for Your House" 77
6. Ezekiel: "I Will Put an End to the Arrogant and the Strong" 93

PART 2
SHIFTING FROM POWER AND DOMINATION
TO POWER AND LIBERATION 113

7. Daniel: "Deliver Us in Accordance with Your Marvelous Works" 115
8. Jonah: "Out of the Belly of Sheol I Cried, and You Heard My Voice" 121
9. Haggai and Zechariah: "I Am About to Destroy the Strength of the Kingdom of Nations" 129
10. Obadiah and Malachi: "The Arrogant and the Evildoers Will Be Stubble" 135
11. Nahum and Joel: "Do Not Fear, O Soil . . . For God Has Done Great Things!" 143

PART 3: SHIFTING FROM "POWER OVER" TO "POWER WITH":
HARMONIOUS RELATIONSHIPS 151

    12. Hosea: "I Will Make for You a Covenant on That Day with the
        Wild Animals" 153

    13. Isaiah 1–39: "My People Will Abide in a Peaceful Habitation" 161

    14. Isaiah 40–66: "I Am about to Create New Heavens
        and a New Earth" 171

CONCLUSION *183*

Notes *185*
Bibliography *203*

Editor's Foreword

THIS SERIES AROSE OUT OF FEMINIST CONCERNS, including the conviction that the biblical texts were produced by men in a patriarchal culture and that the ways in which the texts depict women and men are consequently conditioned by the assumptions associated with patriarchy. But such concerns lead essentially to other concerns. If the culture depicted in the texts is patriarchal, then it is also hierarchical; its way of organizing society is not only to place men over women but also to place free men over slaves, rich over poor, Hebrew over foreigner, as if persons could be appropriately relegated to one or another rung of a ladder depending on their sex, status, or prestige in society.

According to ladderlike or triangular models of social organization, even the lowest-runged humans rank higher than nonhumans, with those living nonhumans commonly identified as animals ranking higher than those living nonhumans commonly identified as plants. According to this scheme, all living beings rank higher than the matter commonly identified as nonliving that inhabits the universe. Although the applications of patriarchy-hierarchy find different expressions at different times in history and in different ethnic cultures, and although the ancient Israelites as hunting and agricultural societies were likely more conscious of their dependence on the nonhuman and therefore less likely to exploit with abandon than contemporary industrialized peoples, nevertheless, the principle of the legitimating of domination is inherent in the patriarchal-hierarchical worldview.

Such a patriarchal-hierarchical paradigm legitimates the domination of others considered of lesser value and depicts as normal an envy of those considered greater, while defining the desire to "climb the ladder" as "healthy ambition," a quality to be cultivated. This attitude stands in stark contrast to forms of social organization that assume the interdependence of the cosmos and posture themselves respectfully before the fragile ecosystem of which human beings are only a part and certainly not the pinnacle. A *Liberation-*

Critical Reading struggles with interpreting the biblical texts in ways that do not legitimate the patriarchal-hierarchical paradigm that permeated the culture that produced the biblical texts. These volumes seek to approach these texts from the perspective of a respectfully interdependent worldview.

I wish here to express my gratitude to Helen and Bill King from whose farm I came to understand the difference between my former, very narrow version of feminism and the ecofeminism to which I now aspire, and the women who have agreed to participate in the series and shared my struggle, to Sharon, Carol, and Dianne. I am especially grateful to Marshall Johnson, former editorial director at Fortress Press, whose patience and faithful encouragement have been invaluable.

ALICE L. LAFFEY

Preface

N THE EARLY 1980S I WAS STUDYING FOR MY MASTER'S DEGREE. I was sitting in Ben Asen's prophets class at St. Louis University, totally enamored of a professor who could make the biblical texts come alive. How I loved the characters to whom I was being introduced. I knew they were my friends, because somehow there was some sort of "connection" between their spirit and my own story.

Years later, when studying for my doctorate, I met Alice Laffey at a Catholic Biblical Association meeting in Washington, D.C. Our first real conversation occurred a year later, when, after I had finished my dissertation on the prophet Micah, I visited her in Massachusetts. We talked for hours about life, biblical texts, hermeneutics, the prophets.

Two years later I sat on a set of bleachers next to Alice in an emptied auditorium after the presidential address at the Catholic Biblical Association meeting. It was then that she described her project to me and asked if I would be interested in writing the volume on the prophets. I was excited and delighted. Here was an opportunity to write about those friends of mine whom I had come to love and know so well. Now that is the story of the seedling that has blossomed. To Ben and to Alice, I am grateful.

In this book on the prophets, I try to approach the texts from a hermeneutical perspective, one that is critical, creative, respectful, and informed by my own religious experience lived in the context of a contemporary world that longs for poet-prophets, history-makers, and story-tellers of a new day and a new vision. This is far from a definitive study; I like to think of it as the beginning of a conversation where all voices are welcomed as we search together for a glimpse of a piece of the truth that burned so deeply in the hearts of our prophetic ancestors. Would that we would set the world ablaze!

I would be remiss if I did not thank many wonderful colleagues and friends who have contributed in some way to this work. I am especially indebted to Christopher T. Begg, who directed my dissertation at The

Catholic University of America. Chris's expertise and continued support have given me not only foundational skills but also the encouragement to move forward with my work and interest in the prophets.

I am grateful to Ehud Ben Zvi, who has been a loyal colleague and conversation partner at various junctures of this project, and who offered many comments on the Micah material in Chapter 2. The material in this chapter is the result of further work done on my dissertation as well as new material gathered for a paper presented at a regional conference of the Society of Biblical Literature. Through Ehud's guidance, this paper received the Society of Biblical Literature National Regional Scholar Award. To Ehud and the AAR/SBL Pacific Northwest Region, I express my gratitude. Chapter 6 on Ezekiel originated from work I had done with Victor Matthews in the Biblical Law section of the SBL and the volume on *Gender and Law in the Hebrew Bible and the Ancient Near East* (Sheffield, 1998). To Vic, I owe many thanks for his enthusiastic support and gracious collegiality. Work done with Anthony Tambasco at the Catholic Biblical Association task force on "Biblical Perspectives of the Poor and Suffering" helped to shape and clarify my ideas on Jeremiah and the Servant Songs in Isaiah 40–66.

I also wish to thank Russell A. Butkus, chair of the Department of Theology at the University of Portland, whose passion for the redemption and liberation of all creation opened the horizons of my mind and awakened in me a kindred desire. To my Congregation of Dominican Sisters of Caldwell, New Jersey, for their clear vision, commitment to justice, and many expressions of encouragement of my work, I owe a hearty thanks.

I also owe a special debt of gratitude to those who helped with the final preparation of this manuscript: Mary Jo Chaves, OSF, Aunjhelle Crooms, Grace Douglas, Brandon Watson, and theology students. I am also grateful to the library staff at the University of Portland for assistance with research; Jay Betandorff for his computer assistance; the Arthur Butine Fund, which helped to support this project; K. C. Hanson, my editor at Fortress Press, for his careful reading of this work and his insightful comments on it; and Noel and Joel, who have been faithful companions during the research and writing process.

I would be remiss if I did not mention here the memory of the four women who died in El Salvador on December 2, 1980: Maura Clarke, MM, Jean Donovan, Ita Ford, MM, and Dorothy Kazel, MM. Bill and Mary Anne Ford, the brother and sister-in-law of Ita, have been personal and special friends of mine for many years. I will always remember in my heart these four women, especially Ita, along with the countless other unnamed women and men who have died living what I am trying to write about: a prophetic way of life that calls for and works toward the liberation, transformation, and salvation of all.

Finally, this book is dedicated to my mother and father, Mary and George, who loved me into life and whose prophetic spirit taught me the relationship between justice and compassion. They have blessed me with the lived example of what it means to act justly, to love tenderly, and to walk humbly with God (Mic 6:8).

MAY 23, 1999
PENTECOST

Abbreviations

AB	Anchor Bible
BTB	*Biblical Theology Bulletin*
CBD	Cambridge Bible Commentary
CBQ	*Catholic Biblical Quarterly*
ICC	International Critical Commentary
FOTL	Forms of the Old Testament Literature
JBL	*Journal of Biblical Literature*
JFSR	*Journal of Feminist Studies in Religion*
JSOT	*Journal for the Study of the Old Testament*
JSOTSup	Journal for the Study of the Old Testament Supplement Series
MT	Masoretic Text
NAB	New American Bible
NAC	New American Commentary
NCBC	New Century Bible Commentary
NICOT	New International Commentary on the Old Testament
NIV	New International Version
NJBC	New Jerome Biblical Commentary
NRSV	New Revised Standard Version
OBT	Overtures to Biblical Theology
OTL	Old Testament Library
OTM	Old Testament Message
VT	*Vetus Testamentum*
WBC	World Biblical Commentary
ZAW	*Zeitschrift für die alttestamentliche Wissenschaft*

Introduction

I N THE FIELD OF BIBLICAL SCHOLARSHIP, there is a variety of approaches related to the study of the biblical text. This particular study of the prophetic tradition has several marks of distinction that differentiate it from other works but also provide a sense of coherence between this work and the other volumes in this particular series. First, this study includes the biblical book of Baruch. Consistent with the principle of inclusivity, the series has embraced for consideration biblical texts recognized by diverse believing communities as deuterocanonical or apocryphal in addition to the traditional canonical books.

Second, the study's central focus is on two main issues in selected prophetic texts: the role of power, with an emphasis on how power can be exercised to dominate and to liberate, and the role of eschatological vision, with an emphasis on how that vision presents a paradigm shift that moves from "power over," that is, domination, to "power with," that is, dominion. A critical analysis of all of the prophetic materials led me to recognize that certain texts demonstrate various power relations and the ways that power can be used: to dominate, to liberate, and to engender harmonious relations. Each section of the book moves through various "shifts" until a new paradigm emerges, one informed by justice, righteousness, and peace, a "new creation" that can be realized only when the relationships between God, humankind, and the natural world are harmonious and interdependent.

Third, the prophetic books are not studied in the order in which they appear in the canon, nor is each book studied in its entirety. Moreover, the study is concerned with the final canonical form of each prophetic book instead of the various stages of the text's transmission, development, and redaction. The discussion attempts to establish a conversation between the world of the canonical text and the world in front of the text.

Fourth, throughout the study, attention is drawn to the role that language plays in the various biblical texts. This study explores how metaphors, similes, imagery, etc., seem to be reflective of certain perspectives, attitudes, and mindsets within a particular culture, and how figurative language not only creates a powerful message that is either oppressive and diminishing or liberating and transformative, but also colors the poetic and religious imagination of its readers in such a way as to have an impact on their theological perspectives and understanding. Central to the discussion is the multifaceted way God is portrayed by the biblical text. What needs to be realized and understood is that the biblical text as a whole has gone through extensive processes, both oral and written, prior to its present canonical form(s). Therefore, one is not hearing God directly but, rather, is hearing the voice of the prophets, redactors, and final editor(s) as they try to communicate their experience of God through the medium of literature. This experience of God and the interpretation of God's ways as represented in the prophetic texts is historically, socially, culturally, and theologically conditioned and remains so throughout the biblical text as a whole and in contemporary times as well. Divine wrath and violence in metaphorical and figurative language are also addressed, specifically in light of contemporary global concerns about violence in its many forms. Particular attention is also drawn to how images from the natural world function metaphorically and symbolically, and how these images have an impact on the text's theological message as well as on the audience's theological imagination.

Fifth, the study represents a holistic approach to the biblical prophets insofar as it deals with issues and a vision that concern not only humankind but also the natural world. Thus, the study is admittedly done from a contemporary perspective that is informed by contemporary ideological concerns. Issues such as anthropocentrism, androcentrism, classism, speciesism, gender, patriarchy, hierarchy, and so forth, which seem to be embedded not only in the prophets' messages and texts but also in the authorial voice(s) behind the texts, are unmasked and critiqued insofar as they relate to the central focus of the book: power. A clear argument is made that the abuse of power affects both the human and nonhuman world.

Sixth, selected biblical texts are examined from a liberationist point of view, one that is informed by my own social location as a white, middle-class, North Atlantic, Christian female who is committed to the search for and dissemination of truth. My social location and life commitment affords me the opportunity to interact with the biblical texts from both a position of power and privilege and a position of powerlessness and marginalization. Although the study proceeds from a reader-centered approach, the approach is significantly informed by the historical, social, cultural, and literary world of the prophets that helped shape the prophetic books as we have them today.

Seventh, in addition to the use of a holistic approach and an informed liberationist point of view, I also use a hermeneutical approach that is sensitive to the theories and thoughts of such scholars as Jose Severino Croatto, Hans Georg Gadamer, Paul Ricoeur, Sandra M. Schneiders, Elisabeth Schüssler Fiorenza, Fernando Segovia, among others, all of whom argue that the biblical text is a living tradition and not merely a historical artifact or a classic work of ancient literature. Thus, the task of a liberation-critical reading is to hold each biblical document up for scrutiny not only to test its coherence with issues of justice, compassion, and grace, but also to point out how certain biblical texts can call into question one's own theological predispositions and attitudes toward life and God.

One final word: it is my hope that this study will contribute to the restoration of the prophetic texts to the believing communities of faith and that the prophetic spirit alive within all of life will continue to be awakened and become the true source of power that liberates and transforms all of creation. For this liberation and transformation, all creation groans and waits with eager longing and hopeful anticipation:

> For, I am about to create new heavens
> and a new earth;
> The former things shall not be remembered
> Or come to mind. (Isa 65:17)

Already this vision is unfolding if only we have ears to hear, eyes to see, and hearts to perceive the divine in the unexpected.

PART ONE

Power and Domination

T HE BOOKS OF AMOS, MICAH, JEREMIAH, Lamentations, Baruch, Habakkuk, Zephaniah, and Ezekiel all have as one of their central concerns justice for those who suffer profound injustice at the hands of others whose inordinate need for power and control has caused unnecessary oppression—when Torah is disregarded, covenant is broken, God is forgotten, and the ways of justice and righteousness are abandoned. Such a situation existed thousands of years ago in Israel and the ancient Near East and continues to persist globally even today. The problem is systemic, and, just as in the times of our ancient ancestors, it calls for a response that is bold, courageous, daring, and passionate on the part of men and women worldwide.

What is particularly significant in the prophetic books as a whole, and what appears to some degree in the first group of texts in this section, is the link between social sin and the suffering of the natural world. The biblical texts portray the suffering as something that is divinely incurred as it relates to divine chastisement: God strikes the land and the natural world in order to deal punitively with those who cause unjust pain and agony. When this happens, both the people and the natural world are recipients of violence. And yet, many readers and believers of the biblical text know that such depictions of God raise all sorts of hermeneutical and theological questions because certain deeds are ascribed to God when, in fact, they appear to be more representative of human projections.

The link between social sin and the suffering of the natural world is, however, a most important one since our current state of environmental distress is due, in large part, to the abuse of power, the need for control, and a blatant disregard for the intrinsic goodness of all creation. This disregard has led to an attitude and a way of life that speak of the "survival of the fittest"—the strong and the powerful. Such an approach violates the natural order and balance of creation and the interdependence of life that was part of the divine vision when all of creation came into being.

In the various selections from the prophetic texts of this section, one encounters two central characters, the prophet and God, who are present in the midst of some of life's most challenging and gruesome situations. At times their voices are heard as one and the same voice; at other times just the prophet's voice is heard. Yet the message is the same: oppression and injustice will not go unchecked. How the various unethical situations are handled is a further issue that is raised in this part but dealt with more specifically in Part Two.

These groups of texts offer hope insofar as the plight of the vulnerable, the poor, and the suffering is revealed. The fact that the prophets in the texts and the texts themselves give voice to the voiceless victims of injustice calls listeners and readers then and now to a deep sense of responsibility and accountability. But would that the voiceless victims be empowered to speak for themselves!

By analyzing the texts in this section, one may come to see that some of history as recorded cannot continue to be repeated. The cycle of violence has to be broken and new metaphors engendered if the seeds of justice and righteousness, loving-kindness and mercy are to take root. Would that all peoples chart a new course so that the ongoing biblical story and tradition may be transformed.

1

Amos

Overview: A Historical, Literary, and Hermeneutical Interplay

RESPLENDENT WITH A VARIETY OF RHETORICAL FORMS expressive of a polished, impassioned, dynamic, and didactic style, the book of Amos captures the imagination of its readers with its straightforward, "in your face" message. The prophet cuts to the chase in order to draw attention to the horrific injustices of his day (1:1—5:3; 5:7-13; 5:16—9:10). But such a message is not without words of encouragement (5:4-6, 14-15) and a vision of future restoration (9:11-15), one that speaks of hope and not of despair, life and not death.

As a literary work, the book of Amos is a historical reflection of what life may have been like in eighth-century Israel as seen through the eyes and experience of one of the book's central characters, Amos, a herder and sycamore dresser (7:14) from Tekoa (1:1) who becomes a prophet by God's choice (7:15).

Scholars such as Norman K. Gottwald and William J. Doorly have tried to reconstruct the historical situation and social climate of the eighth century B.C.E. that would have prompted Amos to preach such a bold message. Gottwald notes that the focus of Amos's attack was the upper classes, who enjoyed a certain degree of prosperity during the reign of Jeroboam II. He comments:

> The greedy upper classes, with governmental and judicial connivance, were systematically expropriating the land of commoners so that they could heap up wealth and display it gaudily in a lavish "conspicuous consumption" economy. Hatred of other nations, military swaggering, and religious rhetoric were generously employed to persuade people to accept their miserable lot because it was, after all, "the best of all possible societies."[1]

Doorly adds that the people being oppressed in Amos's time were the poor, the needy, and even the righteous. Farmers were forced to grow cash

crops such as wine and oil, which they did not need for survival. The powerful in Samaria needed the crops for the sake of cultivating and sustaining
international trade. Laws that governed the passing on of land through the
male line were ignored, and thus families were losing their land, becoming
tenant farmers charged with excessive rents by wealthy landlords. Even the
justice system became controlled by the urban rich, who did not allow for
"justice at the gate" on behalf of the commoners.[2]

Although both the prophet Amos and certain commentators speak of the
upper class in a collective way such that one would assume that all the wealthy
of Israel were corrupt, this may not have been the case. The "corporate sense"
provokes some biblical scholars to the point that they call upon other scholars in the field to critique not only the biblical text but also those who comment in the text.[3] For example, Judith E. Sanderson notes that "Amos specifically condemned wealthy women for oppressing the poor (4:1) but failed
specifically to champion the women among the poor."[4] Furthermore, Sanderson points out that with respect to Amos 4:1, "a survey of modern commentaries . . . reveals the alacrity with which women are blamed for societies' evils,
their relative powerlessness is disregarded, and their accountability for sin is
seen as greater than their circumstances would allow."[5] Thus, one needs to
read the book of Amos (as well as the other prophetic texts and the commentaries) with not only a sense of appreciation but also a "hermeneutics of
suspicion."

Viewing the book as whole, one sees that the Amos text consists of nine
chapters that can be subdivided into five main literary units:

Superscription and Introduction (1:1-2)
1. Prophecies against Foreign Countries (1:3—2:16)
2. Address to the House of Israel (3:1—5:17)
3. Triple Warning (5:18—6:14)
4. Five Visions (7:1—9:10)
5. Promise (9:11-15)

Within each of these literary units there is a wide variety of literary forms,
such as admonition (5:6, 14-15), lament (5:1-17), narrative (7:10-17), as well
as a variety of literary techniques that include the repetition of stock phrases,
such as graded numerical sayings (1:3, 6, 9, 11, 13; 2:1, 4, 6); rhetorical questions (2:11; 3:3-6, 8; 5:18, 20, 25; 6:2, 3, 12-13; 7:2; 8:5, 8; 9:7); similes (2:13;
5:24; 6:5; 8:8; 9:5, 7); metaphors (4:1; 5:2; etc.); antitheses (e.g., 5:4-5); and
quotations (7:1-17). These forms and devices attest to the literary artistry of
the text and support its appeal to the ethical consciousness and theological
imagination of its readers. Many of these techniques have shaped and mis-
shaped attitudes throughout the centuries to the present. Such attitudes can

cause and, in fact, have caused oppression or can be and have been the impetus for effecting a deepening reverence and respect for all of life. Thus, the artistic expression of Amos needs to be appreciated but also approached with a hermeneutics of suspicion.[6]

A detailed study of selected passages from the book of Amos follows. The purpose of the study is to unmask the role of power in relation to oppression as it is represented by the text and embedded within the text and to ascertain how the insights gained might influence the ethical consciousness and theological imagination of readers in relation to life today.

Amos 1:3—2:16
"For three transgressions . . . and for four. . . ." (1:3)

This block of material is a collection of prophecies against eight centers of Syria-Palestine: Damascus (1:3-5); Gaza (1:6-8); Tyre (1:9-10); Edom (1:11-12); Ammon (1:13-15); Moab (2:1-3); Judah (2:4-5); and Israel (2:6-16). Each prophecy consists of three parts: a messenger formula, "thus says the LORD"; an indictment (1:3, 6, 9, 11, 13; 2:1, 4, 6); and an announcement of chastisement (1:4, 7, 10, 12, 14; 2:3, 5, 13-16). In some instances, there is a concluding messenger formula, "says the LORD (God)" (1:5, 8, 15; 2:3, 16). Each prophecy presents heinous examples of violent deeds.

Amos 1:3-5
". . . because they have threshed Gilead." (1:4)

The prophecy against Damascus opens with the standard prophetic messenger formula that sets the stage for the words of divine wrath and also lends "authority" to both the prophetic message and the text. According to v 2, what follows in 1:3—2:16 is not a proclamation made in a "matter-of-fact" way. God is angry, and the natural world knows it and pales in response! What is addressed here is a violent military campaign launched against Gilead, one of Israel's richest territories, near Damascus, the capital of Syria.

The brutality of the campaign is described with metaphorical language: "they [the people of Damascus] have threshed [the people of] Gilead with threshing sledges of iron" (v 3). H. W. Wolff notes that

> the technique by which grain was cut up and crushed gives this metaphor its brutal cogency. Grain was threshed by drawing over it a heavy sledge, the hoards of which were curved upward at the front and the underside of which was studded with prongs; the use of iron knives, rather than flintstones, for these prongs in the iron age sufficiently increased in the efficiency of the sledge.[7]

This metaphor emerges from the context of an agrarian society. Israel and the surrounding countries were agricultural people. Thus, the metaphor speaks directly to the original audience's life experience.[8]

In response to such brutality, God promises a fourfold chastisement: (1) to torch the house of Hazael[9] and the strongholds of Ben-hadad;[10] (2) to break Damascus's gate bars; (3) to cut off the inhabitants from the Valley of Aven,[11] along with the one who holds the scepter from Beth-eden;[12] and (4) to exile Aram's people to Kir.[13]

The text reveals that God does not tolerate injustice. God does indeed deal with the perpetrators of injustice and does so on behalf of those who have suffered injustices. That is good news. How the perpetrators are dealt with, however, is problematic.

The text portrays an extraordinary powerplay. Because Damascus oppressed Gilead violently, Damascus is to reap what it has sown—violence. God will inflict terrible, violent, lethal punishments on Damascus because of the terrible and violent deed it has done to Gilead. Damascus had "power over" Gilead, so God will now have "power over" Damascus; but God will win for three reasons: (1) because God is the "all-powerful" "sovereign one" who acts on behalf of those who have been oppressed;[14] (2) because the injustice is done to Gilead, one of Israel's richest territories, and therefore, God most certainly will act on behalf of that which belongs to God's "chosen people,"[15] especially since God is Israel's God and this is Israel's story, told from Israel's perspective; and (3) because a group of people, expressed collectively through the use of "Damascus," had "power over" another group of people, God will indeed have "the last word." In antiquity, God was understood to be the one who had "power over" Israel and over the other kingdoms. Ultimately, power rested with God. Here, perhaps, is the central issue that underlies all the other issues in the text.

In vv 3-5 God is portrayed as "warrior god" who has "power over" injustice and "power over" other peoples. As "warrior god," God promises to deal with injustice by "conquering" the enemy, the perpetrator of injustice. This image of "warrior god" and its association with the notion of power and having "power over" is due, in large part, to a gender-specific portrayal of and metaphor for God. In the ancient world, and in many circles today, God was and is imagined as a male deity. Furthermore, the historical and cultural times of the prophets were marked by countries in conflict with each other, with Israel being no exception. Consequently, experiences and ideologies of war shaped and informed Israel's self-understanding and self-expression. Also, in ancient times, warriors were, for the most part, male. Therefore, it is not surprising that the "warrior of warriors" would be a male God whose might would make right by avenging the enemy.[16] Lastly, this image of God having power over a non-Israelite country also comes from Israel's self-understanding that its God is the true God who is "ruler over all."

The prophecy against Damascus begins with "Thus says the LORD" and ends with "says the LORD." Prophetic messenger formulae function to lend authority to the prophecy: what the prophet says are the words of God, and from the biblical tradition one knows that when God speaks, the word that God has spoken happens.[17] Both the Hebrew text and the NRSV express the idea of divine chastisement in the future. History records that Damascus did fall to the Assyrians in 732 B.C.E.[18] If so, it would seem that God used another empire, the Assyrians, to accomplish the promised threat. Control is now added to power. Not only does God have power over others, but God "controls" others, and here power and control are for destruction. This perspective surely needs to be called into question.

Despite the text's marvelous statement on the unacceptability of perpetrating unjustified violence against others, the text implies an acceptance of violence that cannot go unnoticed or unaddressed.

Finally, were all the people of Damascus guilty of committing injustice? According to the text, God's stinging chastisement will be all-encompassing. Imminent disaster is to come upon the Arameans. Corporate responsibility and corporate punishment were common motifs in Israel and in the ancient Near East[19] but would not be acceptable today. It would be a further injustice to hold responsible those within a group who are innocent of wrongdoing and who, perhaps, may be victims themselves of power and oppression within the group.

Amos 1:6-8
". . . because they carried into exile entire communities." (1:6)

The second prophecy of judgment is against Gaza, also known as the Philistines. Through the use of metonymy, Gaza represents the entire Philistine empire just as Damascus in vv 3-5 represented all of the Aramean empire. In v 6, God, speaking through the prophet Amos, accuses Gaza of a crime that it committed against defenseless people: Gaza is guilty of slave trade. Entire communities were carried into exile and handed over to Edom (v 6) so that they could serve the interests of the powerful.[20] Verses 7-8 describe the divine chastisement that will befall Gaza because of its crime. The text depicts the commodification of human beings: people using other people for their own gain, an injustice that existed in the ancient world but also continues today. God is again portrayed as "warrior god" who will mete out violent punishment to avenge the victims and to strike at the oppressors. As in the prophecy against Damascus (vv 3-5), the central image of chastisement is fire (v 7).[21] Once again, the text makes clear that injustice is not divinely sanctioned; the powerful will be brought low; however, the means will be violent.

The issues raised here are the same as those raised in vv 3-5. While the text may offer hope to those who suffer oppression, it is clear that this text does not present a model for dealing with the violation of human rights and dignity today. But clearly, the text does reveal that despite all of the world's advancement since the eighth, seventh, and sixth centuries B.C.E. when the experience was being lived and the text being shaped, some human beings continue to be the prey of powerful predators. And, in too many cases, violence continues to be the way to settle disputes.

Amos 1:9-10
"They did not remember the covenant of kinship." (1:9)

The third prophecy of judgment is against Tyre, the chief city of the Phoenicians during the mid-eighth century. This text is similar to the prophecy against Gaza insofar as Tyre stands divinely accused for the same crime as Gaza. Added to the issue of human commodification, however, is the fact that Tyre "did not remember the covenant of kinship" (v 9b). This is a poetic way of saying that Tyre disregarded and violated treaties, with "the covenant of kinship" being a "paradigm of all treaties."[22] Such deeds reap divine anger and the promise of divine chastisement. Justice will be done, but how? The motifs, metaphors, and issues of this passage echo those of vv 3-5 and vv 6-8.

Amos 1:11-12
". . . because he pursued his brother with the sword." (1:11)

In the fourth prophecy Edom is declared guilty of pursuing his brother with the sword without pity. Edom is also guilty of harboring anger and wrath relentlessly. In other words, Edom is in violation of "the customary ethos of kinship obligations."[23] The divine chastisement is, once again, fire. For the fourth time, the text drums home the fact that injustice will not be tolerated and that God will deal with the issue, albeit with violence. Repeated images in the four prophecies can serve to reinforce the message but can, at the same time, imprint in one's imagination a less than positive impression, one that suggests that God sanctions violence as just punishment for oppressors. This is not conducive to a life-affirming transformation of people, culture, history, and society.

Amos 1:13-15
". . . because they have ripped open pregnant women in Gilead." (1:13)

Perhaps one of the most gruesome and violent images in the collection of prophecies against the countries is directed against the Ammonites. They are guilty of ripping open pregnant women in Gilead for selfish reasons: to enlarge their own territory. This atrocity is the abuse of power and war at its worst. Furthermore, women, children, and the poor were considered to be among the most vulnerable members of the society of their day. Sanderson, in contrast to most commentators, makes reference to the heinous injustices women suffered at the hands of male military soldiers. She notes:

> Specifically, in ancient times conquered women were customarily raped and carried off as booty; women already pregnant were butchered on the spot, as were small children who could not make the journey. While they were unfortunately not extraordinary acts, Amos considered the Ammonites' atrocities against pregnant Israelite women at least worthy of God's judgment of conquest and exile.[24]

And yet the punishment promised is as violent as the crime itself. Unbridled, selfish, human power is checked by divine power, but according to the text, the power exercised is violent and destructive. Power is here portrayed as a violent oppressive force whether it is perpetrated against the innocent, exercised unjustly, or exercised justly.

Amos 2:1-3
". . . because he burned to lime
the bones of the king of Edom." (2:1)

The repetitious recital of the countries' injustices continues in Amos 2:1-3, the sixth prophecy, which is addressed to Moab. Moab is guilty of burning to lime the royal bones of the king of Edom. To burn the bones of a human being was considered a severe desecration, especially since within the culture at this time such an act was reserved for the most despicable of criminals.[25] As in the other prophecies, Amos makes clear that such a deed is unacceptable, especially to God, who promises to send fire upon Moab, cut off the ruler from its midst, and kill all its officials with him.

This text presents a devastating and confusing picture indeed. First, it shows the lack of reverence on the part of some people for the remains of another. Second, it highlights a deed that differentiates between human beings at the point of death, namely, that it is acceptable to treat the bodies of criminals but not other human beings in certain ways. While this differentiation may have been culturally acceptable then, it needs to be addressed today. Because of the intrinsic goodness of all of creation, appropriate care of a corpse is necessary regardless of the deceased's race, class, status, condition, or state in life. The desecration of anyone's bones is unnecessary. Third, the punishment that God promises is similar to that of the other texts—fire— and yet the chastisement is even more lethal. God promises to cut off Moab's ruler from its midst and to kill all Moab's officials with him. Such a desire is in complete contrast to God's own law that forbids killing (for example, Exod 20:13). Again, God's response to violence is violence! And again, we ask, "Is this the way of God?"

Amos 2:4-5
"... *because they have rejected the law of the* LORD." (2:4)

This prophecy of judgment against Judah is different from the other prophecies against foreign countries. Judah's crime involves no explicit use of power nor any violence. Rather, Judah has rejected God's law and has gone astray. For Judah, this is a most serious offense because Torah is connected to the people's ethical conduct. Forgetfulness of God leads to forgetfulness of God's ways, leading in turn to political, social, economic, and religious disorder and dysfunction. Such is precisely Judah's condition before the country completely collapses in 587 B.C.E. Where one does find an expressed assertion of power is in v 6. Here, as in former prophecies of judgment, God promises to send fire on Judah "to devour" the strongholds of Jerusalem.

The imagery of fire used in the text reflects the violence of warfare common to Judah, particularly during the eighth to sixth centuries B.C.E. When used in association with God, it presents the image of a God of wrath who desires to use power to demolish a country even when that country has not been indicted for any explicit violent crime. From the text one sees that God makes no distinctions between the expressions of indictment and their respective punishments. All receive the same—fire (1:4, 7, 10, 12, 14; 2:2, 5).

Amos 2:6-16
"... *because they sell the righteous for silver.*" (2:6)

In the prophecy against Israel, one sees God, through Amos, enumerating the many transgressions of the people. Each transgression, in some way, is a violation against other people. First, there is economic exploitation of the righteous and needy on the part of some Israelites (v 6). Second, the poor are abused (v 7a). Third, the afflicted are pushed "out of the way"; in other words, they are denied access to and deprived of fair treatment by the court systems.[26] Fourth, a maiden is sexually exploited by two men—a father and his son (v 7b). Fifth, debtors are exploited, perhaps poor men and widows specifically (v 8a).[27] Sixth, others are drinking in holy places the wine that was obtained from fines they imposed, perhaps on the poor (v 8b). Some Israelites are also guilty of making the Nazirites drink wine, thus forcing them to break one of their vows of consecration (see Num 6:3-4; Judg 13:14); others silence the prophets (v 12)!

Clearly, the text reveals an abuse of power on the part of some of the Israelite people. The victims of such abuse, for the most part, are the righteous, the poor, women, and people following a holy way of life. Within Israelite society, these people would be the most vulnerable in terms of political, social, economic, and religious status, and therefore, the people most easily abused. The idea of "making the Nazirites drink wine" and commanding the prophets not to prophesy admits of a certain overt disregard for the explicit honoring of God. Hence, from the text one can see that the threads of power, domination, and control were part of the fabric of Israelite society. It was these threads that caused others' lives to be torn apart.

Verses 13-16 describe God's response. God will come as a foe among those who stepped all over the vulnerable, and God will push them down. Birch comments: "It is clear in the speech of judgment to Israel that Amos's God is God not only of history but also of the weak, the poor, and the powerless. God's judgment is exercised in behalf of those most vulnerable, most likely to be exploited and manipulated. This is not the God of the powerful and important people of the land. This is the God found among 'the least of these.' . . ."[28] While this is an accurate picture, it must not be forgotten that God's exercise of judgment over the unjust is as violent as the ways of the unjust themselves. Hence, the text legitimates the assertion of violent power in order to eliminate injustice.

Amos 1:3—2:16 in Context

These eight prophecies against foreign countries are a mind-shattering, heart-wrenching, and soul-splitting picture of how power and control, when used violently, results in oppression and destruction even when the intent is to bring about goodness or restoration.

In each prophecy there is a vivid description of a series of unacceptable injustices done to men and women. They are victims of people who have exercised power and control over them. In some instances, the victims are the most vulnerable, the most powerless of society. The oppression done is not explicitly gender- or class-specific.

The fact that each prophecy is pronounced by a prophet through whom God speaks offers a sense of hope to those who are victims of injustice. Their plight has gone unnoticed; something will be done on their behalf to the perpetrators of injustice.

These texts show that in the biblical world there was a hierarchy of power, God being the most powerful and the one who could win out against even the most powerful of human beings. Never once in any of the prophecies are any powerful people named. They are referred to only by third person singular and plural pronouns, "he" and "they." No attention is drawn to them specifically,[29] but unfortunately, none of the victims is mentioned by name or class either. Clearly, each prophecy proclaims that God, not the unjust ones, has the last word, which is a word that carries with it punitive measures that serve to avenge the victims and to make known that God is ultimately the one "in charge"; God does not tolerate injustice.

While positive elements can be drawn from the prophecies, the prophecies also present several serious problems. First, God is portrayed as one whose anger at injustice is so great that the impending action against the unjust is as violent as the injustices themselves. Here, it seems that the principle of *lex talionis* is in full operation: "an eye for an eye, and a tooth for a tooth." God's punitive action is as oppressive as the oppressors' actions. Israel and the other countries were constantly battling; their religious expression and imagination is connected to their lived experience, and their metaphors and literary expressions are also drawn from that same experience.

From the texts, one gets the impression that all of the people of Damascus, Gaza, Tyre, Edom, Ammon, Moab, Judah, and Israel are corrupt and therefore deserving of chastisement. That all, rather than most, are evil, is unlikely and seems an erroneous and an unjust assumption.[30]

As a group of so-called prophecies, these proclamations are prophetic insofar as they herald the role of the prophet as a spokesperson of the Divine who will not accept injustice nor allow injustice to be the final word. Although they may accurately portray how God is understood within the social location of Israel, we must ask if God is a God who exercises power destructively. If God so punishes, then who of us, graced yet imperfect and capable of injustice, can ever hope to survive much less be forgiven of our own transgressions? A community of believers today, called to follow the ways of God, is called to repent of ruthless anger and the desire for revenge.[31] If these texts represent a living tradition that can continue to find a home within the believing community today, then the community needs to be attentive to the worlds, limitations, ideologies, and theological perspectives that shaped the production of these texts. Contemporary interpretation hopefully leads to a re-visioning of a God of justice who can be described with new metaphors that, we hope, have the power to transform.

Amos 4:1-5
"You cows of Bashan . . . who oppress the poor, who crush the needy." (4:1)

Perhaps one of the most famous passages in the book of Amos is the one directed against the well-kept women of Samaria who are referred to in the text as the "cows of Bashan."[32] Bashan was a plain in the Transjordan that was famous for its "plush pastures and robust cows."[33] These women are accused of oppressing the poor and crushing the needy. They are also self-indulgent and seem to have some power over their husbands from whom they order up drinks.

Given the context of this passage, the issue here may be not only that these women are treating the poor and needy very badly but also that they have become wealthy through their husbands' oppression of the poor and ill-treatment of the needy, although the text does not state this explicitly. One needs to be careful about assumptions; some of these women may have married into wealth.[34] Clearly there are power, class, and gender aspects to this text. It seems that some of the wealthy have power over some of the poor and needy, who, in the text, are nameless and genderless. Specifically, it is women and not men who are oppressors. Yet, one wonders whether these women are not just acting according to what is expected of them and what they have observed from their lived experience.

The text could raise several problems for some readers today. The first is gender. Only the women from among "the careless, pleasure-seeking population of Samaria as a whole . . ."[35] are singled out to receive the prophet's indictment. What about the men?

Second, the metaphor compares the women to cows. Because a majority within Israelite society were herders and farmers, many metaphors come from the natural environment.[36] In its own social world context, comparing the Samarian women to the cows of Bashan would, for its hearers and early readers, perhaps, communicate nothing more than a comparison between pedigreed cows and well-kept women.[37] As Sanderson points out, "'You cows of Bashan' was almost certainly not meant as derogatorily as it sounds in English now, though the precise nuance in Amos's mind is not clear. It was common to compare human qualities to animal qualities; whether the application was positive or negative depended upon the context."[38]

When heard in the context of a contemporary technological society that has health and ecological concerns and sensitivities, this metaphor takes on a new nuance. The comparison is heard as derogatory, inferring that the women were "fat and unacceptable." Moreover, referring to a person as an animal is to be guilty of diminishing the human, if viewed hierarchically, because an animal is considered to be of lesser value than a human being. Interlocked in diminution is the eco-ethical issue of speciesism, "the assumption that animals are inferior to human beings and do not warrant equal consideration and respect."[39]

The metaphor of the "cows of Bashan" is used in the biblical context of a prophecy of judgment: the women of Samaria are being condemned. Therefore, when an informed reader hears this metaphor in the context of a patriarchal, hierarchical, ecologically exploited world today, the metaphor is heard as one that mocks both women and nonhuman life. The nonhuman animal possesses a negative image, and when the animal is then applied to women, both share the negativity.[40] What may once have been a neutral metaphor has now become a gender-specific, degrading metaphor. Finally, in vv 2-3 one sees that the luxurious lifestyle of these wealthy women, who are presumed to have no concern for the poor and the needy, will not continue forever.

Amos 4:6-13
"I laid waste your gardens and your vineyards." (4:9)

The poetic story told in vv 6-13 presents a startling picture. God reiterates all the divinely initiated negative actions that were done against Israel in the hope that Israel would return to God (vv 6-13). God withheld rain, struck the people with blight and mildew, laid waste their gardens, had the locust devour fig and olive trees, sent out pestilence, killed the young men with the sword, carried away the people's horses, made a stench go up the people's noses, and overthrew some of them.

In the ancient Israelite world, God's blessing meant fertility, longevity, and prosperity, and God's curse meant famines, plagues, and pestilences. If the people had a lush harvest and plenty of good rain, then they had done something right. If they experienced famine and drought, then they had done something wrong. It was also thought that God would strike the land and other elements in the natural world in order to punish the people for their transgressions.[41] If the grapevines withered by the power of God, then the people had no wine. If pestilence struck a crop of corn, then people had no food. Supposedly, then, they would, in their need, return to God and reform their ways. The text of Amos 4:6-13 reflects these attitudes and beliefs.

In vv 6-10 God is portrayed as intentionally manipulating various elements in the natural world in a destructive way so as to coax the Israelite people to return to God. The God who once saw the natural world as good[42] now turns it into a pawn in an effort to turn human beings from their wretched ways. Even human beings are sacrificed in the course of God's action (vv 10-11).

Some of the concerns that underlie Amos 4:6-13 need to be kept in the forefront of one's reading. Several of them continue to color certain contemporary theological thought. For those working from a creation-centered theology, this text demands comment; at the present time, the natural world continues to be a victim of some powerful human manipulation, domination, and abuse.

Amos 5:10-13

". . . because you trample on the poor. . . ." (5:11)

Amos 5:10-13 portrays other examples of the inordinate assertion of power on the part of some of the people in ancient Israel. Once again, it is the poor (v 11), the righteous (v 12), and the needy (v 12) who are overpowered and become victims of a whole array of injustices. Yet God will deliver justice. Both oppressors and oppressed remain nameless and genderless and therefore "faceless." Had the prophet Amos named both groups, the text would have had greater clarity and the message greater power; the culprits and victims would have been liberated from an impressionistic backdrop that serves to protect the identity of the offenders while keeping those offended in the shadow of anonymity.

Amos 6:1-7, 8-10, 11-14

"I abhor the pride of Jacob." (6:8)

In Amos 6, one sees the prophet railing against those who are complacent in Zion and secure in Samaria (vv 1-7). Although the text gives no mention of the economic status of these people, one can presume that the prophet is delivering a woe prophecy to the wealthy upper class of Israelite society (cf. 4:11, 4-5), who, by its complacent and self-indulgent attitude, allows violence to go unchecked (v 3). Would that the rich had used their power on behalf of justice, but this seems not to have been their choice (vv 4-7).

In vv 8-10, the prophet upbraids the Israelites for their pride, a theme that continues in vv 11-14: they stand condemned for turning justice into poison and righteousness into wormwood and for taking pride in their own strength without due recognition of God's role in their recent successful military campaign (vv 12b-13).[43] The Israelite people are, therefore, guilty of proud self-assertion and a perversion of justice. But are all of them guilty, as the text would have the reader believe? Underlying their pride and perversion is the use of power to obstruct and to oppress. To suppress such attitudes, God promises to raise up a country that will oppress the house of Israel itself.

Once again, one sees a hierarchical power play that begins and ends with oppression. One also sees God's power and control coming to the fore: God will use one country to oppress another. Does this text not reflect attitudes endemic to both patriarchy and hierarchy, characteristic of the culture of the day but likely shared by both the prophet's own theological consciousness and message and those of the text's later editors?

Amos 8:4-14
"Hear this, you that trample on the needy. . . ." (8:4)

With direct candor, the prophet Amos addresses a group of Israelites who have taken advantage of others for economic gain (vv 4-6). As in Amos 2:6-16; 4:1; 5:10-13, those who suffer are the poor and the needy (vv 4, 6). Once again, these people are nameless and genderless. The injustices done against them are twofold: they are cheated out of money (v 5),[44] and they are made into bartered goods (v 6). Such reprehensible behavior on the part of those possessing greater economic and social advantage and "know-how" does not go unnoticed. In vv 7-14, God plans to take action against the culprits of injustice whose ruthlessness stems from apostasy and greed (vv 5, 13-14).[45]

In this series of predicted divine chastisements, God's wrath is depicted in the form of an earthquake.[46] Other retributive measures include: the sun going down, feasts turning into mourning and songs into lamentations (vv 9-10), sackcloth covering the loins and shaved heads (v 10b,c), the famine adversely affecting the people (v 13), and the people deprived of hearing God's words with a resultant aimlessness in their lives (vv 11-12). Injustice will not go without reprimand; unethical behavior is exposed.

This text reveals to people then and now that in a hierarchical society power is, in fact, connected to one's social and economic status. This power can be—and many times is—used abusively for self-serving purposes that deny others their legal rights and human dignity. Yet this sort of domination will not have the last word; justice will be done. God's power will affect the lives of the offenders in most uncomfortable ways. The text suggests that justice will be a corporate experience and not directed solely at the troublemakers. While God's actions here are depicted as less violent and destructive than they are elsewhere, God's wrath is not. The divine wrath and earthquake portrayed here, however, may in fact be symbolic.

Amos in Context

Several points can be gleaned from these selected passages in the book of Amos. Within the ancient biblical world, certain people who had power often used it to oppress others in violent ways. The victims of such oppression were often powerless and usually came from among the poor, the needy, and the righteous. Dominating power and oppression cut across gender, class, and status divisions.

Second, God was perceived as a deity with tremendous power. God is pictured in the texts as one who used power to inflict punishment on those whose abuse of power had caused harm to others. However, God's powerful deeds of chastisement were often themselves violent and destructive. In addition, God is portrayed as one who dominated the natural world to try to win back the cherished but wayward Israelites.

Third, the texts admit to a certain "hierarchy" of power. Certain humans and nonhumans are oppressed by those who are more powerful than they, and the powerful are then punished by an even more powerful God. Furthermore, this type of hierarchical oppressive power is shown to be related to what is understood today as patriarchy. With the exception of the women of Samaria who exert power over their husbands, most of the documented power plays rest with the men. God is portrayed as a male involved in power plays for the sake of justice.

Fourth, the metaphorical language in the book of Amos is replete with violent imagery. Such metaphors and images likely reflect the social location and cultural world of not only the prophet but especially the authorial voice of the text.

Fifth, in the text God and Amos are the "voice" for victims of injustice. Readers are given a portrait of a God who does not just verbally condemn horrendous situations; God will do something about them.

Thus, the texts speak clearly about power, injustice, and the struggle for justice. Many of the injustices recorded in the book of Amos not only occurred in the past but continue to occur today in various parts of the world. Read in the context of this present age, the ancient texts clearly point out that the human community still uses power abusively; it is still in need of much healing and transformation. When the paradigm shifts fully from power over to empowerment, from violent injustice to peace-filled justice, from oppressive hierarchy to liberating reciprocity, then the texts from the biblical story of Amos will be descriptions of the past. New social attitudes will name a reconciling God. Until then, history is repeating itself.

2

Micah

Overview: A Historical, Literary, and Hermeneutical Interplay

WRITTEN IN A CREATIVE AND BLUNT STYLE, the book of Micah presents itself as a word addressed to the people of Israel and Judah in the latter half of the eighth century B.C.E. Micah, the prophet of the text, is seen as both imaginative and bold. With intricate wordplays, clever figures of speech, and gripping metaphors, he condemns the political and religious leaders of his day who, with others, are responsible for ignoring, perpetuating, and causing some gruesome injustices (see, for example, 2:1-2, 6-9; 3:1-3, 9-12; 6:9-16).

The latter half of the eighth century B.C.E. was, some would argue, the most challenging of all ages in Israel's history because it brought the demise of the Northern Kingdom of Israel, an event that, in turn, set the stage for the collapse of the Southern Kingdom. Gottwald notes that Micah

> came from a small town in the Judean foothills, but spoke his condemnations directly to the leaders of Jerusalem. His biting indictments of socioeconomic injustice are similar to those of Amos, who was also from small-town Judah. The prophet knows at first hand about the expulsion of small landowners from their traditional means of livelihood, dishonest business practices, venal priests and prophets, and a royal regime that connives in the oppression of the poor.[1]

Like other texts in the prophetic corpus, however, the book of Micah contains prophecies that point to a new day full of promise and hope (2:12-13; 4:1-10; 7:11-13) and prayers full of confidence (6:6-8; 7:14-17), wonder, and assurance (7:18-20).

As a literary work of exceptional artistry, the book of Micah can be divided into three main parts: chapters 1–3, chapters 4–5, and chapters 6–7.[2] Chapters 1–3 are judgment speeches with the exception of 2:12-13, which is a prophecy of deliverance. Chapters 4–5 speak of future restoration and salvation for Jerusalem and Israel. The two chapters are very hopeful; restoration and salvation will surely occur (4:9—5:9), although some sort of purification is involved (5:10-15). Chapters 6–7 are a mixed collection of prophecies that represent a vacillation of moods and tones but end with words of hopeful assurance.

The book of Micah contains a number of literary forms and techniques that accent and clarify the message. These include judgment speeches (for example, 1:2-7; 3:1-12); laments (for example, 1:8-16; 7:1-7); a lawsuit (*rîb*) (6:1-5); prayers (7:14-17, 18-20); and reflections (6:6-8). Micah's message is replete with metaphors (for example, 1:2-4; 2:12-13; 3:1-3; 4:1-5, 8-13; 7:1), many of which contain images found in the natural world and express both human and divine power and their interplay.

Some of the hermeneutical concerns in the book of Amos parallel those in the book of Micah. For example, God devises evil to counter evil (2:1-5). Yet God is depicted as being less violent than in Amos. Injustice and oppression are the lot of the day for some of the people in Micah's time, and both Micah and God condemn these behaviors, with God promising different forms of chastisement. The impending divine retaliations, are, for the most part, non-lethal. Wicked ones may go hungry, but there is no mention of their starving to death (6:9-14).

This chapter looks at selected passages from the book of Micah that are related to power. In some instances, power is the direct cause of oppression. In other instances, it is not (for example, Mic 3:8). One cannot help being inspired by the character of the prophet himself, who has a deep love for his people and his God.

Micah 1:2-7
"I will make Samaria a heap in the open country." (1:6)

Verses 2-7 are a judgment speech that features the prophet Micah, in robust fashion, calling his listeners and readers to attention (v 2) and describing God's imminent coming and its effects (vv 3-4), a statement of divine accusation against Israel (v 5), and a proclamation of forthcoming divine chastisement upon Samaria (vv 6-7). The verses attest to the power and sovereignty of God.

In v 2 the prophet sends out a universal call: "Listen, O peoples, all of you / Pay attention, O earth and its fullness." Not only human beings but also the natural world are the recipients of the prophet's word.

Verses 3-4 are a description of an impending theophany. God, who resides in the holy temple (v 2), is going out from it to come down and tread upon the high places of the earth (v 3), and the natural world will respond: the mountains will melt, and the valleys will burst open (v 4). The similes, "like wax before the fire" and "like waters poured out on a slope," heighten the imagery of total disintegration. Together, vv 3-4 describe the power of God and the powerlessness of creation before the power of God.

Through two rhetorical questions (v 5), one learns that the capital cities of Samaria and Jerusalem epitomize the countries' transgressions, though what they are specifically is not yet known. God, speaking through Micah, announces a plan to destroy Samaria because of its offenses (v 5b). Verses 6-7 proclaim impending disaster.[3]

Several hermeneutical points arise from vv 2-5 and 6-7 that need comment. First, it is clear that the prophetic message has cosmological consequences. The earth and people will be affected by Micah's word.

Second, the "high places of the earth" (v 2), together with the mountains and the valleys (v 4), provide a metaphor for both kingdoms and specifically for Samaria, the capital of Israel, and Jerusalem, the capital of Judah (v 5). The impending destruction of the natural world is really a metaphor for the fall of the two kingdoms. The double entendre makes the point that God is "lord over creation" and "lord over Israel." This is what the prophet proclaims and what many of the people of his day either believed or came to believe as a result of the historical events that subsequently occurred.

Third, vv 2-7 describe a theology of God and divine power that is both hierarchical and patriarchal. In vv 2-3 God is pictured in "his holy temple." He is the God who sits enthroned in the heavenly court who will "come down." This is a different image from that of the God who walked in the garden in the cool of the evening (Gen 3:8) and from that of the God who talked with Moses as one would with a friend (Exod 33:11). This is the image of a God who is transcendent, who seems to be "above" and "over" all creation, who will come out of his place to tread upon the high places of the earth. This God resembles a king on a throne. This God is not coming to be with Israel; this God is coming to cast judgment on Israel (vv 6-7). Thus, vv 2-7 present a metaphorical picture of God as a powerful king passing judgment on a group of his subjects. This image ascribed to God uses metaphors that reflect the society's organization of power—its social and political structures.

God's power is described further in vv 6-7. God will mete out punishment to Israel because of its transgressions (v 5). God will "level" Samaria, Israel's capital, and dash to pieces all the city's idols. Israel is guilty of apostasy. In v 6, by metonymy, Samaria represents Jacob/Israel, the Northern Kingdom. The fate of the entire kingdom will be that of the capital city.

As indicated by the use of feminine possessive pronouns and nouns, Samaria is personified as a prostitute, a harlot. Female Samaria represents all of Israel; female Zion/Jerusalem represents all of Judah. Therefore, when the people of Samaria are unfaithful to God or Torah, "she" becomes a "prostitute." God, on the other hand, is viewed as a male figure, and because God is God, God can never be unfaithful.

The text seems to allow one's theological and social imagination to distribute power patriarchically, giving affirmation to the male gender while diminishing, in a derogatory manner, the female gender. The use of gender-specific metaphors in v 6 to describe Israel's religious ills has, unfortunately, led to patriarchal assumptions and oppressive practices by the people who have received the biblical text.

Micah 2:1-11
"The women of my people you drive out." (2:9)

Micah 2 conveys a stinging message of judgment. Verses 1-5 contain a woe proclamation[4] spoken by Micah, while vv 6-11 comprise a disputation prophecy, God's words delivered by Micah.[5] Verses 1-3 use vivid verbs to describe concretely the wickedness of some members of his Israelite community.

In v 1, some Israelites "devise wickedness," indicating that their wrongs are premeditated.[6] The phrase, "because it is in their power," connotes both free will[7] and authority. Clearly, the verses are about power. Wolff notes that

> the words of the verse [v 1b] characterize Micah's audience not only according to their deeds, but also according to their potential as [people] of authority. It is therefore clear that Micah makes an accusation against a particular elite. Their power is the basis (*kî*, v 1bβ) for the laying of these plans; it also provides the possibility for the execution of these plans. Power corrupts when it does not follow wisdom's admonition: "Do not withhold good from those to whom it is due, when it is in your power to do it" (Prov 3:27).[8]

In other words, a certain group within the Israelite community is using its God-given freedom and authority to take advantage of others, even to the point of oppression (v 2).

Verse 2 clearly identifies the inequities that the accused have planned, worked out, and performed. The accused "covet fields, and seize them" (v 2). They also covet "houses and take them away" (v 2). Mays notes that

> verse 2 moves from a general characterization of conduct to a specific stipulation of deeds. The powerful are expropriating the property of small landowners through oppression. The engine which drives the enterprise is covetousness, breaking the instruction of YHWH to his people: "You shall not covet your neighbor's house(hold)."[9]

Deuteronomy 5:21 specifically forbids the Israelites to covet another's house or field. Hence, Torah has been violated by some who have taken advantage of others.

Some within the Israelite community are guilty not only of covetousness and stealing but also of extortion: "they oppress householder and house / people and their inheritance" (v 2b).

In summary, vv 1-2 present a picture of and an accusation against certain members of the Israelite community who, through their abuse of power, violate God's commands and ordinances for their personal gain.

Verses 3-5 contain an announcement of judgment comprised of a proclamation of intended chastisement (v 3), a prediction of disaster (v 4), and a threat (v 5). In these verses God is portrayed as a schemer of actions that are going to take place to "get even" with those who have behaved unjustly toward others. Ultimately, those who have taken land will lose their fields (v 4) and be banned from any further acquisition of property (v 5). God uses divine power to act on behalf of those who have been victimized by those abusing their power.

The vignettes contained in the book of Micah may prompt readers to visualize a causal relationship between negative social behavior and divine punishment. The present vignette (vv 1-5) suggests a direct relationship between the harshness of the actions of some and the harshness of the punishment these same people will receive. Thus, those who use power oppressively will experience the punishing power of God.

The picture that the text presents of God is problematic. Just as some people devised wickedness against one another in vv 1-2, so now God in vv 3-5 devises wickedness against those who are unjust. The use of irony intensifies this correlation. Whoever plots and plans evil (vv 1-2) will, in turn, be a victim of future calamity (vv 3-5), and whoever possesses ill-gotten land will also, in turn, be dispossessed of it by God (vv 3-5). The culture of the society that produced the text understood God to behave in a fully retributive manner. The text assumes the acceptability of God behaving in such a manner.

In vv 6-11, God is heard speaking through Micah, quoting the prophet's adversaries in the process.[10] The point made in vv 1-5, that is, that God will not tolerate injustice, is also the central message of vv 6-11. God disputes the delusion of those who think they can take advantage of others without having to suffer retribution.

The readers of vv 6-11 are asked to reflect upon the strained relationship that exists between God and some of the Israelites because of their smug attitude (v 6) and their deeds of injustice (vv 8-9). God expresses righteous anger (v 10) regarding some of the people's inability to discern and accept truth (vv 6, 11). The use of quoted material and the rhetorical questions, followed by divine accusation, divine chastisement, and divine mockery, provide an insight into the nature of a God who is both a God of confrontation in search of justice and a God of mercy who has a particular concern for the trusting and the least powerful. One hears in vv 8-9 a message of divine outrage directed at those guilty of injustice; implied is a message of care and comfort for victims of unethical behavior.

In summary, Mic 2:1-11 is a text whose central theme is power. Certain human beings exert their power over others for personal gain. Yet that in turn would lead to more power. Such an unjust assertion of power does not go unnoticed or unchecked. The text celebrates a God and a prophet who act on behalf of the victimized and powerless. Even though the notion of God devising evil to counteract the evil done by some to others may be off-putting, the divine chastisement fits the crimes. The oppressors will lose their land (vv 4-5) and in other cases will be driven out from the land (v 10).

Hence, while there appears to be a power struggle between God and a group of self-centered people who amass what is not their own, God's power is greater and constructive. The coming of the Assyrians is attributed to God as divinely ordained chastisement; and this derives from Israel's view of God as the fundamental causation in the world. The text would have one believe that the loss of land was the direct result of the intervention of God and only indirectly caused by the Assyrian invasion.

Finally, the text is strongly conditioned by the prophet's and later authors' and editors' social location. One wonders if those guilty of oppression and the abuse of power will ever have their spears turned into pruning hooks. Does justice always have to happen through divine chastisement, or can it happen through transforming grace? The paradigm of domination represented in the text has not yet been shifted.

Micah 3:1-12

*"Hear this, you rulers of the house of Jacob
and chiefs of the house of Israel,
who abhor justice and pervert all equity. . . ." (3:9)*

Perhaps one of the most profound chapters in the entire book of Micah, chapter 3, is comprised of four parts: an address to Israel's political leadership (vv 1-4), a proclamation concerning the prophets (vv 5-7), an interlude (v 8), and another address to Israel's leadership (vv 9-12). In this chapter, one sees that the abuse of power is both overt and subtle. One also sees power redefined. Finally, one observes power used to chastise those guilty of injustices. Thus, chapter 3 presents a comprehensive view of power that includes a revelatory element. The voice of the prophet is strong and unswerving.

In vv 1-4, 5-7, and 9-12 Micah outlines very specifically the injustices and sins of Israel's political and religious leadership. The rhetorical question in v 1 articulates plainly the sin of Israel's leadership: they do not act justly; they are "haters of good and lovers of evil" (v 2a). The use of contrast intensifies the accusation.

The prophet's invective continues with a brutal metaphor (vv 2b-3). Here, Micah compares Israel's leaders to savage butchers and voracious cannibals who treat people like animals ready to be consumed. This violent metaphor, with its graphic verbs—tear, eat, flay, break in pieces, and chop up—and its two similes, intensifies and vivifies Micah's point while stimulating the readers' imaginations to envision a brutal scene. Thus, the metaphor, coupled with the strong verbs and similes, crystallizes for readers the extent of injustice within Micah's community, its leadership in particular, and opens eyes wide to the horrendous wickedness of which political, community, and religious leaders are capable.

Now, to Micah's opponents and to the text's readers, his metaphor might have sounded odd because he first mentions that Israel's leaders and rulers tear the skin and flesh from the people's bones and then eat the people's flesh. Instead of following through on the previous image of people being devoured, he describes how the leaders flay the people's skin, break their bones, and chop up their flesh. Micah's disregard for a linear progression in his vivid description only intensifies the gruesomeness of the individual actions that various leaders have perpetrated against other people.[11] Thus, through Micah one is given a glimpse of an abuse of power that has literally devoured the lives of others.

In response to such injustice, God will not answer the vicious ones when they cry out; rather, God will hide God's face. Not to experience the presence of God in one's life meant, for the Israelite, pain and chaos. Here, God is portrayed as nonresponsive to these people in their time of need. Those who have abandoned God's ways will themselves experience abandonment. For believers, this experience would be devastating and could serve as a call to change one's ways.

Following his attack on Israel's political leadership, Micah verbally assaults Israel's prophets (vv 5-7). They are guilty of leading the people astray by their false prophecies. They have corrupted their prophetic office for personal satisfaction and gain. Moreover, they respond negatively to their own Israelite audience, who fail to provide them with the expected recompense (v 5). God's response is not to punish others with physical harm but to take away the gifts that are part of their prophetic office. Here, power is used to suppress rather than to oppress.

Micah 3:8 gives a clear picture of power as it related to the prophetic office. After two verbal attacks, Micah takes a reprieve. Instead of talking about someone else, he now makes a proclamation about himself. Micah sets himself apart from those he has been attacking, namely, the political and religious leaders of Israel. He appears as the polar opposite to those from whom God's

Spirit is withheld. He boldly states his many gifts. He is "filled with power, with the spirit of the LORD, and with justice and might, to declare to Jacob his transgression and to Israel his sin" (v 8).

The arrangement of this list of gifts is interesting. To be filled "with power" is to be filled with God's Spirit, and to be filled with God's Spirit is to be filled with justice and might. Power, then, can be a divinely given gift that moves one to expose others' injustices to the unjust ones themselves and to those associated with the ones causing injustices. Once the injustices and the ones causing the injustices are exposed, the power of the perpetrators is diminished and oftentimes "usurped." To expose injustices is an act of justice that implies that the unjust and their deeds have no power or control over the one who speaks out.

In the context of vv 1-7 and vv 9-12, power, when rooted in the divine Spirit, becomes an energy that empowers one person to deal with injustice by exposing it (vv 1-7) and confronting those who cause it (vv 9-12). Micah 3:8 shows that the power of the prophet rests not in punitive action but in the prophet's confrontational word. This is quite different from some of the other messages that the prophets speak.

In the last segment of Micah 3, vv 9-12, Micah again attacks the political and religious leaders of his day. In this address, he includes the priests (v 11). Micah lists the wrongs that his addressees are guilty of and then mocks them by quoting their own words. Finally, Micah states directly that it is because of the injustices of the leaders that the symbols of God's presence—Jerusalem and the temple—will be destroyed.

In summary, these texts from Micah 3 present insights into the intricacies of power. One can draw several conclusions. First, power and hierarchy are potentially interrelated. In the case of Micah's society, but certainly not unique to it, some of the political and religious leadership use their power to the detriment of others.

Second, power and patriarchy are potentially interrelated. In the ancient Israel depicted in the Micah texts, male hierarchical leadership abused power, and consequently, the abuse of power depicted was gender-specific. In most developed countries today, the majority of leadership positions are held by men, making men more likely than women to be abusers of power.

Third, power and language are potentially interrelated. Metaphorical language, as in the case of vv 2-3, has the power to describe injustices that are so horrendous that they defy banal vocabulary. Metaphorical language has the power to arouse one's imagination, to sting one's moral conscience, and to move people out of anesthetized mental, spiritual, and emotional states of consciousness.

Fourth, power and religious ideology are potentially interrelated. Israel's belief that it could do no wrong because God was on its side (v 11b) became an ideology. Israel used this particular premise to justify and sanction certain unethical actions. W. J. Wessels comments: "Zion theology undoubtedly became ideological in nature by dominating the mindset of the people of Judah in not seeing the danger of their way of living. It suited the leaders of this society that this was the case, because through the power of this ideology the people supported the establishment and its practices, considering it to be God-given. No critical thinking existed or was tolerated."[12] Wessels further points out that ideology can become an "excellent means to exercise power over people."[13]

Finally, power and empowerment are interrelated. Power can strengthen one to do a task: with the divine gift of power, Micah is empowered to expose unjust people who do unjust things. Here human and divine power coalesce in order to free the truth about people and situations. Micah 3:8 is both challenging and revelatory insofar as it allows one to see how power can be used for the sake of the common good. The power of a prophet can disarm the power of injustice wielded by those who abuse power. Micah, a male prophet, calls to task the male leaders of his day.

Micah 6:9-16
"Your wealthy are full of violence." (6:12)

God, through the prophet Micah, enumerates a list of behaviors of which the Israelites are guilty. Verses 10-12 catalogue "commercial and social vices"[14] that include wicked scales, a bag of dishonest weights; the verses accuse the wealthy of being full of violence and other inhabitants of speaking lies. The victims of such injustices are not mentioned; one can only presume that they are not the wealthy and not people with any kind of social power. A hierarchical social system has left the victims of abusive power nameless—as it usually does.

Verses 13-16 contain a list of the divine actions that are planned for the unjust ones. A punitive God uses the natural world to chastise. Unlike the Amos text, in which God is depicted as striking out against creation in order to win back Israel (Amos 4:7-10), here God is portrayed as withholding fertility; that is, when people sow they shall not reap (v 15).

As in the other Micah texts, this passage reveals injustices related to status and confirms that such injustices are not acceptable. The text implies that all the wealthy are guilty of violence, but this is an unjust presumption. Those among the wealthy who are kind, generous, and truthful need to be liberated from social and collective stereotypes that the text seems to legitimate.

Micah 7:1-7
"The powerful dictate what they desire." (7:3)

Verses 1-7 are a powerful pericope, with their contrasting images creating a dauntingly imaginative picture. Through the use of similes and metaphors created from images within the natural world (v 1), Micah describes the condition of his society: it is a wasteland. The faithful have disappeared from the land and there is no one left who is upright; people hunt each other down; the official and the judge request a bribe; the powerful dictate what they want and so pervert justice. Even the best person among them is like a brier, a thorn hedge. No one can be trusted because even family members turn on each other. The only hope is God.

The passage describes a totally corrupt society. Even the extended family, known to be a "stabilizing and integrating structure within Israelite society,"[15] disintegrates from within as its members topple its hierarchical structure. Here the abuse of power cuts across gender, class, and status. People are at each others' throats. Against such violence, the prophet knows no power other than the power of God, for which he waits with confidence, trusting in God's compassion. The abuse of power can lead to devastating violence that affects a country, a society, and a home. And yet, even though the biblical text, and perhaps one's life experience, would make it seem like all is hopeless and all people are bad, the fact that a prophet like Micah hopes in God is itself a sign of goodness and hope. The transformation of any society rests in the power of its prophets who call on the power of God with expectant hearts, and in God who will indeed act with compassion.

Micah in Context

Looking at these texts as a whole, one can see a wide range of behaviors associated with power within the ancient biblical world, many of which continue to today. While power is related to hierarchy, patriarchy, status, gender, and class, it often penetrates and cuts across these classifications. It is something innate to humankind as part of creation. Power can be used to bring about justice, as Micah used it, or injustice and oppression, as it was abused by those who, with unfair scales and false prophecies, took advantage of others.

The texts also show that power rests in both the spoken and written word. The prophetic word has the power to express the inexpressible through metaphor, to arouse and awaken one's moral conscience, and to give expression to experiences that are absolutely devastating and that might otherwise go unknown. The prophetic word can even make one shudder if, for example, one is a believer and hears about some of the gut-wrenching actions that

God is planning to take in response to injustice. As a written word that is believed to be prophetic, the texts of Micah have the power to influence how people think about other people, how people perceive the ways of God, and even how people perceive God. Thus, the text of Micah has a certain "power over" one's religious imagination, especially when what is proclaimed is said to be "the word of the LORD." Without critical and hermeneutical assessment of prophetic texts, one runs the risk of a distorted view of prophets, prophecy, people in general, and most especially, of God and God's ways.

Finally, the message of Micah, with its multilayered expressions of power, challenges readers to reflect on how power can be used to devastate or to liberate, depending upon how one exercises power—with oppressive force or with transforming compassion.

3
Jeremiah

Overview: A Historical, Literary, and Hermeneutical Interplay

WRITTEN IN BOTH PROSE AND POETRY, the book of Jeremiah captures the historical crisis of the last days of the Southern Kingdom Judah, its capital Jerusalem, and the temple before the kingdom collapsed and the capital and temple were destroyed in 587 B.C.E. The years 627 to 587 B.C.E. were a time of political turmoil and conflict, coupled with religious apostasy. This is the time when Jeremiah, both a historical figure and one of the central characters of the book of Jeremiah, was said to have been active as a prophet.

Assyria, one of the great powers of this time, gave way to a new power, the Babylonians, who were known to Jeremiah and his community as "the foe from the North." With the fall of Assyria, the small country of Judah, which had been in the grips of Assyrian control, was liberated but soon forced to submit first to Egypt and then to Babylon.

Material from biblical accounts and historical documents provides evidence that prior to the collapse of Judah, its political leaders, particularly several of its kings, were corrupt, and many of its religious leaders, specifically from among its priests and prophets, were unfaithful to their vocation. Even though King Josiah, who reigned from 640–609 B.C.E., led a thorough reform that renewed the Mosaic covenant and destroyed all high places of idolatrous worship, this religious focus did not persist after Josiah's death. Many of the Judahite people again took up the worship of other gods and forgot God, covenant, and Torah, causing internal strife. The gradual political, religious, and social turmoil of the country led to its eventual downfall, but not without forewarning and persistent pleas for reform from Jeremiah, God's servant and God's prophet.

Remarkably, Jeremiah survived the Babylonian invasion; but he witnessed the collapse of a kingdom, the demise of a city, the destruction of the temple, and the exile of many of his people. The book of Jeremiah reflects all of these events and reverberates with warnings of doom and promises of hope.

The book of Jeremiah lacks a logical sequence of chronological events. This is due in part, perhaps, to the fact that editors of the final canonical text had several different kinds of collections of varied materials that they had to sort into collections and then weave together. Material included biographical information about Jeremiah; Jeremiah's sermons; historical accounts of Judah's final days; prophecies against kings, false and corrupted prophets, foreign countries; and oracles concerning a new covenant. The book can be divided into four distinct parts: Prologue and Jeremiah's Prophetic Call (1), Sermons of Jeremiah (2–25), a Series of Narratives (26–45) into which is embedded a Message of Hope (30–33), and Prophecies against Foreign Countries (46–51), which conclude with a Review of Jerusalem's Destruction (52). There are four basic types of literary material found throughout the book of Jeremiah: poetic oracles, prosaic narratives, sayings, and discourses.

Some of the material has been attributed to Jeremiah himself, while other material is associated with Baruch, who was supposedly Jeremiah's friend and secretary. Other material has been identified as later additions. In addition to the character of God, the character Jeremiah takes a lead role in the book and deals with several issues of his day, namely, true and false prophecy, transgression and repentance, faith and hope in God, and the vision of a new covenant, etc. Perhaps no other prophet and no other biblical character in the Old Testament is as straightforward and as direct with both God and people as was Jeremiah, a light to the peoples and a herald of both doom and hope. Central to his personal lamentations and sermons is the image of the heart, the place from which Jeremiah responds to both his God and his people with passion and certainty.

This chapter explores selected passages from various chapters of the book of Jeremiah that fit with the theme of "power and domination" in an effort to bring to light a variety of hermeneutical issues, many of which have already been noted in the texts of Amos and Micah.

Jeremiah 2:14-19, 20-28, 29-37

"Now I am bringing you to judgment for saying, 'I have not sinned.'" (2:35)

Verses 14-19, 20-28, and 29-37 are part of a divine prophecy (2:1—3:5). In these selected verses, readers see Judah powerless before foreign kingdoms and God. This is a condition that Israel has brought upon itself because of its wickedness and apostasy (vv 14-19). Images from the natural world describe

Judah's ravaged state (v 15) and are followed by words of harsh indictment with warnings of severe chastisement (vv 20-37). Amid the image of Judah's powerlessness, images of power come to the fore, making for a troubling scenario with a disturbing theological message.

Rich in metaphor, imagery, and rhetorical questions, vv 14-19 portray God challenging Judah for the choices it has made, specifically, its political alliance with Egypt and Assyria (v 18) and the worship of other gods (v 19). In v 14, God confronts with three rhetorical questions. The first two questions pertain to Judah's actual identity as a freed people; the third question pertains to Judah's current state of oppression, a situation that seems incongruous with their identity as a people. In v 15 an animal from the natural world is used metaphorically for Judah's enemies—the Babylonians, with an implied reference to the Assyrians. Past tenses are the tenses of vision that communicate an event in the future as if it has already happened. Hence, the "lions" refer to the Babylonians[1] with past references to the Assyrians. Verse 15 describes the devastation done by Judah's enemies to its land and cities. The reason for all this is that Judah has forsaken God and the exclusivity of that relationship. Apostate Judah has broken covenant, a choice that incites God to anger and judgment (vv 20-37).

These six verses portray Judah metaphorically as a male (vv 14-15); this is an unusual portrayal, since Judah is often and typically engendered as a female. A lion, a creature from the natural world with whom Judah was familiar, serves as a second metaphor. The male lion, known to dominate the animal world, fits the idea of the enemy Babylonian army that eventually does take Judah by force. The lion metaphor can also suggest to readers, however, that in the ancient world power—in this case, power used for destruction—rested in the male species. Judah's land and cities are devastated. Power associated with dominance in relation to the male species continues to create tension today. Viewed in a contemporary setting, the text favors one gender over another with respect to power, and this image does not help to transform attitudes, cultures, or genders from patterns of domination to relationships of mutuality.

Furthermore, Judah is overpowered by its enemies on account of its political alliances and its poor relationship with its God. The land and the cities suffer. The land is devastated by an enemy people, which according to the text is the result of a lack of proper relationship with God. Historically, the Babylonians did ravage Judah; the prophets, writers, and editors of the biblical text seem to declare Judah's defeat as punishment for its apostasy, which was tied to problematic political alliances and all sorts of injustices.

The text seems to create a twofold problem. First, an empire devastates Judah, and indirectly God has a part in this, even though God states that Judah brought the devastation on itself through apostasy (v 17). Second, the text focuses on Judah's land and cities as the recipients of the devastation. Here, land would include the natural world as well as its inhabitants. The Judahites and their land suffer: (1) because of the wickedness on the part of some of their own (v 19; see also v 13), although the text makes it seem all-inclusive; (2) because of the overpowering military invasion of other peoples, and (3) because they did not remain faithful to their God who ceased, as it seems, to protect them and their land.

It seems, then, that one can deduce from the text that God's nonassertive use of power is the indirect cause of the suffering of part of the natural world and a particular group of people; God's nonassertive action allows for another power to emerge to set right and fulfill a theological agenda: that "it is evil and bitter for you to forsake the LORD your God" (v 19). In summary, the text describes interlocking points of power with the natural world's land as a victim of power and domination in the presence of a God who seems somewhat uninterested.

In vv 20-28, God, in a monologue that quotes Judah, indicts the Judahites for their apostate behavior. As in vv 14-19, vv 20-28 present multiple images of power and domination. These verses also contain metaphorical language that evokes images of power.

The first image of power is a vision of a very powerful God in relation to a people who have decided to assert themselves and go their own way instead of walking in God's ways. Throughout vv 20-28, God is the speaker; Judah is the silent partner. God makes a case and also gives a rebuttal. Thus, Judah does not have the power to speak, and readers see that Judah's thoughts are expressed only through God and God's words. One could argue that this is a portrait of God revealing to the prophet Jeremiah the offenses of Judah that he, in turn, proclaims to the people. Thus, knowledge is "being given" to the prophet and to Judah by a seemingly "all-knowing" God. But the fact remains that no real dialogue transpires between God and Judah or between God and the prophet for that matter, as it does between God and Moses (Exod 33:12-23) and between God and Jeremiah earlier (Jer 1:4-10).

The text seems to suggest that in the face of transgression against the Divine, the transgressor is to be "seen and not heard," and that power of speech belongs to God, the accuser and victim of the broken relationship, and not to the transgressor and accused. Of further note is the fact that questions addressed to Judah directly (see v 21) go unanswered; this situation is quite different from what one sees in Genesis, in which Adam, Eve, and Cain are confronted by God and, in spite of their transgressions, are given the freedom to respond (Gen 3:8-13; 4:9-16, respectively). Clearly, the text portrays Judah as belligerent toward God in spite of God's patience and goodness (vv 20-21), and yet one needs to ask: Why do Judah's actions warrant no direct conversation with God, not even through the prophet? Is it because Judah is not persistent enough? Or is it because God is portrayed as the dominant one in the relationship? The transgressor Judah shall be shamed just as a thief, when caught, is shamed (cf. 2:26).

In Jer 2:20-28, God's voice dominates the scene and foreshadows God's dominance over Israel (2:35). What does this text suggest to the one who goes astray today? Is the picture consistent with the God of Genesis 3 and the God of Exodus 4? What does this text say about God and one's interpretation of God and God's ways?

Verses 26-28 declare that the God of Judah is much more powerful than any other god who has no power to liberate or to save. Thus, Judah's God is portrayed as one who has power over all other gods. For contemporary readers, the dilemma continues to be, "Who is the God of Judah?" and "To what extent is the God of Judah as revealed by the prophets a reflection of particular theological constructs, social influences, and cultural mores?" In vv 20-28, then, one sees a hierarchy of power: God is more powerful than all other gods and more powerful than a transgressor.

The natural world and gender-specific images used in vv 20-28 have the potential to evoke the imagination of the text's listeners while impressing powerful images on their minds. The images of Judah (1) as an animal breaking from its yoke (v 20), (2) as a "restive young camel interlacing her tracks," (3) as a wild ass at home in the wilderness in heat sniffing the wind "without anyone being able to restrain her lust," and (4) as a choice vine turned wild all depict vividly Israel's ruthlessness. Perhaps, though, the most offensive images portray Israel as one sprawled out under every green tree, playing the whore, and as the female wild ass in heat whose lust cannot be restrained. Both images make derogatory assertions that admit of a gender bias on the part of the text's writers and/or later editors. Whereas all metaphors and images have the potential power to awaken and condition one's imagination, some metaphors reflect the perverse or biased attitudes of some people in a particular culture at a particular point in time.

The tone and message of indictment in vv 20-28 continue in vv 29-37 and conclude with an image of God passing judgment upon Judah (vv 35-37). God, through the prophet, is the speaker of this passage. Words of indictment against Judah begin in v 29 and conclude in v 35a. In these verses, one is given a rather distasteful image of God and a repulsive image of Judah that is offensive and gender-biased. In vv 29-32, God is self-vindictive, angry, punitive, violent, and verbally powerful, as question after question and image after image is delivered to Israel in order to reinforce that God is faithful and Judah is not.

The image of God striking down Judah's children (v 30) is startling because it gives the impression that God uses violence as a means of chastisement. The text seems to legitimates the use of violence as a means of correction; it clearly reflects a social situation where violence, as a means of chastisement, was sanctioned. For those readers who are victims of domestic abuse, particularly children, this text is not good news.

Equally offensive are the female references (vv 32-35). A "girl" forgetting her ornaments and a "bride" forgetting her attire refer to Judah forgetting God (vv 32-33). Couched in the rhetorical questions, the implied answer is, "No"; neither would a girl forget her ornaments nor a bride her attire, yet Judah does forget its God. The seriousness of apostasy is played off a picture of female frivolity. Verses 33-35a portray Israel as a "hussie," one who was so promiscuous that she even taught "wicked women" her ways. The metaphor continues in v 34 where "the lifeblood of the innocent poor" is said to have marred her skirts. There is no doubt that some members of Israel are guilty of oppressing the poor. Furthermore, if this is not enough, Judah is also portrayed as a dishonest woman who is blind to her own faults (v 35).

The metaphorical language in vv 32-35a presents several difficulties. The text's use of such gender-specific metaphors and descriptions paints a negative and cruel image of women as a gender that is fickle, unfaithful, promiscuous, and glibly dishonest. Moreover, the fact that, according to the text, such an image is pronounced and its referents condemned by God complicates the initial problem even more. Since there are no such male metaphors to balance this one, what might the text be inferring about women from God's perspective? Furthermore, if such images as the whore (see 2:20, 33) are used as a rhetorical device "to expose men's sins,"[2] this is all the more offensive to women insofar as it sets up a negative image of innocent women to counteract the crimes and brashness of malicious men. Women are thus used for the purpose of buoying up and setting straight men who are guilty of offensive crimes. Moreover, Judah is portrayed as one who uses its power for domination. Its own sword devours its own prophets (v 30) and has the blood of the innocent poor on its "skirts." In this regard, the condemnation by God through the prophet is deserved.

In vv 35b-37, God is portrayed as one who asserts power over Judah. God is going to bring Judah to divine judgment that will result in punitive chastisement: Judah will be shamed by Egypt and Assyria and will be exiled. Historically, Judah is brought to its knees and its people exiled. This historical reality gives additional credence to the theological intent of the text, making it possible to see how historical realities shaped and influenced the text's theological views.

In summary, amid shifting metaphors that portray Judah as both male (vv14-16) and female (vv 33-37), vv 14-19, 20-28, and 29-37 present a composite picture of the divine disdain and disgust that are deserved by a once-favored people. The central point of these passages is theological: when Judah forsakes God and God's ways, Judah becomes vulnerable to international powers that devastate it (v 15). The text admits of no divine defense on behalf of Judah because it has turned away from its God. Hence, the texts suggest that: (1) ultimately, God is "in control" of people's lives and destiny, (2) sin leads to punitive suffering, and (3) the power of foreign empires is secondary to God's power that God uses both actively and passively to devastate or allow devastation to occur.

What, then, does one make of a theology that seems to say, "If you are good and remain in right relationship with God and others, then God will reward you; if not, then God will punish you"? It seems that the biblical writers and editors of these Jeremiah passages ascribe enormous power and control to God. For those who are righteous, that could be a hopeful message, but for those who are guilty of sin, it could lead them further and further away from God out of fear. It is one thing to atone for one's transgressions; it is quite another to be "punished" for them.

Finally, Jer 2:14-19, 20-28, 29-37 speak of power, control, and punishment. The texts portray God as one who has power to act passively or aggressively in a way that can be devastating to people and the natural world. The text also suggests a "hierarchy" power. Metaphorical language can facilitate the exercise of power, domination, and control over others. It can either create new and positive attitudes or perpetuate old ones that admit of and reinforce biases still present today. Jeremiah 2:14-37 suggests to readers today that they cannot read biblical texts without careful critique of the texts' historical, literary, and theological limitations.

Jeremiah 5:12-17, 18-31

"They shall eat up your harvest and your food;
they shall eat up your sons and your daughters." (5:17)

Verses 12-17 are both the continuation of an indictment speech (vv 12-13) and the beginning of a divine judgment speech (vv 14-17). The passage draws clear connections between power and domination with respect to Judah and itself, Judah and God, and Judah and the Babylonians.

In v 12, arrogance overpowers the Judahites. Confident in God's love for the people, some of Judah's prophets have smugly proclaimed that God will not do anything to harm the people despite their injustices (vv 1-11). Such religious arrogance blinds some prophets to the reality that God does not tolerate injustice. Indeed, the people will suffer (vv 15-17), an experience that the text attributes to the work of God (v 15).

In v 13, God condemns some prophets for having spoken falsely (see v 12). Ironically, what the Judahites do not realize is that the prophet Jeremiah, who is addressing them, is speaking a word that will be fulfilled. The text portrays

God as one who empowers this prophet, but not with a message the Judahites wish to hear (v 14b). Furthermore, the text describes God as sending the enemies of the North, the Babylonians, against Judah. Historically, Jeremiah predicted this event and then watched it happen. Thus, in vv 12-13 the text makes clear to readers that arrogance can be an overpowering vice that can lead to a false sense of confidence, which, in turn, can lead to unpleasant consequences that come as a surprise.

The traditional prophetic messenger formula in v 14 opens the divine judgment speech in vv 14-17. In this speech, God is going to send a foreign empire against the Judahites to devour their food and children and to destroy the cities in which they "trust." In relation to these verses, three theological points need to be addressed.

First, readers are given a clear understanding that God will not tolerate injustice, apostasy (see, for example, v 6) or falsehood, arrogance, or smug overconfidence on the part of religious leaders who should be calling the people to right relationship with God and to a life of justice and righteousness. The text stresses integrity, particularly when it comes to religious leadership within a community.

Second, readers are given the impression that God has absolute power and control over foreign kingdoms and can use other countries to accomplish a specific divine goal; in this case, the Babylonians will punish Judah violently for its apostasy, transgressions, complacency, and smug attitude. Thus, God is portrayed using power to manipulate, control, and inflict violent punishment. Although the punishment should be aimed at the perpetrators of injustice, the text shows that children and the natural world are to be ravaged by the infiltration of the Babylonians into Judah. The text suggests two questions: (1) Is God someone who causes suffering to the land and children as a way of "getting to" those responsible for injustice? and (2) Is this truly the way God uses power: to control, manipulate, and destroy, all in the name of divine "justice" and "righteousness"? Historically, what is foretold in vv 12-17 does come to pass. Judah is ravished, and many of its inhabitants are exiled. Judah is overpowered by another country that is depicted as being under the power and control of God, who is proclaimed by the text as the ruler of peoples and the lord of history. The picture of God that the text offers appears to be derived from the author's interpretation of historical events in light of specific social and cultural realities and in the context of a particular theological construct, namely, that God blesses those who are faithful and obedient and curses those who are unfaithful and disobedient (see, for example, Deuteronomy 28).

Third, the reference to the destruction of the fortified cities in which the people trust is another assertion of power that has theological overtones. The text suggests that the people are to trust in the strength and power of God and not in things that seem to offer security.[3] Thus, God has the enemy destroy the cities along with the children, animals, and foodstuffs that the natural world produces. The text prompts further questions: (1) Is this a way to teach people a lesson or is it a picture of the arrogant assertion of divine power? and (2) Is this an adequate portrait of God, or does it merely depict a community's, author's, and/or editor's need for an all-powerful God who could insure monotheism, justice, and righteousness with respect to worship and communal life? In a world of religious pluralism that strives toward nonviolence, Jer 5:12-17 seems to legitimate religious triumphalism and justify the inordinate use of power to bring about truth, justice, and righteousness. The text appears to legitimate, unfortunately, manipulation and violence, two ways to use power that continue to be sorely in need of transformation.

Written in prose, vv 18-19 provide a bit of comfort to a community of people that has just been informed of its impending devastation at the hands of a God-sent enemy (vv 14-17). Verse 18 clarifies that the coming devastation will not be total (cf. 4:27; 5:10). In v 19 God, after posing a question, reiterates the reason for the coming disaster: the people have forsaken their God.

Verses 20-31 comprise a prophecy of judgment addressed to the people of Judah. God calls them to attention: "Hear this. . . ." Verse 22 begins with two rhetorical questions in which God confronts the people about their nonchalant attitude: They are not fearful of God, nor do they tremble before God. God then reminds the people of God's creating and limiting powers: placing the sand as a boundary for the sea.

In vv 23-28, 30-31, God lists the people's shortcomings and transgressions: they have a stubborn and rebellious heart (v 23); they are not God-fearing (v 24); they steal from others and have become great, rich, and complacent through their exploitation (vv 26-27); their wicked deeds are unending; they judge unfairly the orphan and the needy, who are the most vulnerable in society (v 28). Even their religious leaders are corrupt: prophets prophesy falsely, and the priests rule as the prophets direct (v 31). Is it any wonder, then, that God determines to punish them (v 29)?

In these verses, readers are given a variety of expressions of power. God is portrayed as one who has creative powers and who expects a response of "fear and trembling" from people. This desired response suggests that God is powerful and great. Furthermore, power is linked to domination and oppression. The impression given by the text is that people are subservient to God. In these verses, readers see the expression of righteous anger on the part of God who is aggravated by a people's lack of fidelity. The covenant relationship between God and God's people has been broken, and the outcome is social and religious chaos—especially hurtful to the most vulnerable and those of little or no status in the community—the orphans and the needy. Religious arrogance has led to the abuse of power, which in turn has led to further religious corruption, particularly among the prophets and the priests. As certain members of the community take advantage of others, the priests act as the puppets of those prophets who have corrupted their prophetic office and have misused their God-given power. Given these circumstances, it would be a further injustice if God did not confront such social and religious injustices and then do something to rectify the situation. While readers see in the text the powerful voice of God confronting such injustices, what cannot be ignored is the way the text portrays God as dealing with the injustices (i.e., vv 15-17).

In summary, vv 12-17 and 18-31 suggest to readers that the power of injustice, whereby some people use power to oppress and dominate others, is an egregious and unacceptable offense that demands justice, especially divine justice. The content of vv 12-17 and 18-31, however, provokes several questions. Must divine justice be expressed through violence? The text would have one think so. Or does the text mirror an inevitable historical situation of further human aggression and power over a weakening group of people—namely, the Babylonians over Judah—a situation that has been attributed to God by the text's writers and later editors? Hermeneutically, just as the power plays within the text need to be examined closely, so do the theological and ideological attitudes of the world behind the text and the world of the text. These attitudes have helped to shape the text into its present form. Were all powerful people in Israel corrupt? Were all prophets false and all priests puppets? The universalizing nature of the prophetic discourse would have one think so. Yet the universalizing attitude embedded in a text cannot go ignored because prophetic texts have the power to influence a reader's imagination and thoughts toward accentuating the depravity of the human condition and to continue to be labeled "the word of God."

Jeremiah 6:13-15

"For from the least to the greatest of them,
everyone is greedy for unjust gain." (6:13)

Jeremiah 6:13-15, part of a prophecy of judgment (vv 9-15), cites the social and religious corruption of the Judahites (vv 13-15a) and God's intent to punish them severely (v 15b). W. Brueggemann points out that "Jeremiah 6:13-15a makes the general indictment of v 10 more specific. All persons, but especially the religious leaders, are indicted for their unprincipled economics."[4]

These three verses bring to the fore several points for hermeneutical consideration. With respect to power, the text shows that the Judahites have used whatever power they had for self-serving purposes that led to widespread injustice toward one another. R. P. Carroll points out that the phrase "unjust gain" "hints at violence and plunder but may in this rhetorical setting simply refer to the eager pursuit of profit at the expense of others, cf. 22.17."[5] Whatever the case, it is obvious from the text that the inordinate use of power is connected with domination and oppression—injustice.

In v 15b God declares that the people will suffer divine retribution—God will overthrow them—because of the malicious deeds they have done. Divine power is asserted over human power in order for justice to overcome injustice. Historically, the southern kingdom of Judah was overthrown when taken by force and demolished by the Babylonians. The phrase "at the time I punish them, they shall be overthrown, says the LORD" harks back to Jer 5:15-17. The punishment will be massive; all will suffer to some degree. Divine power asserted to put in check abusive human power is a point in the text that calls for celebration. On the other hand, that this assertion of divine power takes the form of violence (a point that seems to be condoned by the text and that goes without comment by later commentators on the text[6]) calls for hermeneutical reflection on the just use of power.

Specifically, Jer 6:13-15 proclaims to readers that the power of justice is to prevail over the power of injustice. Yet the image of God about to "overthrow" the people, and the historical reality that actualizes this image, also show readers that violence begets violence, but when done for a divine purpose and the common good, it is acceptable. On the contrary, without the understanding of biblical metaphor that emerges from the social and cultural realities of the ancient world, readers could be left with a distorted view of God. This view could then color one's theological understanding to the extent that violence for the sake of justice becomes theologically acceptable. In the context of contemporary reality, is not the point that violence will remedy injustice a rather superficial solution to the overbearing problem of aggression that existed in the ancient world and continues to exist today?

Finally, the merism of v 13, "from the least to the greatest of them," followed by the accusation that "everyone is greedy for unjust gain," which is then followed by a divine judgment to be inflicted upon all, gives the reader a picture of generalized punishment. This view put forth by the text prompts further questions: Was injustice and corruption as pervasive and all-consuming as the text reveals, or is this an exaggerated image derived from the historical event of the complete demise of Judah? And is not the notion of "corporate punishment" that one hears in the text evidence of an underlying deuteronomistic theology of retribution that speaks of corporate responsibility and corporate punishment? If this is so, then readers of Jer 6:13-15 need to grapple with this and recognize that such a theological framework has shaped the writers and editors of the text and may continue to shape some people's theology today. If such a theological principle goes without critique, then the religious praxis and preaching that follows from one's reading could engender more social and theological problems for the human community that continues to struggle with injustices today.

Jeremiah 8:4-12, 13-17
"Therefore I will give their wives to others
and their fields to conquerors." (8:10)

Jeremiah 8:4-12 is a prophecy of judgment. Verses 4-9 are an indictment; v 10a cites the impending divine punishment; and vv 10b-12 give the reason for the punishment in words identical to 6:13-15. Images from the natural world are used to point up the foolishness of the Judahites (vv 6-7). In v 7, the birds seem to have more sense than the people. From the text, it seems that the Judahites have become overpowered by their own stubbornness: they hold fast to deceit; they refuse to return to God; they do not repent of their wickedness; and they stay their own course (vv 5-6), an action that eventually leads to their defeat and that of their country. In v 8, the wise are condemned and will receive their just desserts. An invading enemy will capture them. Readers also see that their wives will bear the consequences along with their land as it is turned over to conquerors. Presumably, the "wise" refer to the male Judahites given the fact that in the culture of the ancient world, men, for the most part, were given some sort of training and education. What becomes disconcerting is that the women—the wives of the wise men—are made to suffer on account of their husbands' deeds (vv 8-9). Furthermore, the land will be ravished by conquerors on account of the wickedness of the wise.

Readers see how certain vices can overpower one's choices and distort one's ability to reflect on one's actions and how the misuse of one's power can lead to the misuse of another's power; this could, in turn, result in undeserved suffering for parties not directly involved in the situation. God meting out chastisement, not only to the wise ones, but also to their wives and their land is indicative of ancient Israel and Judah's collectivist thinking.

The images and metaphors in Jer 8:13-17 speak of power that causes oppression and defeat. The entire passage envisions the invasion by the enemy empire that is soon to overtake the Israelites, leaving them powerless in the face of their enemies and their God. Verse 13 uses imagery from the natural world to portray God's expressing remorse over the Judahites' lack of responsiveness to positive divine initiatives. In vv 14-15 the beleaguered Judahites speak out, fully conscious of their ill-fate that they attribute to God because of their sinfulness. Readers can see in these verses a glimmer of the theological beliefs of the Judahite community that were, I suggest, beliefs similar to the writers' and editors' beliefs and operative when they shaped the text into its present form.

The main metaphor in vv 16-17 is a military one cloaked in natural world imagery. These verses envision the actual invasion of Judah; images of being overpowered by the enemy empire shift from "a massive rush of power to slow, creeping terror."[7] All of this is because of the Judahites' choice to forsake God and God's decision to teach them that it is "evil and bitter" to forsake the Lord their God (Jer 2:19). Whether or not one sees God as a jilted lover, a betrayed husband, or a father disobeyed, the text portrays God as a "get-even" God trying to bring the Judahites back to the fold. The gruesome images in this text raise the question, Is punitive violent action the best way to accomplish the task, even when violent injustices accompany betrayal? The text would have readers think so if critical thought and theological discernment are not part of one's reading and interpretative process.

Jeremiah 10:23-25

"Pour out your wrath on the foreigners that do not know you,
and on the peoples that do not call on your name." (10:25)

Verses 23-25 are a reflective prayer that shows the power of the prophet, the power of God, the power of other kingdoms, and the perceived powerlessness of human beings in general and the Judahites in particular. The prophet Jeremiah speaks on behalf of himself and his community and begs God to act against the nations that are about to treat the Judahites so horribly.

In v 23 Jeremiah acknowledges the lack of power that human beings have over their own actions, lives, and destinies. God, who is Lord of creation and Lord of history, directs people in the way they should walk, even though the Judahite community has failed to realize this. In v 24, Jeremiah pleads with God to correct him—but not with divine anger, for that would bring him to nothing. Here, Jeremiah, on behalf of the community, both acknowledges the need for divine reproof and also the power of God's wrath that can completely destroy human beings. In v 25, Jeremiah petitions God to use divine power to stop the powerful force of those countries that have devastated the Judahite people and their land. Reduced to a state of powerlessness, the only power that remains within the community is that which its prophets possess—the power to plead with God for mercy. Jeremiah's prayer in its entirety acknowledges that, ultimately, all power belongs to God; ironically, Jeremiah does not realize that the power of God rests within his spirit and that with God he has the power to help shape the future of his community.

In these verses, readers see that, even though God has power over humankind and events in history, human beings, through the example of

Jeremiah, also have a voice in the shaping of human life and its history. The text portrays a hierarchical image of God. It speaks of a God who controls and manipulates life from afar without interacting with it in the midst of its unfolding events. This is a different image from that of God in the Exodus texts where God journeys with the people in a cloud by day and a pillar of fire by night (Exod 14:21). And yet common to the Exodus tradition and Jer 10:23-25 is the person of the prophets, Moses and Jeremiah respectively, whom God empowered (see Exod 3:11-12; 4:1-9; and Jer 1:1-19) to do God's work, which is essentially the work of liberation (Exod 3:7-10) and restoration (Jer 1:10).

From a hermeneutical perspective, Jer 10:23-25 presents a multilayered picture of human and divine power that reflects certain cultural, social, and theological influences germane to its day while offering a challenge to contemporary readers: like Jeremiah, human beings have the power to help shape the future direction of life on the planet. Riddled with pockets of warfare, terrorism, and escalating ecological disasters, creation is being devoured by human sinfulness that is the work of human beings and not the doing of God. Would that people everywhere would rise up, like Jeremiah, to seek the God of justice whose power lies not in wrath but in transformative love that is present in the midst of life, working for the good of all creation despite all obstacles.

Jeremiah 14:1-9, 13-16

"The wild asses stand on the bare heights,
they pant for air like jackals;
their eyes fail because of no herbage." (14:6)

This divine proclamation is a lament. In vv 1-6, Jeremiah sketches a picture of what life will be like when the drought strikes Judah. It will be a time of great distress for farmers as well as nobles, for the animals as well as the land. Human beings and the natural world both will suffer. One of the curses for disobedience that God is said to have threatened the Judahites with is a drought (Deut 28:22). It seems that the warning is now being fulfilled. The text presents the drought as a result of God's judgment on the Judahite community.

Images of powerlessness abound in this passage. The nobles, with all their power, and their servants, can do nothing about the lack of rain except be ashamed and dismayed, mourn and cover their heads. W. Holladay suggests that "the shame of the nobles arises from their sense of weakness, from the withdrawal of Yahweh's blessing, from the devastation which the disaster works on the community."[8] The ground cracks; the land is unable to produce grass or herbage. The doe can do nothing else but abandon her newborn fawn—there is no food. The wild asses stand on bare heights and pant in the heat—there is no herbage, no shade, no water. Even the farmers can offer no help to remedy the situation. They too are dismayed and cover their heads.

Readers receive an impression of how overpowering a natural disaster, such as a drought, can be for people, the land, and animals, rendering them all powerless in the face of such a deprivation. There is nothing anyone can do. As an act of divine judgment against the Judahites' wickedness, the drought exemplifies the power of God over creation, over injustice, and over humankind. Here, God has used divine power to afflict the human beings with suffering. They have no water. When the ground no longer produces food, then the animals will die from starvation and lack of water. When the earth's fruits and the animals all perish, then not only the water supply but also the food supply will be cut off from human beings, and they too will die. This has all come about because of the Judahites' apostasy and wickedness. The passage gives clear testimony to the fact that God will not tolerate being forsaken or wickedness; injustice will not prevail.

The situation of the drought raises several hermeneutical points. While the punitive chastisement of human beings by God is bad, what is worse is that nonhuman forms in the natural world are made to suffer and die on account of human sinfulness. What kind of a God strikes at the land and animals in order to make people suffer? Is this action justice for all concerned? Are the innocent to be punished with the guilty?

Droughts were common experiences in the ancient Near Eastern world. They were a natural occurrence in a climate as hot and dry as that of Judah. They often brought havoc to humans, animals, and plants. With one eye on the text and the other on the social, historical, cultural, and theological milieu of ancient Judah, one wonders whether, when Jer 14:1-6 was being shaped into its present form, certain ecological as well as distinct theological traditions and beliefs did not affect the writers and later editors. Thus, because of tradition and various social realities, disaster occurring in the midst of human depravity would be attributed to God as a sign of God's judgment when, in reality, it may not have been the work of God at all.

Readers can draw a connection between Jer 14:1-6 and today's global situation. Although the drought is a natural disaster that, in reality, is not caused by God in response to human sinfulness, creation suffers today from ecological disasters precisely because of a lack of concern for the planet and its resources by some human beings. Ecological devastation cries out for ecojustice.

Verses 7-9 make clear that the drought is tied to divine judgment and the Judahites' wickedness. Jeremiah calls on God to act on the suffering Judahites' behalf. One sees that God has become like a stranger to Judah. With power,

Jeremiah acts on behalf of his community, confronting God, whom he knows has the power to intervene in the midst of this horrific experience. Jeremiah pleads with God not to forsake the people—even though the people have forsaken God. God's power has been exerted to cause oppression; now the prophet wants God to use divine power to alleviate the Judahites' suffering.

The passage leaves the reader with the impression that with God rests all power. This impression is quite problematic since God is envisioned throughout the book of Jeremiah as a male deity. Power then becomes gender-specific and engenders patriarchy.

In a dialogue between God and Jeremiah, the prophet complains to God about false prophets (vv 13-16). God, in turn, tells Jeremiah to inform those prophets that death will come to them and their families because of their wickedness. Here one sees that in the society of their times, the Judahite prophets had considerable power over the community. They were the community's religious leaders, and ultimately, people believed in them and their prophecies without question or doubt. In v 13, the prophets proclaim false prophecies that are leading the people into further deception. Thus, the text points out that religious leaders have the potential power for leading people astray.

Prophets are people empowered by God to reveal God's presence and to act on behalf of justice, righteousness, and loving-kindness. The are sent by God. The prophets in vv 13-16, however, are false ones "not sent" by God. They have usurped religious power and distorted it, which, according to the text, aggravates God to the point that God vows to use divine power to do away with them. God will pour out "their wickedness upon them" (v16), which will result in their deaths.

In Jer 14:13-16, readers see how the abuse of religious power can have adverse effects on a believing community and on those themselves who misuse their gift. The image of a God who wields and uses power for the purpose of destroying those responsible for religious injustices is an image fraught with theological problems, many of which have been discussed above. The text portrays God as acting on behalf of the vulnerable in society but at the expense of others' lives.

Jeremiah 22:13-19

"But your eyes and heart are only on your dishonest gain,
for shedding innocent blood,
and for practicing oppression and violence." (22:17)

Jeremiah 22:13-19 contains a prophecy directed against Jehoiakim.[9] Verses 13-17 comprise a woe proclamation, a form used most frequently in the prophets to denounce social injustices done to the community. Here,

Jehoiakim is guilty of building large houses without paying his laborers (vv 13-14). He is also accused of shedding innocent blood and practicing oppression and violence (v 17). Jeremiah compares Jehoiakim to his father, Josiah, who was a king who practiced justice and righteousness, especially on behalf of the poor and the needy (vv 15-16). The most dramatic statement appears in v 15a, in which Jeremiah cuts to the heart of what constitutes leadership and appropriate power, asking Jehoiakim, "Are you a king/because you compete in cedar?"

Readers see the blatant abuse of power by leadership. Clearly, Jehoiakim has used his power to dominate, control, and oppress others for his own self-interests. In the context of the contemporary world, Jer 22:13-17 reminds readers that some people in leadership positions continue to act like Jehoiakim, and that unjust situations caused by the abuse and misuse of power cannot go unchecked.

Verses 18-19 comprise a prophecy of judgment. God makes known Jehoiakim's lot because of his wickedness: he shall die and be buried unceremoniously, the worst insult for a king. The text has "dethroned" a king. His abuse of power is unacceptable and cannot be legitimated. On a more historical and somber note, Carroll points out that Jehoiakim died a "routine death" with a "routine royal burial" (cf. 2 Kgs 24:6), and concludes that this fact does not detract "from the powerful assertion of this poem that kings as agents of injustice are sure to be dismissed as ignoble, irrelevant, and not grieved or remembered."[10]

For those readers who attest to the sacredness of all creation, the description of the donkey's burial in v 19 could be troublesome. The comparison may work well when the focus is on Jehoiakim, but it does not work well when one considers how the animal is to be buried. No care is given to the animal; it is simply dragged and thrown out beyond the gates of Jerusalem, presumably so that it could become food for the wild animals. While this act may conform to "the laws of nature," it is still a stark image.

Jeremiah 34:8-22

"Each of you took back your male and female slaves,
whom you had set free according to their desire,
and you brought them again into subjection to be your slaves." (34:16)

Jeremiah 34:8-22 can be divided into three parts: vv 8-11, a description of a proclamation of liberty; vv 12-16, a prophecy of judgment; and vv 17-22, a proclamation of impending divine chastisement. In vv 8-11, Jeremiah recalls how King Zedekiah had made a covenant with the people on behalf of the slaves, namely, that they should be set free and not enslaved again. He next describes how the people broke the covenant and enslaved their slaves again. In vv 12-16 God describes the Exodus events, which serve as a reminder to the people that a covenant was made with their ancestors regarding slaves. The Judahites are now no better than their ancestors: both have broken the covenant, and the slaves are made to bear the brunt of the break; they are once more enslaved. Verses 17-22 describe what God will do to the people for having broken covenant. They are to endure a variety of punitive chastisements that will end in the complete chastisement of Judah (v 22).

Looking at vv 8-22 as a whole, one can see the liberating effects of power gone sour. A people once freed are again enslaved. Furthermore, the breaking of the covenant is not acceptable in the eyes of God who asserts power for woe over those who break covenant. In these verses, as elsewhere, God asserts power on behalf of the enslaved, but the outcome of such assertion is deadly. Chastisement is severely punitive.

Jeremiah 46–51

"The people of Israel are oppressed, and so too the people of Judah;
all their captors have held them fast and refuse to let them go." (50:33)

Chapters 46–51 are a series of prophecies against foreign countries. The prophecies depict Jeremiah as a prophet to the foreigners and proclaim God as the God of all peoples, who is responsible for their destinies. In these oracles one sees the universal breath of God's power, the sovereignty of God, and an emphasis on all nations having to worship and honor God's sovereignty. The texts also deliver the subtle message that God's laws have universal validity, and therefore, all nations are called to the practice of justice and righteousness. The prophecies are outlined as follows: 46:1-25, against Edom; 47:1-7, against Philistia; 48:1-47, against Moab; 49:1-6, against Ammon; 49:7-22, against Edom; 49:23-27, against Damascus; 49:28-33, against Kedar and Hazor; and 50:1—51:58, against Babylon. Given the great length and scope of these prophecies, only two are studied in this chapter: 49:23-27, against Damascus, and 49:28-33, against Kedar and Hazor. From these two prophecies, one can glean the central theme of all the prophecies with respect to God's sovereignty and power.

In 49:23-27, Damascus, a city northeast of the Sea of Galilee, provides a geographical reference that implies all of Syria.[11] The text gives readers a view of Damascus as feeble, panic-stricken, in anguish and sorrow, soon to experience even more distress. God will enkindle a fire at its wall that will destroy the strongholds of Ben-hadad.[12]

The prophecy against Kedar and Hazor[13] refers to a military invasion and the devastation that will result (49:28-33). Verses 28-29 address the enemies of Kedar who are called to attention and assigned a task. The inhabitants of Kedar, under siege, are urged to seek shelter and security in out-of-the-way places (v 30). Verses 31-33 describe what will become of Kedar. While King Nebuchadnezzar of Babylon seems to be overpowering Kedar's "enemy," the text indicates that God will bring Kedar to its knees. Kedar is an insignificant place; one wonders why God would pursue this group of people. R. B. Huey suggests that "perhaps the purpose for including these relatively insignificant peoples was to show that no one, however unimportant by our standards, would escape God's judgment."[14] This echoes an attitude heard in Jer 6:13 and 8:10 pertaining to the people of Judah: "from the least to the greatest. . . ." Now it applies to the other countries.

In summary, both poems offer an image of God's power and sovereignty. God is to be not only Judah's God, but also God of the other countries as well. No reason is given for either Damascus's or Kedar's destruction; one might speculate about the historical events behind these texts. While the "God of All Peoples" here uses divine power for destruction, an image fraught with problems, readers need to remember that elsewhere in the prophetic corpus, divine power is used to restore the countries one to another and all to the Divine (see, for example, Isa 2:1-4 and Mic 4:1-5).

Jeremiah in Context

The above passages from the book of Jeremiah all display a vivid and multi-layered picture of how power can be used to dominate, control, and oppress others. Such power tries to correct injustice on the one hand but causes it on the other. Moreover, the texts suggest that the use of power to oppress and dominate others is egregious and unacceptable. The texts raise several theological points for discussion and problems that need further unraveling. The image of a God who uses power punitively and violently "on behalf of justice" needs to be understood in the historical, social, and theological context of its day. Readers are challenged to understand that the texts themselves reflect the social realities and attitudes of their writers and editors. Despite how the selected texts present a disturbing portrait of God, one thing is certain: God does not tolerate injustice; it is confronted and dealt with. Finally, the texts proclaim a God not only of Judah but also of creation and of countries, a God who will in time bring all creation to salvation through a process of liberation and restoration.

4

Baruch and Lamentations

BARUCH AND LAMENTATIONS HAVE A COMMON historical setting: each one reflects a painful yet significant time in the life of the Judahite people—the Exile. The fall of Jerusalem, the destruction of the temple, the demise of the Southern Kingdom, and the deportation of so many people led to bewilderment and grief on the one hand and hope and encouragement on the other. Both texts reflect this mixture of sentiments; both capture the listener's and reader's imagination with their poetical, metaphorical expressions; and both raise questions about issues concerning power, control, and the image of God.

Baruch

Overview: A Historical, Literary, and Hermeneutical Interplay

A collection of many distinct pieces, the book of Baruch has as its backdrop both the fall of Jerusalem in 587 B.C.E. and the exile. Although it is not part of the Hebrew or Palestinian canon of sacred texts, Baruch is known to Catholics and Greek Orthodox as one of the seven deuterocanonical books and to Protestants as one of the apocryphal texts. Baruch belongs to the Diaspora Judahite people who, exiled from their homeland, settled, for the most part, in Egypt and Mesopotamia. The many historical references are not to be taken as history or facts based on history. Rather, they are references intended to capture the experience of exile, with its sense of separation, so that the Judahite people of the Diaspora might find a sense of strength and encouragement as well as comfort and hope.

The authorship of this book has been attributed to Baruch, Jeremiah's noted secretary, but, in fact, the actual author is unknown. The book can be divided into four main parts:

- an introduction followed by Baruch's confession and penitential prayer (1:1—3:8)
- a wisdom poem (3:9—4:4)
- a prophetic address that functions as a response to 1:1—3:8 (4:5—5:9)
- a letter of Jeremiah (6:1-73).

Both the first and fourth units are prose (narrative); the second and third, poetry. Among the themes that emerge from Baruch are monotheism, transgression, repentance, consolation, encouragement, and hope. Baruch 1:1—3:8 and 6:1-73 are written in a descriptive, reflective style, whereas 3:9—4:4 and 4:5—5:9 are written in a hortatory style characterized by a series of commands, often in direct address (for example, 4:5, 21, 30; and 5:5).

Hermeneutically, a few points need clarification. The Judahite people are referred to as "children" (see, for example, 4:21, 25, 27) despite the fact that, for the most part, the exiled community was comprised of adults. While such a term can be a term of endearment, it also admits of a certain hierarchy; the prophet is somehow over and above those being addressed and therefore in a more powerful position. God is portrayed in the text as sovereign, all-powerful, regal, kingly, compassionate, and just. God also, however, uses power to inflict certain chastisements on some of the Judahite community members (for example, 2:1-10). Baruch 3:9-19 identifies some of Israel's transgressions that resulted in the people's being exiled, including several that involved the abuse of power. The use of the term "Israel" (for example, 3:9, 24) in the corporate sense, as well as other related terms such as "my people" (4:5) and "my children" (for example, 4:19, 21, 27), assumes that all Israelites are guilty of some sort of transgression. Such a sweeping generalization is most likely inaccurate. Some of them were, perhaps, innocent.

Another point for discussion is the incidents of cannibalism. Among some of the exiles, hunger became so great that they even turned to eating their own children, who were the most vulnerable of human society.

The use of gender-specific metaphors and personifications for ancient cities, particularly Jerusalem, is both liberating and oppressive. Personified as a woman, Jerusalem speaks out about her miserable state. Even though the prophetic text allows its readers and listeners to hear the voice of a woman through the use of metaphor and personification, the truly liberating power rests not in the woman being empowered to give voice to her experience but in God, who is personified metaphorically as a male deity.

Finally, various passages in chapter 4 depict the ruthlessness of Israel's "enemy," one that was sent by God (4:15-16). Here the blatant use of oppressive power is perceived to be divinely sanctioned.

This segment of the chapter examines selected passages of the Baruch text in order to shed fuller light on the hermeneutical issues raised above. One sees both human and divine power used oppressively.

Baruch 2:1-10
"So the Lord carried out the threat." (2:1)

Baruch 2:1-10, part of the book's first main division (1:1—3:8), is a narrative that recalls from the exiled Judahites' perspective the suffering they endured on account of their transgressions. Following the words of a confession (1:15-22), whereby the exiled Judahites acknowledge their disobedience to God, their disregard for God's statutes, and their apostasy, is a description of divine retribution.

In vv 1-5, the Judahites attribute their former calamity, the fall of Jerusalem in 587 B.C.E. and the degradation of the entire country, to the fulfillment of a divine threat that had been spoken against them, specifically against the judges, the kings, and the rulers, and the people of Israel and Judah (v 1). Because of their disobedience and apostasy, many of the Israelites were forced to engage in cannibalism (v 3), and later they were made by God into an object of scorn and a desolation that God would "scatter" (v 4).[1]

In vv 6-10, members of the exiled Judahite community affirm what they understand to be God's just retribution. They sinned and therefore deserved to be chastised: "the Lord our God is in the right. . . ." In these verses there is also the admission that despite God's reprimands, they still have not had a change of heart. Hence, these verses highlight the people's stubbornness.

Baruch 2:1-10 raises several hermeneutical points. First, the text asserts that what God threatens to do, God does. Historically, Jerusalem was destroyed in 587 B.C.E., marking the fall of the Southern Kingdom, Judah. Prophets such as Micah, Ezekiel, and Jeremiah warned the Judahites about such a disaster. In this text, the promised divine threat has already come to pass.

The common theological question that emerges is: Was the demise of Jerusalem and Judah the direct result of God's plan, or was it an inevitable historical event that was given religious significance before and after it happened? I suggest that possibly it is the latter. Without question and critique, contemporary readers and believers could be left with the impression that God's justice is punitive and vindictive: "Obey me, follow my statutes, or die!"

In some societies and cultures in which capital punishment is operative or where the religious philosophical idea of "an eye for an eye and a tooth for a tooth" is prevalent, the text could serve as a divine sanction for violent human acts done, in the name of justice, to those who have committed injustices. Moreover, the notion of God sending in another country to overtake one that is guilty of injustice perpetrates an attitude that justifies aggression as a means of dealing with injustice. Such an attitude has resulted in behaviors that cause bloodshed, and these have even been labeled Holy Wars.

The vision and ways of God and God's implementation of justice need penetrating discernment, especially in light of the prophetic eschatological vision that speaks of a time when nation will not lift up sword against nation and will learn war no more.[2] Then, perhaps, the statement in the text, "The LORD our God is in the right . . . ," as once understood by the Judahite community to refer to the calamities that have befallen them, can be read differently. And for contemporary readers of the text, national aggression, both ancient and ever new, will be seen as neither divinely mandated nor religiously sanctioned.

Verse 3 continues a second hermeneutical point that needs to be addressed. The reference is to children as victims of cannibalism. In a hierarchical society, as Israel was, children, along with the poor, widows, and the fatherless, are considered to be the most vulnerable of all of society's members. Verse 3 recalls how they became food for some of the hungry exiles. While cannibalism may have occurred in some cultures, here it is children who are victims of others' needs.[3] While there are laws and admonitions to safeguard parents, laws that safeguard children are lacking.[4]

Third, the dominant use of the first person pronoun throughout vv 1-10 suggests excessive inclusivity and therefore inaccuracy. Did no one entreat God? Did no one obey God's voice? Were there no righteous people behind this corporate personality of Judah?

Finally, vv 1-10 acknowledge transgression. Here, the text bears witness to the fact that the exiled Judahite people were a community that took responsibility for its offenses insofar as they admitted their guilt. A change of heart has not yet taken place, however (2:6-10). Furthermore, God is just in all that God commands the people to do; God is "in the right" (v 6).

In summary, this passage presents a particular image of God as exercising power over a country that is made "to pay" for its crimes and offenses. Divine power is used as divine retribution. The text also shows how certain people in desperate situations used their power over others; for example, sons and daughters become victims of cannibalism. Finally, the admission of guilt on the part of the exiled community is an act that eventually does empower them. It becomes the first step that will lead to a change of heart and the restoration of a breached relationship with God. Subtle as it is, the text does offer hope despite its pervadingly somber tone.

Baruch 3:9-19
"You are defiled with the dead." (3:10)

With a command to listen and be attentive, the speaker of this beautiful prayer addresses the Judahites as a whole and in particular the Diaspora.[5] The tone of the passage is reflective, and from the speaker's exhortations and rhetorical questions, one is able to see images of both power and powerlessness.

The poetic prayer in praise of wisdom opens with gusto: "Hear the commandments of life, O Israel; give ear, and learn wisdom!" (v 9). Verses 10-11 comprise a rhetorical question addressed to Israel, who is in exile, landless, homeless, "defiled with the dead" (v 10), "counted among those in Hades" (v 11), and therefore powerless. The reason for Israel's powerlessness is given in vv 13-14: Israel did not walk in God's ways (v 13) and seems to have lacked the wisdom that comes from God; the passage next exhorts its audience to learn where wisdom is (v 14).

Verses 15-19 contain a series of rhetorical questions that are used to point out to Zion the folly of human power. This power appears to be both hierarchical and anthropocentric. The rhetorical questions are addressed to "rulers" and to those others who: (1) lorded it over the animals on the earth, (2) made sport of the birds of the air,[6] (3) hoarded up silver and gold continuously, and (4) "schemed" to get silver. Here, one sees a situation of humankind's "domination over" the natural world. Moreover, the hoarding of silver and gold with "no end to their getting" suggests that there is little concern for sharing the wealth with others, particularly the poor. One wonders where all the silver and gold were coming from in the first place, especially since "there is no trace of their works" (v 18). The text suggests that there might be something devious going on among people who have a certain amount of power because of their position and economic status. And, although they go down to Hades, others arise in their place, and the cycle of hierarchy, androcentrism, and domination continues.

In sum, this passage is a lesson for Judah and humankind in general about the folly of human power in relation to the power and wisdom of God.

Baruch 4:5-20
"For he brought a distant nation against them." (4:15)

Verses 5-20 are part of a lengthy prophetic address (4:5—5:9), which is a response to 1:1—3:8. In vv 5-8, the prophet both encourages (vv 5-6) and admonishes (vv 7-8) Judah's exiles. In vv 9-16, the prophet, through metaphor and personification, allows grief-stricken Jerusalem to give voice to "her" grief. The city is portrayed as a mother (vv 10-11) and a widow (vv 12, 14-16); in vv 15-16, she speaks, in third person reflective style, about her experience. Verses 15-16 conclude with personification and metaphor. In vv 17-18 the prophet responds directly to Jerusalem with a dubious rhetorical question (v 17) that leads into words of hope, assurance, and comfort (v 18). In vv 19-20, the prophet once more personifies Jerusalem who encourages her children—those Judahites soon to be exiled—to go from her because she has been left desolate (cf. v 12). The image of Jerusalem as a widow suggests that the perceived abandonment by God was, for the Judahite community, comparable to the pain and loss experienced at the death of a spouse.

In vv 5-8, the speaker encourages the Judahites while more specifically reminding them that they went into exile because of their infidelity to God. This exile of Judah's "sons and daughters" is said to have been brought about by the "Everlasting." In these five verses, one encounters the powerlessness of Judah in the hands of a powerful God whose perceived method of chastisement is oppressive in response to the infidelity and arrogance of the Judahite people (vv 7-8).

Judah's apostasy and arrogance are further described in v 13, and then God's chastisement is made explicit:

> For he brought a distant nation against them,
> a nation ruthless and of a strange language,
> which had no respect for the aged
> and no pity for a child.
> They led away the widow's beloved sons,
> and bereaved the lonely woman of her daughters. (vv 15-16)

In these verses, one sees the power of God and the powerlessness of Judah. Judah is at the mercy of another, more powerful empire, Babylon, sent by God to conquer Judah.

In vv 15-16, there are several points for discussion. The Everlasting (v 8) God (v 10) is said to be the initiator of the Babylonian invasion of Judah that resulted in the exile. Here, one sees divine power used aggressively, resulting in oppression and pain: many Judahites will die when the Southern Kingdom is attacked; many other Judahites will be exiled.

In addition, the use of the third person masculine pronoun, "he," with reference to God in v 15 indicates clearly that a male metaphor for the Divine was one of several metaphors identifying God in ancient times, especially within the Judahite community. In the context of vv 5-20, this male metaphor for God used in conjunction with the image of aggressive power raises two concerns. As the text stands, it presents and legitimates a picture of God as one more powerful than any empire or group of people, who is able to control nations and peoples even to their detriment (vv 15-16). Moreover, the fact that this God is a male deity could legitimate for the male segment of society, then and now, the use of aggression against aggressors.

Complementing the image of a male deity, throughout vv 5-20 in general and vv 15-20 in particular, a feminine metaphor is applied to Jerusalem. From a contemporary perspective, this relationship could express a bias against women on the part of the Judahite community and could suggest that the bias was shared by those authors and editors who shaped the text in its final canonical form. As mentioned earlier, Jerusalem is personified as a

mother and a widow—two gender-specific images—who is grieved, sorrowful, and in contrite mourning. Mother Jerusalem suffers because of the transgressions of her children. Here and throughout the Bible, Jerusalem is classi-
fied as a feminine noun; cities as well as countries were often associated with
the female gender in the ancient world.[7] Surprisingly, this trend still continues today in certain cultural and social settings. In this particular context,
Jerusalem is portrayed as desolate, but later on, the city is depicted as one that
is about to be restored, one in which God takes delight (see, for example, Bar
4:36—5:9). It would not be accurate, therefore, to assert that the text posits a
completely negative bias toward women, in spite of certain negative imagery
associated with cities personified as female. According to the text, however,
Jerusalem becomes beautiful and desirable only when God, portrayed as a
male deity, takes care of her directly. Given the metaphorical language associated with both God and the city of Jerusalem, it is possible to hear a patronizing, patriarchal, and hierarchical tone inherent in the passage. And even if
one were to argue that the suffering and future glory of Jerusalem express a
theological message, namely, that life is nothing without God, the message
still does not speak of a mutual relationship. Clearly, God is portrayed as one
who controls Jerusalem's life and destiny.

While one is given a picture of sorrowful Jerusalem and hears the voice of
widowed mother Jerusalem, who laments both the pain suffered on account
of her children and their captivity, nowhere does one hear the voice of the
children's other parent. Jerusalem portrayed as a woman is allowed to speak.
Hence, both the prophet and the text liberate and give power to the female
voice through the personification of Jerusalem as a woman. This is noteworthy, but it does not add balm to the problem of domination and control
in relation to most gender-specific metaphors.

Finally, in vv 17-20, the power of God is trumpeted. One is given the
impression that God is able to make weal and woe for people by controlling
the course of events. The God who delivered Israel into the hand of its enemy
will now rescue Israel from the enemy's hand. Again, one needs to question
this punitive image of God and understand it in its historical context.

In summary, vv 5-20 are a proclamation of mixed images. The God who
uses powerful, controlling, and oppressive measures to chastise Israel (vv 6,
15) becomes the source of Israel's hope and deliverance (v 21). The gender-
specific female metaphor for Jerusalem can be taken as both patriarchal and
liberating. The choice of metaphor and imagery is obviously influenced by
cultural, social, historical, and religious events, perceptions, and norms, but
it also remains fluid.

Baruch 4:21-26, 27-29

"They were taken away like a flock carried off by the enemy." (Bar 4:26)

Verses 21-26 contain the second of five exhortations (vv 5-16, 21-26, 27-29, 30-35, and 36-37) and the second of four that begin with the command "Take courage. . . ." The speaker is mother Jerusalem who offers words of comfort to her estranged children. Clearly this passage has power as its theme.

Words can be used to empower people. As in previous verses, Jerusalem is here portrayed as a mother who offers words of encouragement to her children who have transgressed the law and incurred the wrath of God. Set in the context of prophecy, readers and listeners can conclude that words of comfort and encouragement are very much a part of the prophetic tradition and spirit that carry with them the potential to effect change.

The word of God is spoken by a deity designated by a male metaphor through a prophet who is also male. Yet the prophet Baruch has chosen to personify Jerusalem as a woman. The reader consequently hears a personified female voice spoken by a male prophet for the benefit of Jerusalem's and Baruch's addressees. Such words of encouragement and comfort appease the Divine who brought about the disaster and exile in the first place. Text and prophet attest to the strong faith and voice of one woman, mother Jerusalem, who represents all mothers, all women, even all parents, then and now, who grieve or have grieved for the oppression of their children, whatever form such suffering did and may take.

Against this image of grieving, comforting, and encouraging Jerusalem as woman and mother, is God, a male deity who brought up the Israelites (v 8) but who, in wrath, chastised them severely and punitively (see vv 15-16, 21). In vv 21-26, God is depicted as someone with incredible power who will use it to deliver the Israelites from their oppressed state and empower them to overtake the enemy who once overtook them.

Thus, in vv 21-26 one sees a variety of images associated with power. Even though personified woman Jerusalem speaks, the ultimate power rests with God, a male deity. While the text liberates the female voice somewhat, it is the male deity who can fully liberate the Israelites. Thus, while a female's words may be comforting emotionally and psychologically, a male holds the power to oppress or liberate. In this sense, the text participates in patriarchy.

Verses 27-29 are spoken by Jerusalem and addressed to the children of the personified city. The theme of power as presented in vv 21-26 continues in vv 27-29. Once again, Jerusalem encourages her children to "take courage" (v 27), to cry out to God with the assurance that God will hear and remember them. As in vv 21-26, God is depicted as one who is capable of causing both oppression and liberation.

Baruch 4:30-37

"Wretched will be those who mistreated you." (4:31)

In Bar 4:30-37, God exhorts Jerusalem through the prophet Baruch to "take courage" (v 30). The underlying theme is power. Here the text portrays God as using divine power on behalf of Jerusalem and the Israelites. God who once oppressed Israel will now oppress those who enslaved and mistreated the people. Babylon and "her" cities will feel the negative effects of God's power (vv 31-35), whereas Israel will be liberated. The city of Babylon is also personified as a female.

In vv 36-37, the focus shifts from the impending execution of God's wrath on Babylon to words of encouragement for Jerusalem. The text attests to the power of God's word (v 37) for, at the word of the Holy One, the exiles return. Throughout chapter 4, a question emerges: Does the powerful word of God lead to oppression, liberation, or both? The text would have one convinced that it leads to both.

Lamentations

Overview: A Historical, Literary, and Hermeneutical Interplay

Like the book of Baruch, the book of Lamentations also has as its historical backdrop the fall of Jerusalem in 587 B.C.E. and the exile. Comprised of five poems that are recorded in five chapters, Lamentations captures, reflects, and responds to the emotional, social, political, economic, and religious crises that the Judahite people experienced at the collapse of the Southern Kingdom and the painful exile that occurred thereafter.

One wonders how a person could write so poignantly. The author of these five poems remains anonymous, although the book has often been attributed to the prophet Jeremiah. Unlike Baruch, the inspiration and canonicity of the book of Lamentations has never been questioned; nevertheless, no one is quite sure where to place Lamentations in the canon, since the Hebrew tradition places it among the Writings, and the Greek and Latin tradition place it among the Prophets. I have chosen to include Lamentations among the Prophets. In its final canonical form, Lamentations is passionate poetry that exudes a sense of spontaneity while at the same time reflecting a highly skilled and technical hand that uses acrostics, numerical patterns, and parallel line structure. Most scholars keep the inherent five-poem structure, with each poem assigned to a different chapter in the book,[8] though a more elaborate and detailed structure is possible. Regardless of the structure, the book of Lamentations is organized on a rhythmic 3+2 pattern and is a potpourri of literary types[9] that express some of the deepest sentiments of human pain and frustration. And yet at the center of such heart-wrenching emotion lies a personal message that is profoundly reflective; it is somewhat hopeful and reassuring for the Judahite exiles and for anyone who experiences turmoil or dislocation.[10]

Hermeneutically, the book of Lamentations raises several points for thought and discussion. The poems present a God who, to some of the Judahite people, is powerless, unable to intervene to liberate them from their miserable state. For some other Judahites, God does have tremendous power; God used this power to create the devastating situation of exile. Still others view God as the one who has abandoned them. Furthermore, the Judahites express their feeling of being completely overpowered by God and other countries, both of whom have become, in some people's perceptions, the "enemy." Such a multifaceted view of God leaves the reader and the believer in a quandary: Is this passive-aggressive person really God?

Moreover, the book of Lamentations uses gender-specific metaphors that do not present the female gender in an attractive light. The city of Jerusalem is compared to a woman: once a bride, now a widow; once a princess, now a vassal. Other gender-specific female images also raise questions. Yet, toward the end of the book, the devastating effects of power are not gender-specific; male and female alike experience oppression.

The poetic technique of comparing the rage of God to that of animals who can be ferocious when cornered or hungry accentuates the violent behavior of certain animals and presents God in an odd way. While the metaphorical language gets the point across, how one sees and treats certain animals in creation can be conditioned by how the animal has been presented down through the centuries.

The passage illustrates the folly of putting full confidence and trust in ideologies. People allowed themselves to be brainwashed by the "Zion tradition" (Yahwism), only to have the table turned and the tradition fail them.

Finally, the texts contain both hierarchical and patriarchal elements that will be explored in the following section, which looks at specific passages selected from chapters 1, 2, and 3. Because chapters 4 and 5 contain many of the same themes as Lamentations 1–3, they will not be dealt with in this chapter.

Lamentations 1:1-22
"The LORD has handed me over
to those whom I cannot withstand." (1:14)

Lamentations 1:1-22 can be divided into two segments: (1) a lament over Zion (vv 1-11b) and (2) a lament of Zion (vv 11c-22). In vv 1-11b, the poet laments the condition of Jerusalem, as well as Judah and the roads to Zion (Jerusalem). The central metaphor personifies Jerusalem as a woman (widow), a metaphor that recalls the figurative language of the book of Baruch where Jerusalem is also personified as a woman (widow). In vv 1-22, one learns how agonizing both the destruction and the exile were for many of the Judahites. Elements of power and gender color both segments of this poem.

A. Vv 1-11b:
"Her foes have become the masters,
  her enemies prosper." (1:5).

The text presents a picture of powerless Jerusalem. A widow,[11] Jerusalem is one no longer espoused; she sits lonely, "she that was great among the peoples!" (v 1). Once a princess, she is now a vassal. She has been "demoted"; she is forlorn and scorned. Her lovers offer her no comfort and have become her enemies.[12] In v 5, her "foes," perhaps those who were once her friends turned enemies or perhaps other countries, have now become the "masters," and "her enemies prosper"; they "have stretched their hands over all her precious things." The countries whom she forbade to enter her congregation have invaded the holiest of places, her sanctuary (v 10).[13] Even her children and her princes, who might have been able to help her, have either been taken captive or fled in the face of the pursuer." From daughter Zion[14] has departed/all her majesty" (v 6a); her people are left powerless as they groan, searching for bread. They have had to trade their treasures for food.[15]

Not only is the city Jerusalem powerless but so also is Judah. The southern kingdom of Judah, of which Jerusalem is the capital (v 3), has gone into exile and experiences "suffering" and "hard servitude." The fact that Judah has no "resting place" symbolizes that the country has fallen out of favor with God. "Rest" was considered a gift and was related to Judah's identity as God's people. "Her pursuers have all overtaken her/in the midst of her distress" (v 3) expresses the utter powerlessness of Judah.

This state of pain and vulnerability evokes a response. "The roads to Zion mourn" because there is no more celebration (v 4).[16] Zion's gates are desolate; its priests groan; its young girls grieve. The city's and kingdom's inhabitants, its priests and maidens in particular, experience misery as do the nobles and children (vv 6, 11b). In v 9, Jerusalem cries out: "O LORD, look at my affliction for the enemy has triumphed!"

A city and a country that were once strong and great have now become vulnerable to the scorn and domination by other countries, rendering the city and the country powerless. The ones most affected are the children, because within the social structure, they are at the bottom of the ladder and are, therefore, the most vulnerable; they cannot defend themselves. Such a situation is not so unfamiliar to people today. Whether in situations of poverty, famine, abuse, or other forms of violence, the ones most affected are often children.

Jerusalem's state of powerlessness raises the question, "What did Jerusalem do to experience such pain and tribulation?" Although the text does not state it directly, one can glean from the reference to "all her lovers"(v 2) and the description of her nakedness and uncleanness that Jerusalem/Daughter Zion is guilty of adultery (vv 8-9).[17] Jerusalem has sinned grievously. And, for this and other transgressions, God causes Jerusalem/Daughter Zion to suffer.[18] The phrase "because the LORD has made her suffer/for the multitude of her transgressions" (v 5) expresses a theological and ideological belief at work during the Exile, prior to it, and even in some circles today. The text presents the image of a God who will use all sorts of violent means, including raising up nations to act with violence or turning allies into enemies, to chastise a people who has gone astray. In this case, it is the Judahites. The hermeneutical issue that arises from these verses is one that pervades these texts: such a depiction of God and God's deeds is a reflection on tragic historical events given a theological interpretation in tune with a theology of divine retribution.

B. Vv 11c-22:
> "The Lord has trodden as in a wine press
>   the virgin daughter Judah." (1:15)

Verses 11c-22, a lament of Jerusalem/Zion, present a variety of images. In these verses, Jerusalem: (1) complains to God directly about "her" miserable state; (2) addresses her passers-by, commenting about the terrible things God has done to her and bewailing her pitiful state; (3) affirms God's terrible deeds of chastisement and then proceeds to address people collectively in order to share with them the suffering that both she and her inhabitants are experiencing; and (4) reverts back to addressing God directly in order to grieve before God. Jerusalem's address includes a heart-wrenching confession of guilt, an expression of anguish over her enemies' jubilation at her beleaguered state, and a demand that God deal with these evil enemies as God has dealt with her. The predominant image is the powerlessness of Jerusalem before God and the other nations, and the city's own personified feeling of vulnerability that is exacerbated by its admission of guilt.

In summary, vv 1-22 sharply contrast the power of God and the punishment of Jerusalem/Judah. The text gives the impression that God uses some countries to go after another country in order to chastise that country for its transgressions.

Jerusalem/Zion is deferential toward God, specifically when Jerusalem acknowledges its wrongdoing after affirming God's punitive actions, which had caused Jerusalem to experience personal and public humiliation. These actions result not only in Jerusalem's being humiliated but also in Jerusalem's increased sense of vulnerability. The city's response is to express to God "her" desire that God also deal with "her" enemies in the same manner that God has dealt with Jerusalem. Hence, Jerusalem invokes God to assert punitive power.

God has power over Jerusalem/Zion and Judah, and power over countries that, in turn, have power over Jerusalem/Zion and Judah. Furthermore, God uses such power to bring justice. The text seems to suggest that violence that begets the desire for violence can be a means to true justice.

Dominating power and gender-specific metaphorical language are inter-related. Jerusalem/Zion and Judah are feminine Hebrew nouns: this may have been the reason that the text's author and editors personified the city and the kingdom as a woman, a widow, who is sorrowful and vulnerable because she was unfaithful to God.[19] Verses 1-22 illuminate both the positive and negative aspects of Jerusalem/Zion and Judah portrayed as a woman. In the face of calamity, "she" does not remain silent. She even dares to address God directly to express what she wants to see done on account of the behavior of her ene-mies. The female voice, often silent in the biblical texts, is empowered through the personification of Jerusalem to speak out boldly.

Jerusalem is described, however, as a widow, a vulnerable state. She has also been unfaithful to God. Jerusalem—"virgin daughter Zion"—is literally brought to her knees. This image of Jerusalem is uncomplimentary to women and especially problematic in many societies today.[20]

Finally, Lam 1:1-22 attests to the power that a certain theological and ide-ological perspective and belief can have over the shaping of a narrative. While Lam 1:1-22 reflects the historical event of the demise of Jerusalem and the Southern Kingdom Judah by enemies, the passage focuses on the theological meaning of historical events. Are the historical circumstances being recorded in such a way as to fit in with a certain theological agenda and belief? If so, then the author's theological ideology dominates and colors historical reality. A theological belief or construct is imposed and shapes the telling of events themselves. For this reason poetic biblical narratives like Lam 1:1-22 need to be read against the grain, with an understanding of the cultural, social, and theological attitudes that were present in the ancient world that likely influ-enced these texts.

Lamentations 2:1-10, 11-22

"He has cut down in fierce anger
all the might of Israel." (2:3)

Chapter 2 continues the description of the Judahites' painful suffering during the exile. The chapter can be divided into two main sections: a description of

God's day of wrath (vv 1-10) and a response (vv 11-22: Zion's in vv 11-12, 20-22; the poet's in vv 13-19). The overall tone of the entire passage is bleak.

Behind vv 1-10 is the collapse of the Southern Kingdom of Judah. In these verses, God's merciless anger has led to divine deeds that have humiliated Zion completely, leaving a people staggering, a city and a kingdom in ruins, and a faith in shreds. These verses again raise the issue of how God is portrayed in the text.

Verses 1-10 give a clear picture of how power and gender-specific metaphors work together to create a devastating picture of both deity and people. God is depicted as a powerful warrior who has destroyed both a city and many of the kingdom's people. For those who survived the devastation, God becomes someone who has forgotten those for whom God has had a special love, namely, "his footstool" (v 1). In the ancient world, to be God's footstool would have been considered an honor: Zion was considered a sacred place and sacred soil. In a contemporary setting, however, the idea of Zion being God's "footstool" may suggest an image of servitude, demotion, and hierarchical utilitarianism rather than respect and honor.[21]

As a warrior, God is seen to be ruthless, one who destroys "without mercy" and who in "his wrath . . . has broken down the strongholds of daughter Judah" and "brought down to the ground in dishonor the kingdom and its rulers" (v 2). The reference to being brought down in dishonor admits of an image that pertains to a particular social and political class: Judah no longer enjoys an elevated status of preference; "she" has been stripped of honor and royal status.

The fact that "Daughter Judah" is depicted as experiencing this pain and suffering from God sends mixed messages to readers. While the phrase "daughter Judah" implies a term of endearment, it might also be heard patriarchically: Daughter Judah is being severely chastised by father God. But brutal punishment seems inappropriate for a child who has not been attentive to a parent's expressed wishes.

"Daughter Judah" communicates to contemporary readers an unhealthy paternal attitude. Judah is a fully developed kingdom, hence, "a grown woman," and yet she is being treated by God as if she were a senseless child. In social, political, and religious structures that are hierarchical and patriarchal, this paternalistic attitude from the one "in power" can be psychologically, socially, and emotionally debilitating for the one not in power. When punitive chastisement is preferred to conversation, mutual reverence and respect are diminished. Additionally, while a female metaphor is used for Judah here and throughout the chapter, a male metaphor is ascribed to God. Hence, a male figure uses aggressive power over a female to chastise her for her transgressions.

The fact that the male figure is God could be grounds for some males to legitimate their unrestrained aggression toward those females with whom they share a relationship. Thus, one could argue that the text appears to legitimate demoralizing violence, in addition to heralding a metaphorical image of God that inspires fear and hatred instead of reverence and love.

What does such a portrayal of God do to one's religious imagination and sensibilities? Might such a depiction be the basis for rejecting God, especially if one has been the victim of aggression and violence? And, for the perpetrator of such aggression, might the text encourage a further running away from God who is "going to get you and make you pay"? One's social location in relation to one's cultural, social, political, and religious world is key to how one hears the text and its impact on one's personal life as it is lived in relationship with others in society, church, and world.

The metaphor of God's "right hand" (vv 3-4) being the hand of power is a common motif in the biblical text.[22] From a contemporary perspective, this image of God as a human person who has hands and who, figuratively, uses the "right" one to assert power could help one to make the claim that the right hand is the preferred one. The right hand has more power to it than the left. For the majority of people, the right hand is the stronger one. Therefore, the metaphor of God's "right hand" accentuates God's power and strength. In a world of human beings where the right hand is often the dominant one, what does such an image communicate to left-handed people? Are right-handed people preferred? Surely all one has to do is to note how many things are crafted with right-handed people in mind. Furthermore, what is the preferred place, to God's right or to God's left?[23] The text suggests a bias that is cultural, social, and religious.

Not only is Jerusalem/daughter Zion humiliated because of God's power over "her" but so are the political and religious leaders of the people. Apparently, they did not act in accordance with God's ways and failed to assume the full responsibilities of their office (see 4:14). Zion's king and princes "are among the foreign countries" (v 9); political guidance has ceased. The prophets are bereft of divine vision and therefore are powerless. Thus, political and religious leadership has crumbled; God's power has exiled some and ceased to empower others. Furthermore, the elders "sit on the ground in silence" (v 10) in dust and wear sackcloth, profound expressions of humiliation.[24] Although the image of the young girls mourning helps to form a merism and may even reflect an older tradition, hermeneutically, the text presents a selective image of mourning. What if a young boy were to mourn, then and now? Would this be culturally, socially, and religiously acceptable? There seems to be very little ancient evidence for this, and few biblical models for it, at least in the Old Testament. Or would such behavior equate young boys with young girls, who have a lower social status? Certain acts can become stereotypical of a particular gender or religious position and can have adverse effects on all parties involved—those being stereotyped and those assigning the stereotype. Truly, human emotions of pain, sorrow, and grief know not gender: both genders need continued liberation from stereotypes of all sorts.

The second half of Lamentations 2 opens with a personal statement by Zion. Zion, in excruciating agony, now laments the destruction and suffering of her own people, in particular infants and babes. Historically, such pain and suffering are the result of the Babylonian invasion and possibly also a famine.[25] The ultimate source of the pain is said to be God (see 1:5, 15; 2:1-8). All of this suffering is because Jerusalem has sinned; "she" has been unfaithful to God who, like an uncontrollably enraged and jealous lover, lashes back for revenge. The most vulnerable and the most powerless—infants and babes—suffer most, indirectly, because of Zion's transgressions. It is often true that those who suffer most, especially in nations where there is civil unrest and ever-increasing violence, are children.

In the context of contemporary life, vv 11-12 provoke reflection on some rather tragic projections. As droughts and famines increase because of global warming and changes in atmospheric conditions that are related to the ecological and environmental crises, more people, especially children, will suffer and die. The planet's condition, socially and environmentally, is less than healthy because of carelessness, greed, the interrelated problems of over-population and overconsumption, human commodification, and utilitarianism.[26] From a theological perspective, one must ask: What kind of God causes disasters that make "infants and babes faint in the streets of the city," that causes lives to be "poured out on their mothers' bosom" (v 12)? Is God the culprit here, or is it an enemy empire and/or a natural disaster that has caused such pain and destruction? A particular theological construct that understands God as all-powerful and directly in control of nature attributes disaster to God and understands it as divine retribution. This theological construct seems to pervade many of the biblical texts, particularly the prophetic texts.

In v 12 suffering infants and babes cry to their mothers, "Where is bread and wine?" Here, mothers are the ones who provide food for children. The text celebrates the role of the female as nurturer and sustainer of life. But where are the fathers? Perhaps they were killed in battle. Or was it the mother's role and not the father's to provide food (see, for example, Prov 31:15)? Whatever the situation, this verse represents either a social and political reality or, perhaps, a social stereotype. Today many families have moved beyond the stereotype to an arrangement in which both mother and father assume the care for children. In fact, in many countries, a father may become the primary caretaker of children or even the sole caretaker in circumstances of divorce or where women in the military are called to active duty.

Verses 13-17, a narrative reflection told from the poet's perspective, contain many of the same hermeneutical concerns as Lamentations 1 and 2:1-12.

Again, Jerusalem/Zion, the guilty party, is personified through the use of a gender-specific metaphor, specifically, as a female, a "daughter" and a "virgin." Today, this metaphorical language could connote patriarchy, paternalism, and hierarchy that are offensive to some contemporary readers and may even have been offensive to some ancient biblical listeners and readers as well.

Some prophets who could have helped Jerusalem/Zion did not because they were corrupt. The depraved social, political, cultural, and religious climate of the day had power over certain prophets who compromised their own God-empowered vocation. This situation demonstrates that even though a prophet may be divinely commissioned, God leaves the prophet free to choose whether to obey. Some prophets, like Micah (for example, 3:8) and Jeremiah (for example, 20:1-12), choose God's way; others do not (Lam 2:14; see also Mic 3:1-7).[27]

Verses 15-16 describe how one group of people can take advantage of another group, especially when the second group is in a very vulnerable position. That was Jerusalem's situation in relation to some other countries. One person or person(s), or for that matter, one country, one company, one group, can literally destroy another that is perceived to be weak (see, for example, v 16). The text of Lam 2:16 puts forth this attitude with no judgment whatsoever from either poet or later commentators.

The one responsible for the havoc Zion has experienced along with the consequential pain and suffering is God, who not only threatens to chastise those who do not keep Torah and covenant, but who also carries out the threat. God can be violent (see, for example, 2:1-8). Furthermore, God uses other people to execute destructive threats. God uses Zion's foes. Thus, God has tremendous power and uses it to achieve a purpose that is both destructive in its planning stages and in its effects. Through God's power, enemies come face to face to crush the one who has enraged God the most. Verse 17 is likely to leave many contemporary believers dismayed at the ways of God, if in fact, these are God's ways.

The poet encourages Zion to express sorrow to God continually (vv 18-19; see also 1:20-22) and then to beg God to come and help in the midst of such suffering for the sake of the children. Here one sees that for Zion power for weal and for woe rests ultimately with God. The God who created such havoc is now entreated to offer relief. Seeking divine aid, particularly for the children fainting with hunger,[28] demonstrates that the biblical writers/editors hoped that an appeal to God on behalf of innocent victims might receive a positive response, since God was known to act on behalf of those who suffered oppression unjustly.[29] Furthermore, Zion is encouraged to voice the pain of her children, who, perhaps, cannot express it themselves because they are so weak and voiceless except for cries and whimpers. Thus, there are elements that speak of asserting one's energy and power for the sake of liberating and saving the lives of others who, though innocent, suffer and are powerless.

In vv 20-22, Jerusalem addresses God directly, taking God to task for all the hurtful and harmful deeds God has done through the maliciousness of Jerusalem's enemies. Jerusalem confronts God outright by means of rhetorical questions and then describes for God an excruciating scene of suffering. One is able to glean an insight into Jerusalem's state of affairs after its siege. Children were victims of cannibalism; priests and prophets were being killed; people—young and old—were strewn all along the streets; and young men and women were murdered, perhaps as a result of enemy warfare. All of this Jerusalem attributes to God's anger, which God acted upon mercilessly. The phrase "you invited my enemies from all around . . ." (v 22) makes God's power seem even more insidious and manipulative. It is horrific to "invite" people to act viciously. Children suffered even greater violence than hunger. They were being eaten by those who had borne and nurtured them, their mothers. Children, society's most vulnerable, became the prey of their mothers, who were overcome by a force greater than their power to resist—hunger.

Yet both poet and text empower Jerusalem, a woman—a widow despised—to give voice to her tragic situation despite God's seething animosity toward her. Jerusalem has responded to the poet's encouragement and speaks out directly, strongly, and boldly. Empowered, she confronts her "enemy" God (1:4), who has used power against her, and indirectly challenges God to remember "his footstool" (v 20).

Verses 20-22 present a repulsive view of the effects of God's power. The verses do offer hope, however, to those, particularly women, who have been engulfed by violence, who witness its effects, and who can no longer remain silent. Jerusalem speaks out when the violence she suffers as restitution affects those who are not directly guilty of the injustices, especially children. Jerusalem confronts God, whom she understands to be responsible. The metaphorical woman stripped of her integrity and strength confronts, metaphorically, the powerful metaphorical man who has chastised her. The poet portrays a model of assertiveness, not aggression; Jerusalem deals with God assertively and not aggressively as God has dealt with her. Which model is more fitting for dealing with injustice and conflict today? Jerusalem's or that depicted as God's?

In summary, Lamentations 2 is a passionate, provocative text that reflects the aftermath of a major historical event in the life of the Judahite community, specifically the exile. Having a theological agenda and perspective, the text raises many contemporary hermeneutical concerns that invite consideration and discussion. The text describes the suffering of Jerusalem/Zion at the hands of enemies, particularly the Babylonians. Because God was outraged by Jerusalem's unfaithfulness and other transgressions, God wanted Jerusalem's enemies to bring about disaster.

The metaphorical language and personifications of Lamentations 2 create a bone-chilling image of God as a warrior and a heart-wrenching image of the city Jerusalem as a faithless woman and a widow. Once a strong city, Jerusalem, and by extension, Judah and the Judahite people, have become vulnerable as a result of God's punitive chastisements. These punishments affect not only the guilty but also innocent victims, especially children.

Lamentations 2 provides readers with a picture of how domination, control, hierarchy, patriarchy, and paternalism can generate oppression, particularly when these attitudes and behaviors are exercised in male-female relationships. Gender-stereotyping is also evident in this chapter, though the widow Jerusalem's assertive behavior is commendable.

The chapter illustrates how certain theological constructs, perspectives, and ideologies can influence the understanding and interpretation of God in relation to life events and can also shape a text's production and interpretation. Finally, Lamentations 2 may make some readers uncomfortable because of its violence. Those who attempt to use the text in liturgical and pastoral settings must take this aspect of the text into consideration.

Lamentations 3:1-20, 43-54
"He is a bear lying in wait for me,
a lion in hiding." (3:10)

In Lam 3:1-20 and 43-54, a person, perhaps the poet,[30] perhaps a prophet, perhaps one of Judah's inhabitants for whom the poet speaks, laments bitterly in a deliberate tone what a powerful God has done to him and the people in his city with whom he stands in solidarity.[31] The deliberateness of the tone is evident from the list of deeds that God has done to cause suffering. Both poet and text assign a male metaphor to God. Divine power is once again associated with a particular gender, but sadly, this power is violent, aggressive, and oppressive. God is clearly an "enemy." Such power and imagery raise many of the same hermeneutical questions discussed in relationship to Lamentations 1 and 2.

Verses 10-11 and 12-13 introduce two new images of God. Verse 10 metaphorically describes God as a "bear" who lies in wait and a "lion in hiding." In the great chain of being, the lion, the male lion, is the king of the animal kingdom. These two animals are often mentioned together and commonly associated with danger.[32]

God, like a bear and a lion, has attacked a victim, tearing it to pieces and leaving it desolate. In the ancient world, the use of metaphors from the natural world was most effective, since the culture was predominantly agrarian and involved in animal husbandry. From a contemporary hermeneutical perspective, though, one sees a savage God. From a hierarchical perspective, God has become "less-than-human"; God has become like an animal.

In vv 12-13 God is a hunter, specifically, a skilled archer who shoots and hits the mark, the victim's vitals. God is no longer acting like an animal; instead, the speaker has become like an animal, someone to be shot with arrows and hunted down by God. The violent hunter-archer image projects a theological impression of God as one who has "power over" people and uses it as a hunter, an archer. Today, this image of God challenges the intrinsic goodness of all of creation, especially since, from a theological perspective, it violates the belief that all life is holy.[33]

After an interlude (vv 21-42), the speaker's lament resumes in vv 43-54. The text focuses on what God has done to the speaker and the people, collectively. In the aftermath of war and exile, the Judahites try to make sense out of their experience, and once again a historical event is interpreted from a theological perspective.[34] God is depicted as both disinterested and enraged; God's anger leads to pitiless killing, accomplished by Judah's "enemies," who have brought devastation and destruction as well as public humiliation.

Verses 48-54 give readers a poignant view of the speaker's personal pain and suffering that is the result of having experienced (1) the people's devastation (v 48), particularly the young women of Jerusalem; (2) the lack of a response from God to this devastation; and (3) unjustified personal oppression and persecution caused by "enemies." Although the speaker stands in solidarity with the devastated community, his voice represents both those who have been faithful and yet have suffered the consequences of "God's wrath" as well as those who have been unfaithful.[35] An image from the natural world, a bird, becomes the impetus for a metaphor. The enemies hunt the speaker down "like a bird." How vividly this metaphor conveys the impression of powerlessness. Finally, the speaker receives some comfort from God, who is then entreated to assert power over the enemies.

Looking at the text as a whole, one again sees a disconcerting image of God who lashes out against a community, causing pain and suffering to the guilty and the innocent alike. The text legitimates the use of violence to address injustices.

The suffering of innocent victims who are part of a collective whole needs to be explored. Jeremiah knew such suffering; he was thrown into a cistern by his enemies (Jer 38:1-13). The infliction of suffering on the innocent has continued from ancient times to the present. On November 2, 1989, for example, Sister Dianna Ortiz, a member of the Ursuline Sisters, experienced a similar trauma in Guatemala, along with other innocent victims.[36]

Lamentations 3:52-54 beckons to the human community never to forget the senseless acts of violence—whether by means of pit, gas chamber, landmine, or toxic waste—done to both innocent people and to nonhumans as well. The text stands as a powerful reminder of what human power, at its worst, can do—deeds that do not flow from the Divine and should not be projected onto God.

Baruch and Lamentations in Context

Passages from the books of Baruch and Lamentations continue to raise for readers today critical questions of both a theological and an ethical nature. The texts call readers to understand how metaphorical language developed and functioned in the ancient world and then to assess critically the images in light of contemporary understanding. They call readers to a new awareness and consciousness with respect to violence, injustice, and the evolving responsibility of the human community to assure a quality of life for all of creation. Finally, the texts call readers to liberate God from the power of past destructive theological images. God is forever doing something new and therefore needs to be discovered anew in the midst of creation's transformative process that speaks of life, beauty, and harmonious relationships.

5

Habakkuk and Zephaniah

WRITTEN WITH BREVITY AND CANDOR, the books of Habakkuk and Zephaniah deliver chilling words of judgment upon the people of Judah prior to the destruction and collapse of the holy city of Jerusalem, the temple, and the Southern Kingdom as a whole. In the book of Habakkuk, the prophet pleads with God to do something about the rampant injustice that plagues Judah, and then receives a divine response: "Alas for you who heap up what is not your own" (Hab 2:6). Divine judgment continues in Zephaniah where foreshadowed woes become imminent promises of divine action against injustice: "The great day of the LORD is near, near and hastening fast" (Zeph 1:14). In both books one sees a variety of expressions of power that are brought to light in this chapter.

Habakkuk

Overview: A Historical, Literary, and Hermeneutical Interplay

A dialogue between the prophet Habakkuk and God provides readers with a glimpse into the seventh century B.C.E. Like the century before, this period was a time of social, political, and religious unrest; but now the southern kingdom of Judah and its inhabitants stand on the brink of ruin and exile; the fall of Jerusalem and the destruction of the temple are imminently on the horizon. Injustice plagued Judah in the seventh century B.C.E.; the law proved ineffective; and the prophet Habakkuk thought that God was unconcerned and insensitive to the wickedness that prevailed—greed, theft, embezzlement, extortion, debauchery, and idolatry. Such a perception by the prophet leads not only to his complaining to God but also to a series of heated confrontations. During these times of trial and uncertainty, however,

God is not insensitive to the local and international situations. God responds to the prophet, and the prophet concludes with a prayer that ultimately speaks of hope in God.

The book of Habakkuk consists of three chapters and can be subdivided into two parts: chapters 1:2—2:20, the prophet's pronouncements, and chapters 3:2-19, the prophet's prayer. These two divisions can be subdivided into a series of smaller units: Habakkuk's complaint to God (1:2-4); Habakkuk's confrontational address directed to God (1:5—2:1); a divine response from God to Habakkuk that takes the form of a vision statement that incorporates a series of woe-sayings (2:2-20; vv 6-8, 9-11, 12-14, 15-17, 18-19); and Habakkuk's prayer (3:2-19). Verse 1 of chapter 1 is a superscription; 3:1 also functions as a superscription. Habakkuk 3:1 introduces the prophet's prayer and shifts the reader's focus away from God and back to the prophet, who closes the book on an upbeat note of hope and faith rooted in God.

As a whole, the Habakkuk text moves at a lively pace due in large part to the unabashedness of the text's two speakers, Habakkuk and God. The addresses and exchanges that take place are brought to life by the repetitive use of such literary techniques as direct address (see, for example, "O LORD" in 1:2 and 3:2), which is also achieved by the use of the pronoun "you" (see, for example, 1:12, 14; 2:10, 16; 3:9, 13); rhetorical questions (see, for example, 1:3, 12, 17; 2:13, 18, 19; 3:8); the use of imperative verb forms (see, for example, 1:5; 2:2b, 4); and the cataloguing of a series of woe prophecies (2:6-8, 9-11, 12-14, 15-17, 18-19). Metaphorical language presents a multifaceted picture of God as "Holy One" (1:12); "rock" (1:12); one who not only listens but also responds (1:2—2:1; 2:2-20); one who is radiant (3:3-4), powerful (3:5-7), and like an enraged warrior who will act on behalf of justice (3:2-15), though according to the prophet Habakkuk, not in the same direct way as may have been perceived at other junctures of Israel's and Judah's history. This time, God is seen not so much as a warrior but more like a "commander-in-chief" who will send the Chaldeans (1:6) to deal with the people and the land of Judah.[1]

From the book of Habakkuk, then, four dominant themes emerge: (1) a concern for rampant injustice; (2) an effort at presenting God as powerful and just in the face of injustice; (3) an assertion that righteousness and faith are inseparable; and (4) God as one's hope and salvation in times of trouble.

From a hermeneutical perspective, the book of Habakkuk raises questions about the use and abuse of power, a topic that could engender and invigorate further scholarly discussions on the text. For instance, the use of power is sometimes an assertion of dominance and control rather than a means to empowerment with liberation as the ultimate goal. Specifically, the text portrays God in 1:5-11as one who raises up the Chaldeans, "a fierce and impetuous country," for the purpose of meting out divine punitive justice to

Judah because of its apostate and lawless ways (for example, 1:2-17). This God is capable of reducing people to fish and crawling things (1:14), as the wicked "swallow" the righteous (1:13). And yet this is the same God who empowers the prophet Habakkuk by giving him a vision that is horrible for the Judahites who oppress others but hopeful for the victims of injustice (for example, 2:2-19).

Habakkuk 3 gives a mixed view of power. In vv 2-15, the prophet's prayer provides a clear yet metaphorical portrait of God's power in relation to all of creation, for example, how God shook the earth and made the foreigners tremble (3:6), how the mountains saw God and writhed (3:10), how God came forth and asserted power to save the anointed ones (3:13), and so forth. According to Habakkuk 3, God has power over heaven, earth, kingdoms, the natural world, and people; all of these pale before or on account of such power, with the exception of the prophet, for whom God is his salvation and strength (3:19).This chapter explores the use of power with an eye to highlighting some of its devastating effects.

Habakkuk 1

"Destruction and violence are before me;
strife and contention arise." (1:3)

Perhaps no other prophet except for Jeremiah interrogates God like Habakkuk, who with passion and an "in-your-face" style repeatedly asks God, "Why?" Why does God make him look at trouble and wrongdoing and watch the innocent be overcome by the injustices of the wicked (vv 2-4)? Why does God observe the treacherous and keep silent (v 13)? And yet God is not silent; the prophet receives a response (vv 5-11) and gets a glimpse of what God is planning in response to the wickedness occurring in Judah.

Chapter 1 is a dialogue between God and Habakkuk. In vv 2-4, the prophet complains to God; in vv 5-11, God responds with a vision of doom; in vv 12-14, the prophet complains to God a second time and then concludes his lament with a description of the Babylonians' violent deeds and continual ruthlessness (vv 15-17).

Following a superscription (v 1), chapter 1 opens with the prophet Habakkuk complaining to God (vv 2-4). In two rhetorical questions, Habakkuk asks God why he, the prophet, is not being answered when he cries out for help, and why God is not saving him when he shouts out, "Violence!" One can appreciate the prophet's perplexity, especially since he knows from his religious tradition that God has rescued the innocent from the hands of the wicked in the past. Habakkuk poses a third rhetorical question (v 3a), this time asking why he must see wrongdoing and trouble. In vv 3b-4, the prophet describes the internal state of affairs of Judah: destruction, violence, strife, and contention.[2]

The verses reveal many dimensions of power, including (1) the power of the prophet: he squarely confronts God, who gives the impression of being totally unconcerned about the injustices occurring in the community; and (2) the power that the wicked have over the righteous: even the legal and judicial system is ineffective. Contemporary readers in a global situation spotted with violence, injustice, and oppression need to consider whether Habakkuk's questions are appropriate, real, and timeless. One also sees in Habakkuk's complaint the prophet's conviction that God has the power to rectify the present situation. In this regard, Habakkuk's view of God is hierarchical; he expects God to overpower the wicked who seem to be overpowering the righteous. Thus, the text presents a model of power that is hierarchical: justice would finally be realized when God intervenes and gets control of the situation by exerting power over the wicked. This is foreshadowed in the next section of the prophecy.

In vv 5-11, the speaker in the text switches from Habakkuk to God. God responds to Habakkuk's three questions (vv 2-3). The power and boldness of Habakkuk's lament has evoked a divine response. Habakkuk and his readers learn that God will act on behalf of the suffering righteous. But God will act indirectly through the Chaldeans,[3] whom God is raising up to deal with Judah. This presents readers with quite a disturbing picture of God, who, according to the text, uses divine power to conjure up an empire known to be one of God's "enemies" in order to fight against and overpower the wicked among God's own people Judah, for the sake of justice.[4]

Verses 6-11 describe the Chaldeans/Babylonians vividly, and readers are made aware of their great prowess and power. They are fierce, impetuous, and without a sense of justice. They use their power to oppress others: they "seize dwellings not their own" (v 6). They are dreaded, fearsome, and a people who make up their own rules (v 7). The animal images associated with them— horses, leopards, wolves, eagles—denote both speed and ferociousness: they all come for violence (vv 8-9). No one and nothing will render them powerless (v 10), for "their own might is their god!" (v 11).

What a frightening picture readers are presented with in vv 5-11. The use of power for oppression and devastation is obvious. The text confronts readers about God: What kind of a God would use an empire, especially a violent and unjust one, to deal with another kingdom's injustices? In this text, God is someone who can control the fiercest of countries to incur punitive justice on the unrighteous. Historically, this prophecy foreshadows the Babylonian invasion of Judah and its demise, a devastating event that the people believed was caused by God on account of their transgressions. This event did indeed take place in 598 B.C.E.

In vv 12-14, Habakkuk, with two more rhetorical questions, again reproves God for God's silence and inaction. While God has designated the Babylonians to act against Judah's wicked ones, Habakkuk's question suggests his discomfort with God's plan (v 13). Are not the people of Judah more righteous than their Babylonian enemies? Yet God is silent, allowing the Babylonians to overtake the people of Judah. Habakkuk suggests that they are like fish and crawling things that have no ruler to deliver them (v 14).

In these verses a fearless and powerful prophet confronts God about the forthcoming Babylonians and challenges God, as ruler, to do the work of justice. The images of the people "like the fish of the sea" and "like crawling things" suggest the powerlessness that, on the one hand, the innocent feel in the face of wickedness, and that the country as a whole may feel with respect to the Babylonians. God's "silence" seems to give more power to the wicked ones.

In vv 15-17, Habakkuk metaphorically describes how the king of Babylon treats people—he is like a fisherman who keeps dragging his net again and again to catch more and more fish so that he can increase his own lot (vv 15-16). The fisherman attending his net and seine in v 16 symbolizes the Babylonians' trust in their military power that brought them great wealth at others' expense (see also vv 6, 10). Habakkuk persists in questioning God: "Is he [the Babylonians] then to keep on emptying his net and destroying countries without mercy?" (v 17)

The passage as a whole gives readers a composite view of power. The prophet uses his power to move God from silence to speech. God's silence and inactivity have given power to the wicked, allowing them to overpower the righteous. Moved to respond, God reveals to the prophet the divine plan to use an unjust, overpowering, and violent empire against Judah because of its injustices. For Habakkuk, however, this does not seem to be the solution; power used to destroy another is not a way to bring about justice (v 17). Thus, in this chapter, power is presented as a destructive force except when the prophet uses his power not to attack physically but to confront verbally.

Habakkuk 2:6-20:
"Alas for those who build a town by bloodshed,
and found a city on iniquity!" (2:12)

Habakkuk 2:6-20 is a series of woe-sayings. To whom they are directed is not clear. They could be addressed to Judah or to the Babylonians, or to other foreign countries, or to the wicked in general. The sayings can be divided into several smaller units: first woe (vv 6-8); second woe (vv 9-11); third woe (vv 12-14); fourth woe (vv 15-17); a statement about idols and the fifth woe (vv 18-19); and a statement of affirmation (v 20). Common to each smaller prophecy is an overarching theme: God will not tolerate the abuse of power that overwhelms and overpowers others. Furthermore, trust in idols is foolish. The speaker in this passage is God, who quotes four woes people have said against the wicked.[5] Each of these woes begins with "alas" (vv 6, 9, 12, and 15). After each woe, God offers a reflection. Verses 18-19 differ slightly from vv 6-17. Verse 18 opens with a comment by God about idols and is followed by the fifth woe that God delivers (v 19). The whole pericope closes with a self-reflective statement by God that sets up a contrast between the idols (vv 18-19) and Judah's God, the true God.

The first four woes present a picture of how some people have used their power to benefit themselves at the expenses of others. The first woe casts judgment on those who rob and cheat others (v 6); the second, on those who exploit others to set up houses for their own personal security (v 9); the third, on those who build towns and cities with violence and injustice (v 12); and the fourth, on those who dominate others who are essentially helpless.[6] The fifth woe is different. Here people are upbraided for their trust in idols that are speechless and breathless and therefore cannot "wake up" or get up when addressed because they are lifeless (vv 18-19). This image is contrary to the God of Judah, who, ironically, is speaking in vv 6-19, and before whom all earth must keep silent (v 20). Verses 18-19 and 20 foreshadow Habakkuk 3 where the prophet recalls what God has done in the past as he waits for the day of calamity to come upon the wicked (v 16). This day will be the Day of the LORD, a time when God will assert divine power on behalf of the righteous. The four woes suggest a picture of how some people, or perhaps another country or countries, have dominated and oppressed others by means of power that overwhelmed others unjustly. The fifth woe presents a contrast between the powerlessness of idols and the power of God.

The comments offered after each woe develop further the picture of just how overbearing the ruthless are. For example, they have loaded themselves with "goods taken in a pledge" (v 6); they have devised shame for their house by cutting off many peoples (v 10); and they have shed human blood and have done violence to the earth (v 17). None of these deeds, however, will go unnoticed or unchallenged by the spirit of justice that God makes known to them. Creditors will make the wicked into booty (v 7); the survivors of the wicked ones' plunder will, in turn, plunder their plunders (v 8); contempt will satiate them instead of glory, as the LORD's cup comes around to them (v 17); and their idols will be of no use (vv 18-19). Thus, the wicked who once overpowered others with their deeds of cruelty will themselves be overpowered.

In v 13, the reference to God as the "LORD of hosts" in the verse's context conveys a powerful message that could be understood in two ways: (1) that the Babylonians' oppression of peoples and countries was God's work, God's way of dealing with injustices, or (2) that "the building of a city and its protection depends on Yahweh of Hosts."[7] What is clear here is that any effort involving evil will not be successful.

In v 16, the "cup in the LORD's right hand" that will come around to the wicked ones is a powerful metaphor. Although it is not clear from this text what kind of cup it is, the book of Obadiah speaks of a cup of God' wrath. Those who made others helpless and defenseless before enemies will themselves be given a taste of their own brew.[8] Just as God will deal with injustice indirectly by sending forth a conquering enemy, the Babylonians, so now God's cup is passed around to those who, in their wickedness, have overpowered others. Thus, the powerful will become the powerless, and the powerless, the powerful.

In summary, vv 6-20 present a multifaceted picture of power. When it is used to dominate, control, and oppress others, it causes egregious acts of violence and injustice and will not be tolerated by God. While wickedness may overpower people for a while, justice and righteousness will eventually overpower corruption, often at the cost of pain and suffering and even death to the oppressors. The use of power for the sake of oppression and/or domination that eradicates injustice through violence mirrors a law that was part of Judah's religious and social culture: the *lex talionis*. This was a law of retaliation whereby a guilty party suffers the same harm that the party has incurred on others. Perhaps the text does portray a God of justice and mercy but in a way that some may see today as biased and violent. Thus, while the text is informed by and reflects its culture, it is itself in need of ongoing interpretation by those cultures trying to shift paradigms from justice through violence to justice through nonviolence.

Habakkuk 3:1-16
"In fury you trod the earth,
in anger you trampled nations." (3:12)

Chapter 3 of Habakkuk is the prophet's prayer to God, as the superscription indicates in v 1. The prophet begins in a reverent yet friendly posture toward God in which he acknowledges God's great deeds, asks God to do such deeds again, but now requests God to do these great deeds of wrath with a spirit of mercy (v 2). In vv 3-15, the prophet recalls with God in prayer the various powerful deeds that God has done in the past and then admits his present uneasy state as he waits for the day of calamity to come upon the wicked (v 16). Habakkuk imaginatively and confidently ends his prayer to the God who is his strength and who makes his feet like a deer's to tread upon the heights (vv 17-18).[9] This chapter is an important one because of its images of power and the prophet's plea for God to remember mercy.

Verses 3-15 portray God as warrior, great in strength and powerful over all of creation, whose glory covers the heavens, whose brightness is like the sun, and in whose hand power lies hidden (v 3). Embedded in the warrior God image is the storm god, who often is pictured in Syria-Palestine standing with a lightning bolt in hand, ready to blaze forth. Verse 5 describes warrior God's military cortege: pestilence is in the front lines and plague in the rear guard. Elsewhere in the biblical texts, one sees that pestilence is what God has used to launch an attack against injustice (see, for example, Jer 14:12; 21:9; 38:2). The text presents a view of God as commander-in-chief, one who turns the natural world into adversarial forces to be used against those people guilty of wickedness and injustice.

Verses 6-12, 15 describe the effect that God's power has. Here, it is not only anthropological but also cosmological. The mountains, the tents of Cushan and tent curtains of Midian, the rivers and sea, the sun and moon stand in awe of and, in some instances, are afflicted by, God who comes with power to save "the anointed"—God's own people who suffer under wickedness. The warrior God comes to the rescue of an oppressed people, powerless, in need of a God who will fight for justice on their behalf.[10] God crushing the head of the wicked house and laying its roof and foundations bare suggests the destruction of Judah, which historically does happen when the Babylonians invade it. If the house is Judah, then one sees the prophet speaking here of a punishment corporate in nature, which was a familiar idea and commonly held belief among the Judahites with respect to divine chastisement. This makes the prophet's plea for God to remember mercy in the midst of wrath all the more poignant, dramatic, and prophetic (v 2).

Before the memory of such divine power, the prophet turns queasy and physically uneasy as he awaits the coming of the day of calamity—the Day of the LORD—when God will overpower the people who attack those on whose behalf the prophet speaks (v 16). God has power over a human being as exemplified by the prophet's reactions. Images from the natural world suggest what will happen to the wicked of Judah and the land and its fruits and the animals when the Babylonians invade. Verse 18 foreshadows the coming of God who will not only free the righteous from oppression, but who will also free those who will be exiled to Babylon and Egypt. Embedded in v 18 is an eschatological message of hope as the prophet stands in the midst of his struggling community. His hope is for the moment and the future. The establishment of justice is not a once and for all experience; it is an ongoing process.

The warrior God is an image in the text in need of ongoing theological reflection and evaluation, particularly when this text is heard in a contemporary social setting that is plagued by violence. Brueggemann hits the nail on the head when he states:

> The image of Yahweh as warrior, however, goes well beyond judge and king, both in its assurance and in its problematic. Its assurance is greater than that of the other images because Yahweh as warrior is one who actively and vigorously intervenes with decisive power. The warrior is not simply a king who issues decrees or a judge who renders verdicts. This is an agent forcibly engaged.
>
> To the same extent that this is poignant, palpable assurance, the image of Yahweh as warrior is also problematic because it puts violence into the middle of Israel's speech about God, and it evidences that Israel celebrates God-sponsored, God-enacted violence.[11]

In the discussion that follows, Brueggemann puts the warrior God image and violence in the context of Judah's history and tries to explain how one needs to understand these ideas in their historical and literary settings. If the biblical text is to have any transformation power for contemporary life, theology, and praxis, however, then what Brueggemann has uncovered as "problematic" needs ongoing study lest readers take the text literally and act as God does in the text or use the text to justify violence for the sake of justice. For contemporary readers, the metaphor of warrior God, the text's culture, and the text itself evoke the need for discernment and discussion in light of today's world and cultures.

Zephaniah

Overview: A Historical, Literary, and Hermeneutical Interplay

The book of Zephaniah opens with a superscription (1:1) that links one of the text's central characters, the prophet Zephaniah, during the period of king Josiah. Josiah reigned in Judah from 640-609 B.C.E.; he was noted for his profound loyalty to God and for his efforts to purge Judah and Jerusalem of all their idolatrous high places and cultic objects. He is best remembered, however, for discovering the Book of the Law in the temple, leading in turn to a series of religious reforms in Judah that he initiated. These reforms occurred almost concurrently with the outbreak of civil war in Assyria.

Following in the prophetic tradition of Isaiah and Micah, Zephaniah began preaching just prior to Judah's religious reformation, when Judah was riddled with social injustices and religious abuses. God pronounced through him the coming of "the Day of the LORD," which was to be a time of devastation not only for Judah and Jerusalem, but for other countries as well (see, for example, 1:2—3:8). Eventually, however, the prophet's message of utter devastation changed to one of hope as a new day was anticipated, one that bespoke of joy, reconciliation, and restoration, especially for the people of Judah (3:9-20).

The book of Zephaniah is composed of three chapters and can be divided into two main parts: (1) prophecies of judgment and imminent disaster (1:2—3:8) and future purification (3:9-13); and (2) a prophecy of hope, salvation, and restoration (3:14-20). The opening verses of chapter 1 present a disconcerting picture of an enraged God who promises first to sweep everything from the face of the earth, including people and animals (1:2-3). Later in the chapter and continuing to the opening lines of chapter 2, God promises to chastise sharply the people of Judah and Jerusalem on account of their idolatrous ways and various deeds of injustice (1:4—2:3). In 2:4-15, God's anger has not abated; next on the list to receive judgment, condemnation, and chastisement are the foreign countries. In 3:1-5 the scene shifts back to Jerusalem, which stands accursed because of its overall faithlessness. In 3:6, focus is on deeds done to countries in the past; in v 7, the focus shifts back to Jerusalem. In vv 6-13 as a whole, the chastisement to be inflicted on Judah and the other countries is God's way of purifying the people. Verses 14-20 are directed to the people of Jerusalem, metaphorically, "daughter Zion." (v 14). The people's suffering and lamentation will be turned into a time of celebration and a song of joy. The final word of the book is not doom; it is hope.

The book moves at a quick pace as readers are kept enwrapped in God's fury that comes to life through the use of a variety of images, descriptions, and metaphors. The repetitious use of the phrase "on that day" (1:9, 10; 3:11) adds cohesion to the series of prophecies of destruction while providing an element of surprise: the Day of the LORD is a time of destruction (1:9, 10) that will give way to a time of restoration (3:11). In this prophetic book, the word of God comes across with great power; God, speaking through the prophet Zephaniah, is the only speaker in the entire text.

The book as a whole features several elements associated with power that need to be considered and evaluated. The text presents an image of an all-powerful God who wants to inflict chastisement on the people of Judah and the people of other countries without any expressed concern or care for those who might be innocent of injustice. All the earth, even the animals, will suffer on account of Judah's and the countries' sins. The text shows that social sin has the power to affect the natural world adversely. Furthermore, while corporate punishment was part of the ancient Near Eastern world, this form of chastisement could be seen as problematic today, especially when it is attributed to God and God's ways. Moreover, ideology has the potential power to blind people to reality. In the case of the inhabitants of Judah, their belief in the Zion tradition inhibits them from just and responsible action on behalf of others.[12]

Furthermore, in ancient Judahite society (as in most societies) money played a prominent part in gaining, securing, and ensuring power. One also sees, however, that money becomes powerless in the face of divine justice. Both perspectives pose strong challenges for those cultures, societies, and people who pride themselves on having a certain amount of economic power.

Zephaniah 1

"I will sweep away humans and animals;
I will sweep away the birds of the air and the fish of the sea." (1:3)

The Day of the LORD that Habakkuk was quietly awaiting was drawing near. It was a day most fierce and terrible, a day of destruction that was total for Judah—for the country and the land, for human and nonhuman life. Zephaniah describes a God who is coming with power to deal with the country's and Jerusalem's idolatrous and unjust people. God's power is about to overshadow and overpower an entire country. The historical backdrop is the invasion of the Babylonian enemy whom God is raising up against the Judahites. Following a superscription, the chapter can be divided into five sections: a judgment prophecy (vv 2-6); an admonition (v 7); a prophecy of impending doom (vv 8-13); a description of the Day of the LORD (vv 14-16); and a statement of impending divine chastisement (vv 17-18). The predominant theme of the chapter is divine power directed against Judah.

In vv 2-6, the prophet Zephaniah describes the extensive destruction of life that will befall Judah, especially those who have disregarded God and God's ways (v 6). The use of power will be indiscriminate on God's part, and the judgment will be more inclusive than the primeval flood. For many contemporary readers, God's image and use of power may be unsettling.

On a more positive note, what vv 2-6 do suggest is that there is a relationship between human sin and the suffering of all creation. From an ecological perspective, how human beings live has an effect on the natural world, on all of creation. How human beings live will either sustain and nurture other forms of life or bring about death. Thus, a rereading of vv 2-6, one that is informed by a contemporary socio-ecological perspective, can call readers to a greater awareness of their responsibility for life on the planet.

Verse 7 contains an admonition to be silent before God, who is close at hand, and is followed by a description of what transgressions some members of Judah are guilty of and what God intends to do to those guilty of transgression. The officials and the king's sons who wear foreign attire are most likely guilty of Baal worship (2 Kgs 10:22) and therefore apostasy (v 8). Those who leap over the threshold are guilty of a superstition that holds that evil spirits lurk at a doorway, waiting to enter if one steps on the threshold, an act that would let them in. Because these two acts are associated with apostasy, those who engage in them will experience divine punishment. The wealthy who smugly believe that God is indifferent will also experience God's punishment: their wealth will be plundered, and their houses and vineyards will come to nought (v 13). Hence, the Day of the LORD will be a day of divine wrath, sadness, wailing, and economic distress (v 11).

The description of the Day of the LORD continues in vv 14-16. Hastening ever closer, it will be a day of wrath, distress, anguish, ruin, devastation, darkness, gloom, and clouds, with the sound of battle directed against Judah. The description begun in vv 8-9 of what God plans to do to some people continues in vv 17-18: the inhabitants of the land will lose a sense of direction for their lives and will be slaughtered (v 17). Money will not buy them any security, for the whole earth will be consumed.

These verses draw an extremely graphic picture of how the Day of the LORD will overpower Judah in its entirety. The complete annihilation of the earth is hyperbolic. It symbolizes God's extraordinary rage over the central sin of some of the people: apostasy. God will not tolerate Judah worshiping other gods. The warfare language emerges from the social location of the Judahites—they are about to be destroyed by the Babylonians. What vv 17-18 present, then, is an image of God as someone filled with an uncontrollable rage, who lashes out verbally proclaiming a series of punitive actions that are about to take place upon all of creation because some people have sinned.

The text as a whole portrays God as a violent and somewhat unjust God who will, hyperbolically, sweep everything from the face of the earth. This proclamation symbolizes the forthcoming Babylonian invasion and suggests a theological assertion by the authors and editors: that God is LORD of both history and creation and has power and control over both—power even to effect punitive action for transgression.

Zephaniah 2:8-11, 13-15
"He will make Nineveh a desolation,
a dry waste like the desert." (2:13)

Zephaniah 2:8-11, one of several prophecies in chapter 2 against the foreign kingdoms, features God, through the prophet Zephaniah, denouncing the actions of the Moabites and the Ammonites. Both people have poked fun at the Judahites—"God's people"—and have gloated over their territory. Therefore, "the LORD of hosts," "the God of Israel," will deal terribly with these two groups; and ironically, the plunderers will be the ones despoiled by those they have attacked.[13]

Zephaniah 2:13-15 is another prophecy against a foreign country, Assyria, one of the countries that had invaded Israel, and specifically against the country's proud capital city, Nineveh. Animal imagery reinforces the city's total destruction. Once a secure and exultant city, it will become a wilderness for the animals.

One sees in these texts an ethnocentric view of God, who comes with power to defend Israel by overpowering those countries who have taunted and conquered "God's people." Here, power is used to overpower, and violence gives birth to more violence.

Zephaniah 3:1-8
"Ah, soiled, defiled,
oppressing city!" (3:1)

In Zephaniah 3:1-8, focus shifts from prophecies against foreign countries to a prophecy against Jerusalem. Verses 1-5 portray God taking Jerusalem to task for a variety of reasons: it is obdurate, belligerent, and distant from God (v 2). Animal imagery metaphorically describes the city's political leadership: officials and judges are ferocious and fierce; they prey on those under their authority (v 3). Its religious leaders are just as bad: the prophets are reckless, faithless persons; its priests have profaned the sacred and have done violence to the law. The one who stands in sharp contrast to all of these persons is God, who acts justly every day (v 5). Verse 5 contrasts the unjust with God, imaged metaphorically as a judge: "every morning he renders his judgment, each dawn without fail" (v 5).

Verse 6 recalls the type of judgments God has meted out in the past. God has cut off countries, turned battlements into ruins, laid waste streets, and made cities desolate. Historically all these events reflect the Assyrian devastation of Judah during Hezekiah's reign. The invasion was attributed to God on account of the people's wickedness.

More significantly though, God now hopes that in its present state, Jerusalem will recall this past experience, take note of what happens when one acts wickedly, "take heed to fear him," accept correction, and not lose sight of all that God has brought upon it (vv 6-7). God hopes that Jerusalem will learn from the past and fall in line under God's authority and leadership lest it too have to suffer more punitive consequences. God, however, observes that Jerusalem's inhabitants "were the more eager to make all their deeds corrupt" (v 7). Because of this, then, God is about to pass judgment on Jerusalem (v 8). Those commanded to "wait" for God's justice are the powerless, the oppressed, and the victims of injustice (see also Hab 2:3, 6-20; 3:16; Zeph 3:11).

In vv 1-8, several points emerge about power: (1) power can affect people adversely, making them insensitive to any word of advice or warning, whether from another person or from God; (2) power can lead to the domination of others, as in the case of Jerusalem's leadership, and it can cause others to abuse their authority, as in the case of some of Judah's religious leadership, the prophets and priests; (3) the exercise of power can be punitive, leaving the party with less power in shambles; and (4) the assertion of power by the party who is more powerful, as in the case of God, is usually for the purpose of getting control over a situation. Hence, Zeph 3:1-8 speaks of a hierarchy of power with God depicted as the one most powerful who will take charge of people and a situation to bring about justice. The problem, however, is that God is depicted by the text as using power aggressively and violently. Now, even if this picture is one that has been colored by the culture and interpretation of its authors and editors, it must be recognized as problematic for praxis in the modern world, in which some people try to assert power in violent ways, to confront aggressive violent power that has been used to dominate, control, and oppress both human and nonhuman life forms.

Finally, one should note that God is depicted as a male deity (v 5), and the ones being indicted are Judah's officials, judges, prophets, and priests—for the most part, all male figures. The hierarchy of power, control, and domination is thus linked to one specific gender, with God metaphorically portrayed as male, and suggests that in ancient Judah, aggressive power was, for the most part, linked to gender, hierarchy, and patriarchy, a cultural situation that continues to exist in the world today. The human situation has changed somewhat but is still in need of paradigm shifts so that justice can be achieved through nonviolence, which indeed can become the hallmark of compassion.

Habakkuk and Zephaniah in Context

The books of Habakkuk and Zephaniah focus on power and justice. In both texts, the prophets proclaim a God of justice who will, in due time, exercise power to overcome the injustices that have resulted from the abuse of power by some who, because of their misuse of power, have caused pain and suffering to others undeserving of such oppression and domination. While the texts celebrate God as a God of justice who acts on behalf of the oppressed, the texts' portrayal of how God deals with injustice can be problematic when viewed from a socio-ecological perspective that tries to link theology to praxis and praxis to theology with the overarching goal of reverence for all creation. Clearly, these two books are prophetic and revelatory insofar as they give an insight into the historical, social, religious, and political times of ancient Judah just prior to its destruction by the Babylonians. The texts reflect their culture, as well as how the culture understood God and the ways of God. Situations of power, domination, control, hierarchy, patriarchy, violence, oppression, and so forth existed centuries ago and continue to exist in present times. Thus, the books of Habakkuk and Zephaniah can be a lens through which one can view life today: what needs to be transformed, and what needs to be written anew to shift the paradigms of power from domination to liberation to restoration and re-creation with God at the center of all, freely empowering all of creation with reverent justice and compassionate righteousness.

6

Ezekiel

Overview: Historical, Literary, and Hermeneutical Interplay

One of the most intriguing, disconcerting, highly symbolic, and wildly bizarre books in the prophetic corpus is Ezekiel. Throughout the text, Ezekiel, a prophet and one of the text's leading characters, leaves his fingerprint, "I, Ezekiel," among other personal references.

Ezekiel prophesied from around 593 B.C.E. to about 571 B.C.E., years that immediately preceded the fall of Jerusalem, the destruction of the temple, and the collapse of the Southern Kingdom of Judah, as well as the years that immediately followed. Political disarray that occurred during the reigns of kings Jehoiakim, Jehoiachin, and Zedekiah left the people of Judah in a weakened state, which, in turn, allowed the Babylonians to make continual advances upon Judah. These advances, under King Nebuchadnezzar, eventually turned what was once a strong kingdom into a smoldering ash heap. Judah's suffering inflicted by foreign countries, especially Egypt and Tyre, was perceived by its inhabitants and by Ezekiel himself as God's way of chastising them for their transgressions, apostasy, and injustices done to others. Thus, the book of Ezekiel provides readers with a vivid account of the last days of Judah and the first days of captivity.

The book of Ezekiel can be divided into three main sections: (1) prophecies of judgment against Israel (1–24), (2) prophecies against other countries (25–32), and (3) prophecies of salvation, hope, and promise (33–48). Several literary and structural devices create a continuity and cohesion throughout the text while advancing its narrative action. For example, Ezekiel's commissioning scene occurs twice, once in chapter 3 and once in chapter 33. Throughout the book, visions of the divine presence recur (see, for example, chapters 8–11). Stock phrases such as "the word of the LORD came to me" (see, for example, 6:1; 7:1; 12:1; 13:1; 15:1; 16:1; 17:1; 18:1) link one set of ideas to another.

Other main literary techniques that contribute to the overall style, tone, and message of the book include both apocalyptic and nonapocalyptic metaphors, similes, imagery, the use of formulaic expressions, a divine oath formula, alliteration, assonance, chiasmus, and the prophet's symbolic actions. An extensive variety of literary forms also add to the fabric of this rich text. Some of these include diatribe speeches (16:44-52; 22:3-12); legal disputations (18:1-32; 33:34-39); extended allegories and parables (15:1-6; 16:1-63; 23:1-49; and so forth); a fable (17:1-24); and a funeral dirge (19:1-14).

Several themes emerge from the text including: (1) the centrality of the temple and God's relationship to it; (2) God's power and awesome presence; (3) personal responsibility for one's actions and transgressions; (4) lasting and effective interior transformation; and (5) divine justice in relation to compassion, comfort, liberation, and restoration. The book of Ezekiel proclaims that God will not abandon covenant and will restore it with the Israelites as they begin to rebuild their temple.

Given the length of the book of Ezekiel, there are many elements of the storyline that are ripe for hermeneutical discussions. These include the use of gender-specific metaphors, particularly in chapters 16 and 23, both of which are offensive to the female gender. In present time, they are unacceptable metaphors because they have negative sexual overtones and are degrading. This metaphorical language is linked directly to God and therefore raises serious theological problems with respect to how the biblical text portrays God interacting with the female gender. There are also animal-related metaphors and images that when heard today could admit of diminution on the one hand, and a failure to see the intrinsic holiness and goodness of all life on the other hand.

Central to the book of Ezekiel is the use of power. Power becomes a means to dominate, control, and oppress others, both human and nonhuman species alike. The assertion of power also paves the way for liberation. This study of Ezekiel 5, 16, and 19 focuses on power and domination. Ezekiel 34:1-10, 25 focus on power for liberation, and Ezek 36:1-15 focuses on power for liberation that hints at the use of power for restoration.

As with the other prophetic texts discussed thus far, Ezekiel's portrayal of God and God's use of power is critical to the text's theological assertions and how one then appropriates such assertions. Some of the concerns are political, religious, and social.

This chapter looks at a variety of selected passages from the book of Ezekiel in order to evaluate critically these texts from a hemeneutical perspective. The goal is to raise key questions and bring certain points to light that can no longer be left masked or unaddressed by today's readers of the biblical text, who are challenged to interpret and understand the text responsibly.

Perhaps from the study of these selected passages, readers can begin to see the shift of paradigms in the biblical text and, by extension, how the texts suggest that such paradigms have been shifting throughout history. This present time experiences an urgency for the paradigm to shift more radically given the severity of the socio-ecological injustices and crises that currently confront the entire cosmic community.

Ezekiel 5:1-17

"And because of all your abominations, I will do to you
what I have never yet done, and the like of which I will never do again." (5:9)

Ezekiel 5:1-17 is one passage among many that presents a bone-chilling picture of divine judgment. The text's metaphorical language is disturbing because it creates a male-imaged God ruthlessly angered at female-imaged Jerusalem who has been disobedient. Such disobedience merits the severest of punishments by God for Jerusalem, so that the people will know that God has spoken in jealousy (5:13). The text's metaphorical language also creates a picture of a God whose out-of-control anger becomes lethally abusive. What does this text say about a relationship with God, and what does this text say about God?

Ezekiel 5:1-17 can be divided into two main parts: a symbolic narrative (vv 1-4) and a prophecy of judgment against Jerusalem (vv 5-17). The prophecy of judgment can be further subdivided into three smaller units: an accusation (vv 5-6), a statement about impending divine chastisement (vv 7-12), and a statement of divine rage and further chastisements (vv 13-17). The speaker of the entire passage is God.

In vv 1-4, God commands Ezekiel to shave his head and his beard and then to divide the hairs of his head into three equal portions, which he is to burn with fire, strike with the sword, and scatter to the wind, respectively. This action may seem peculiar, but it is meant to symbolize and foreshadow what God will do to Jerusalem and all its inhabitants on the day of divine judgment (vv 11-12).

Verses 1-4 portray the power that God has over the prophet and the potential power that the prophet could have for his people. Historically, when God commands the prophets to do something, they do it. They are the true prophets and not false ones, if they have not corrupted their prophetic office by going their own way or delivering a message other than the one received from God. In vv 1-4, Ezekiel is the recipient of God's command; the text does not indicate a response on the prophet's part, but in the context of Ezekiel's actions in the book as a whole, one can presume that the prophet does as he is told. Thus, the text suggests that prophets are under the power of divine compunction, but this compunction is not power for the sake of domination and self-serving control on God's part; it is for the good of others.

God commands Ezekiel to act for his community, a sign of what is going to happen to them for their transgression of the law—if they do not turn from their ways. The text suggests that prophets like Ezekiel have the potential power to help their struggling communities, if only people would have ears to hear and eyes to see.

In the next section, vv 5-17, God describes Jerusalem's future, a message that Ezekiel in turn delivers to his audience. God personifies Jerusalem as a woman whom God has placed at the center of the countries (v 5) and in eye's view of all the countries (vv 8, 14-15). Jerusalem has a place of privilege because "she" has been given the divine law and ordinances and has been especially chosen by God.[1] Herein lies the problem that sets the rest of the narrative in motion: God declares to Jerusalem that "she" has rebelled against and rejected the divine ordinances and statutes and thus become more wicked than all the countries around "her" (v 6). "She" has also defiled the divine sanctuary with "her" detestable things and with "her" abominations (v 11). Thus, Jerusalem is guilty of disobedience, disrespect, and idolatry.

The text presents a vision of the social and religious corruption that existed in Jerusalem, God's city, where the temple—God's dwelling place—was located. It also presents the image of woman as unruly, depraved, and faithless. Typically in the ancient world, and in many cultures today, cities are personified as female. With respect to the Israelite culture, what is embedded in the feminine references for Israel, Judah, and Jerusalem is the notion of covenant: Israel, Judah, and Jerusalem were God's beloved, often depicted as God's wife or God's daughter, with God described as lover, husband, or father. Since God is divine and Jerusalem is human, a gender bias arises when Jerusalem sins—and sins in the guise of a woman. All sorts of additional problems arise because of this one gender-specific metaphor in relation to God portrayed as a male deity. Thus, the initial metaphor of God as a male deity who enters into covenant with Israel/Judah/Jerusalem is part of the problem that underlies the female metaphors ascribed to Israel/Judah, and in vv 5-17 Jerusalem, that are patriarchal and hierarchical. These two attitudes undoubtedly have influenced the social and religious thinking, attitudes and experiences of the writers and editors of the biblical text in general and the book of Ezekiel in particular.[2]

Not only does Ezek 5:5-17 give a depraved image of the female gender, female Jerusalem stands accused by God without giving any response or being afforded any opportunity to do so. This situation is reflective of many women's situations in the ancient world, and it is also reflective of the patriarchy and power structure associated with it. Women were often given no voice. It was the men who had a voice in social and religious matters. This situation continues to exist in many cultures today. Thus, vv 6 and 11 of Ezek 5:5-17 present a less than positive historical situation, a metaphor that offends, and a cultural attitude still in sore need of transformation today.

Verses 5-17 serve as a metaphor to express the historical tragedy that will and does befall Jerusalem when the Babylonians destroy the city. Judahite society, influenced by the deuteronomistic theology of retribution, and the text, written by writers and editors influenced by this theological construct, ascribe this inevitable event to God. The people sinned, so God uses divine power to devastate and exile them, destroy their kingdom and its capital, and demolish their temple. Furthermore, these verses depict God as one who has power over injustice, who will use such power to do things that are thoroughly oppressive, demoralizing, abusive, unjust, and blatantly out of control in order to chastise the Judahites and let them know that this God has spoken in jealousy (v 13). These deeds also serve the purpose of divine self-satisfaction (v 13) and teach the other kingdoms indirectly a lesson through Jerusalem's humiliation (v 8).

What is the horrendous judgment that God is about to level on Jerusalem? The text gives readers a vivid description: (1) parents will eat their children and children will eat their parents—cannibalism (v 10a);[3] (2) survivors will be scattered to every wind (v 10b); (3) they will be cut down without pity (v 11); (4) one-third will die of pestilence or be consumed by famine (v 12); (5) one-third will fall by the sword; (6) one-third will be scattered to every wind and liable to death (v 12); (7) they will become desolated and an object of mocking among foreign countries (vv 14-15); (8) they will experience famine and wild animals that will rob them of their children (v 17); they will experience pestilence, bloodshed, and the sword (v 17). Israel wavers on the brink of total destruction by an extremely angry God who, according to the text, states, "My anger shall spend itself, and I will vent my fury on them and satisfy myself; and they shall know that I, the LORD, have spoken in my jealousy, when I spend my fury on them" (v 13).

When this theological picture is united to the historical events that do, in fact, destroy Judah and Jerusalem, the resulting picture is disastrous. God speaks of death and not life, destruction and not mitigation, wrath without compassion, and anger without reconciliation. This jealous, self-interested God even manipulates the forces of creation, namely, rain and the animals and insects, to get even with faithless, sinful Jerusalem. Furthermore, innocent children (v 17) will get caught in the crossfire, and indirectly, so will the land, animals, and plant life when the pestilence and drought comes. God wields power unrestrainedly. The text forces the questions, "What kind of God is this?" and "Is this any way to treat a woman?—or any person for that matter?"

One might well ask if such deeds are representative of God's justice and righteousness in response to injustice.

Ezekiel 16

"I will judge you as women who commit adultery and shed blood are
judged, and bring blood upon you in wrath and jealousy." (16:38)

Perhaps one of the most graphic and metaphorical pieces in the entire book
of Ezekiel, chapter 16[4] makes many startling theological assertions and brings
into question whether or not Ezekiel's message is truly inspired or revelatory.
The picture of God overpowering Jerusalem, portrayed as a female, is far
worse than the picture presented in Ezek 5:1-17. Through its metaphors and
imagery, the prophecy conveys to readers a derogatory, discriminatory, harsh,
and violent message.[5]

Central to the passage is the image of a sinful woman, portrayed by and
symbolic of Jerusalem, in need of redemption and restoration. Verses 1-2 are a
message-reception formula and a command, respectively, that set the stage for
Ezekiel's address to Jerusalem. The passage can be divided into three parts: (1)
vv 3-43bα—a judgment speech comprised of three subunits, including a
description of Jerusalem's origin and growth (vv 3-14), a series of accusations
(vv 15-34), and a statement of intended chastisement (vv 35-43bα); (2) vv
43bβ-58—a diatribe[6] that consists of a comparison (vv 43bβ-52) and a promise of restoration (vv 53-58); and (3) vv 59-63—a prophecy of deliverance.

In vv 3-14, an allegory, God speaks through the prophet Ezekiel. In vv 3-5,
the reader learns of Jerusalem's origins (v 3) and painful first few days of life
(vv 4-5). Jerusalem (1) came from the land of the Canaanites, (2) had parents of a mixed ethnic background, (3) did not have her navel cord cut at
birth, (4) was not cleansed and rubbed with salt, (5) was not pitied by anyone, and (6) was thrown out in the open field because she was abhorred on
the day she was born.

Verses 3-5 contain several points for hermeneutical reflection. The image
of Jerusalem as a female provides some information as to how children, particularly female children, were treated in some ancient societies.[7] The focus
on Jerusalem's mixed ethnic background, coupled with the fact that "she" is
guilty of abominations, suggests that like Jerusalem, some people are "bad
seeds" from the beginning because of their ethnic background. The idea that
Jerusalem's abominations are related to "her" ethnic background recurs in
43bβ-52. The fact that the child Jerusalem was not cared for at birth presents
a negative picture of women: in the ancient world, care of an infant after birth
was the mother's and/or midwife's responsibility. The fact that no eye pitied
the abandoned child to care for it out of compassion can be seen as a serious
indictment against the human community and, by extension, an indictment
against the child's father. The focus on the absence of care for the child, however, keeps the image of the woman in the forefront. This picture of the abandoned child, together with the overtly ethnic reference and the use of gender-

specific imagery, has the potential to enrage readers. Finally, the status of Jerusalem as a "foundling child" opens up several legal points. In the ancient world, whenever a person or an object was cast out, the one doing the casting out relinquished all rights and obligations to the person or object cast out.[8] The law safeguarded the one who cast out and not the one being cast out. The scenario is a sad one: voiceless infant Jerusalem is unprotected by the law after being rejected by her parents (vv 3-5). The text begs the question for contemporary times: Is not Jerusalem's early life situation still happening today, especially where female children are involved?

Verses 6-7 depict God's first encounter with Jerusalem. Here, the metaphorical language gives readers a mixed picture of God. God is (1) compassionate, taking notice of small, insignificant outcasts in their struggles; (2) attentive to the growth process; and (3) efficacious when God commands the foundling child to live and "she" lives.

Two points, however, put God in a less than positive light. First, although God watches the growth process attentively, God comments, "Yet, you were naked and bare." In Gen 3:7, nakedness is associated with transgression and shame; in Deut 28:28, it is part of a divine warning of chastisement; in Ezek 16:39 and 23:29, it is associated with divine judgment and violent actions; and in Ezek 18:7, the one who covers the "naked with a garment" is considered "righteous" (cf. Ezek 18:16). What are readers to conclude? Second, that God does not pick up baby Jerusalem, who is flailing in her birth blood, is troublesome. Why did God not bathe "her," swaddle "her," and hold "her" close? Did God not do these things because Jerusalem is, metaphorically, a little girl and not a little boy (cf. Hos 11:1-4)?

In vv 8-14, God reiterates all the good care that God has offered to Jerusalem. Jerusalem was chosen by God; "she" belonged to God because of God's pledge to "her" and because of covenant; and all that "she" is and has, both materially and physically, is on account of God. On the one hand, God's gestures seem to be kind; on the other hand, they could be seen as patronizing, especially since there is no response from Jerusalem. Further, the relationship between God and Jerusalem is not a mutual one: the woman has no identity except what God has turned her into—the resemblance of a queen who would be fit for him, "the king." In these verses, a woman's fame is equated with her beauty (v 14a), a beauty that is "perfect" only because of the "splendor" that a man, in this case, God, has bestowed on her (v 14b). Beauty, then, in the eyes of a man, is equated with the outward appearance of a woman who is valued not for her own person, but rather for what she has become through the man's care. In sum, the woman has become a product of her husband's care.

Verses 8-14 depict God as a powerful husband who controls the relationship between himself and his wife and who is, essentially, in control of his wife. The regal adornment of Jerusalem and the title "queen" suggest royalty.

For the reader, the question that emerges is: Does Jerusalem have to become "regal" to continue to be loved by God? Verses 15-22 portray God accusing Jerusalem of a series of crimes: "she" has trusted in her beauty, played the harlot, and misused the clothing, jewels, and food God gave her (vv 15-19); she has sacrificed their children to idols (vv 20-21);[9] and she has forgotten that it was her husband, God, who rescued her from death in the days of her youth (v 22). On one level, Jerusalem is guilty of harlotry, idolatry, murder, and forgetfulness. On another level, God's "regal bride" has become an unfaithful, idolatrous, murderous, and absent-minded wife.

The invective against Jerusalem continues in vv 23-29. God accuses Jerusalem of playing the whore (vv 23-25), names all her lovers, (vv 26-28), and points out her insatiable lust (v 29). Jerusalem's "enemies" are also, metaphorically, females—Philistine daughters—whom Jerusalem has shamed by her conduct.[10]

Verses 30-34 give a very dramatic view of the husband and wife relationship between God and Jerusalem. God launches a most bitter attack against "his" Jerusalem: her heart is sick (v 30); she is an adulterous wife; she takes strangers instead of her husband (v 32). She is worse than a whore because she bribed her lovers to come to her instead of receiving their payment. Furthermore she solicited them; they did not come after her as would be the usual practice in prostitution in ancient days (vv 31, 33-34).

In summary, vv 15-34 name Jerusalem's four abominations as adultery, idolatry, child sacrifice, and forgetfulness of God. All of these transgressions are punishable by the law. Both male and female adulterers are sentenced to death either by stoning or the sword (Lev 20:10; Deut 22:21-24; Ezek 23:47; cf. Exod 20:14). The punishment for idolatry is also death (Deut 13:12-16; cf. Exod 20:2-6), as is the punishment for child sacrifice (Leviticus 18–21; 20:1-5; Deut 12:30-32; 18:10-12). Forgetfulness of God receives a strong word of caution (Deut 6:10-12; 8:11-20).

Verses 15-34 give Ezekiel's readers a very disturbing picture of God and, because of the husband-wife metaphor operative throughout much of Ezekiel 16, a distressing portrait of a husband-wife relationship, not to mention a horrendous profile of a woman. God is portrayed as controlling, possessive, angry, and abusive. God loves "his" spouse, is justly angry at his wife, but is verbally abusive in his accusations and physically abusive in his punishment (v 27). Jerusalem, a once silent, passive woman, is turned into a "queen" by her husband, God, to become an initiator of harlotry, a "hussy" incapable of being sexually satisfied. She has violated several laws, and in the case of adultery, both she and her partner(s) deserve to be put to death. The text does not indicate that her lovers are punished or rebuked.

The action of Ezekiel 16 progresses, thus far, at the expense of a woman, and this situation raises three questions: (1) Are readers being asked to sympathize with God, the "victim" of a disastrous marriage? (2) Are the woman's deeds being portrayed horribly in order to accent the strength and power of God's judgments and chastisements? (3) Are the readers being asked to assume that the woman is going to get what she deserves, especially since her transgressions warrant death (see vv 35-43)? Jerusalem is silent throughout the accusations hurled at "her." Does this imply that this is her appropriate stance before God, or a wife's before her husband? With a male metaphor for God and a female one for Jerusalem, the image of the woman will always be discolored, and she will always be the one needing to be redeemed. This metaphor that has shaped Ezekiel 16 can continue to shape theological imaginations today in a way that would be offensive and unacceptable from a liberation perspective.

As the story progresses, readers learn what God is about to do to his adulterous wife (vv 37-41). God intends to: expose her to all her lovers (v 37), judge her according to judgments of adulteresses and murderers (v 38), and then deliver her into the hands of her executioners, who will execute judgments on her "before the eyes of many women" (v 41a). God is handing his wife over to the death penalty.

Next follows a series of self-reflective statements that God directs at Jerusalem. God's aim in punishing "her" has a threefold purpose. God wants: (1) to stop her from playing the harlot and from making payments; (2) to satisfy "his" own fury and jealousy so that he can return to a calm, no-anger state; and (3) to return to her what she deserves (vv 41-43).

In vv 35-43bα, one sees a vengeful, angry God who desires to appease his own feelings at the expense of another's life. Through the use of metaphor, the text suggests that the fate of a wife is in the hands of her husband. The text depicts God as someone who is capable of devising wicked deeds against someone who acts wickedly. The text raises the question: Does violence inflicted by a victim on a perpetrator make right the violence done to the victim? Furthermore, the idea of the woman's nakedness is associated with transgression (v 36), shame (v 37), and humiliation (v 38). The nakedness harks back to vv 7 and 22, which, together with vv 36-38, may contain a subtle tone of disdain toward the female body. The metaphorical language of these verses, and the text as a whole thus far, has a strong bias against women. One thing seems certain, however; God will not tolerate injustice. This strong ethical message put forth by the text cannot, however, silence the question: To what extent does the text itself communicate a truly ethical message?

God's judgment against Jerusalem continues in vv 43bβ-52 and vv 53-58. In these two subunits judgment is couched in a harsh, gender-specific simile and related metaphors, all of which accent Jerusalem's corruption. In vv 43bβ, God tells Jerusalem that all who see her now will ascribe a particular proverb to her: "as [the] mother, [so] her daughter" (v 44). In v 45, God unpacks this simile for Jerusalem, pointing out that "she" is like the Hittite woman, an unnamed woman in the text who "loathed" her husband and children (v 45), and is the sister of her sisters who also "loathed their husbands and children" (v 45). Jerusalem's older sister is Samaria; her younger sister is Sodom (v 46); and the children that both loathed were their daughters (v 46). Thus, Jerusalem is the "middle child" in the family surrounded by familial women who all acted corruptly, yet, as God points out, she acted more corruptly than Samaria and Sodom and therefore made her sisters look "righteous" (vv 48-52). Readers see, then, that Jerusalem was corrupt from birth onward, and that the seeds of her corruption were given to her by her mother, who also infected her two sisters. This corruption was not "learned behavior," because Jerusalem was abandoned at birth. The suggestion is that Jerusalem's internal make-up was corrupt (cf. 16:30). While v 45 mentions Jerusalem's father as an Ammonite, there is no comment about his relationship to Jerusalem. Clearly, the blame for Jerusalem's corruption is her mother—a female.

The metaphorical language of this section (vv 43bβ-52) presents to readers a description of Jerusalem that highlights the corruption of her family members, which is symbolic, historically, of the city's own state of affairs. The fact that the message of vv 43bβ-52 is spoken by God gives the impression of a distinct disdain for Jerusalem and, by extension, for women. Verses 53-58 shift the focus from accusation to promise. Here, God promises to restore all of Jerusalem's and her sisters' fortunes (vv 53-54) and to return the sisters, their daughters, and Jerusalem's daughters to their former states (v 55). Surprisingly though, there is no mention of God's benevolence to Jerusalem for herself alone. Her restoration is so that she can become a consolation for her sisters (v 54). Most detested Jerusalem will finally be shown some sort of mercy. This gift could make her an object of disdain for Sodom, whom she mocked earlier (vv 56-57), and most certainly an object of mockery for her neighbors, who already despise her (vv 27, 57). It seems, then, that God's restoration of Jerusalem is meant to make her feel guilty and ashamed.

Verses 59-63 draw the story to a close. Here, God continues to promise Jerusalem that she will pay for her infidelity (v 59) but that "he" will also now establish an everlasting covenant with her. One sees, however, that the reestablishment of covenant is meant to make Jerusalem feel ashamed (v 61) and to assert God's power and control over Jerusalem (vv 62-63), all in the name of divine forgiveness. Are the readers being asked to accept the fact that there is no mercy without severe justice (see vv 35-43bα) and humiliation first (see vv 43bβ-58)? What readers do see is that covenant and its restoration are for God's self-serving purposes rooted in sensuality (vv 8-14) and the need for domination (vv 62-63). God's loving-kindness (cf. Hos 2:21; Mic 7:19-20) seems nowhere present. Also, are readers being given a model that bespeaks of a tit-for-tat relationship with God? If this is a model for covenant and marital love, should not wife Jerusalem ask her husband God to apologize for his abusiveness? Jerusalem's silence looms large, especially for feminists and liberationists.

In summary, Ezekiel 16 is an intricate and artistic piece of writing whose metaphorical language is simultaneously engaging yet disturbing, vivacious yet offensive. The text's metaphors are symptomatic of underlying ideological, theological, and gender-biased assumptions on the part of the text's writers and later editors. The text represents these assumptions as well as the culture that influenced the thought and writing of the authors and editors. Clearly, the text admits of a bias against women that flows from male–female metaphorical covenanted language, which itself is formed by a patriarchal society and culture. While the text speaks of a forgiving God who is faithful to covenant and to its restoration, the text is revelatory insofar as it sheds light on many ancient and oppressive attitudes and actions, some of which are still present today. These attitudes and actions continue to shape and misshape people's lives as many try to live out life in relationship with God and with one another. Ezekiel 16 portrays a marriage in sore need of transformation by both parties, and a patriarchal God's power, control, and abusiveness toward another human being cry to heaven for justice as loudly as the unfaithful, silent wife.

Ezekiel 19

"She raised up one of her cubs;
he became a young lion,
and he learned to catch prey;
he devoured humans." (19:3)

Continuing in the vein of Ezekiel 16, Ezekiel 19 is also allegorical and metaphorical. The passage consists of two units, vv 2-9 and 10-14; v 1 is a divine statement addressed to the prophet Ezekiel. The text features God giving Ezekiel a message to be delivered to the princes of Judah. Central to the allegory is a female character—a mother—who is compared to a lioness (v 2), who is later compared to a vine (v 10). Two other characters are male—sons of the mother, who are compared to lion cubs. The poem is a narrative about what took place during the reigns of Judah's last two kings after the death of King Josiah. Rich metaphorical language and images interlock historical figures and events to create an amazing picture of power.

The poem opens in v 1 with God telling the prophet Ezekiel to raise up a lamentation for the princes of Israel. Verses 2-14 are a lament spoken by God to the prophet. A short prose phrase at the end of v 14 closes the lament. Verse 1 and the prose phrase of v 14 frame the lament.

In vv 1-4, the focus is on Hamutal and Jehoahaz. The lioness in v 1 refers to Hamutal (2 Kgs 24:18), the wife of Josiah and mother of the two lion cubs, Jehoahaz and either Jehoiachin or Zedekiah,[11] brothers and kings after Josiah's death. Verse 2 gives a clear picture of Hamutal through metaphorical language. Hamutal was a "lioness" among "lions." The phrase and comparison imply that she was an extraordinary person, especially among the men: strong and perhaps very beautiful; it is implied though not stated. She was also a woman with maternal instincts who fulfilled her role as a mother, rearing and raising her cubs—her children. One of her cubs became a young lion—Jehoahaz—who "learned to catch prey and devour humans" (v 3). This young lion soon met with tragedy: after a short reign (2 Kgs 23:31-34), he was captured and taken as prisoner to Egypt by Pharaoh Necho in 609 B.C.E.

In vv 5-9, the focus shifts from Jehoahaz to another cub, either Jehoiachin or Zedekiah. Just as Hamutal had helped to form Jehoahaz into a young lion, she did the same with the other one, who is either Jehoiachin or Zedekiah.[12] Like his brother, this other son "learned to catch prey." He also "devoured people" and exerted great power over their strongholds, towns, and land. Such deeds resulted in his demise: he was dethroned and exiled to Babylon.

Verses 2-9 give a picture of power in relation to the female gender. A female, Hamutal is someone who has strength and beauty and who fulfills a role most often associated with females in the ancient world: motherhood. She nurtures and cares for her offspring. The lion/lioness is considered to be the most powerful of all animals in the hierarchical animal kingdom. In the ancient Near East, the lion/lioness symbolized royalty; for Judah, it was a symbol of rule.[13] The symbolism makes clear that power in ancient times was connected to status and to the royal class, who were the ruling class. As for the role of motherhood, the text features the "Queen Mother," a title given to Hamutal by the royal court of Jerusalem,[14] focusing her attention on two of her sons who eventually became kings. Here, one sees the power that a woman of royalty had with respect to shaping a country's future leadership.[15] One wonders if those cubs who were female received as much attention and care as the male cubs. Furthermore, while a female could have power and influence, ultimately it was the males who ruled the country. Thus, these verses reveal two characteristics of power in the ancient world: (1) it was held by the elite, and (2) it was gender-specific, patriarchal, and noninclusive: the males became the leaders despite the powerful influence of the elite females of royalty.

Verses 2-9 also show the abuse of power in relation to patriarchy. Both "cubs"/sons "learn to catch prey; they devoured humans" (vv 3, 6); the second "cub"/son ravaged people's strongholds and destroyed their cities (v 7), leaving the land and its inhabitants stunned. Here, one sees males using power to dominate and oppress. But these two sons were reared and raised by their mother. What is the reader to extrapolate from this scene about women and the raising of their sons? Is this an indirect invective against women,[16] or particularly mothers of sons? Might the text suggest that mothers, influenced by their culture, raised their sons in a manner that reflected the norms and culture itself, namely, that males aspire to leadership and use their power aggressively? Another example of power is found in vv 4 and 8-9. Those sons who once used their power to oppress others are now oppressed themselves by other countries, specifically by the pharaoh of Egypt and the king of Babylon, who use their power to take captives. Here again, one sees the exercise of power by elite males.

Finally, vv 2-9 as a whole foreshadow what will happen to Judah: the country will be defeated and captured by countries greater than itself, and the people will be exiled to Egypt and Babylon. In the world of power there is also a hierarchy of aggression. The more aggressive one can be, the more powerful one can become. The Judahite leaders used their power to overpower their own people; the Egyptians and Babylonians used their power to overpower the Judahite leaders. The text makes clear that those who use their power to overpower others become themselves victims of others' abuse of power.

The allegorical picture changes in vv 10-14. Here the text portrays mother Hamutal as a lush vine in a vineyard. The double image of the mother and the vine symbolizes Judah. The plant's stems would be her sons, and thus, the reference in v 11 to the vine's strongest stem that became a ruler's scepter is a reference to one of Hamutal's sons, specifically, Zedekiah.[17] To whom "it" refers in v 12 is not clear. Blenkinsopp argues that the reference is to Zedekiah;[18] Clements suggests that the reference could be to Hamutal since "she had herself been taken to Babylon, along with others of the royal household (Jer 9:2)."[19] This reading would then lead to a new interpretation of the poem, specifically, that it is not about the fate of Judah's last king, but rather, about the fate of Judah as represented by the mother—lioness Hamutal.[20] This interpretation, in fact, would point up the folly of the mother's ambition for her sons that resulted in their downfall. All these female images, then, of the mother lioness turned vine, all representative of Hamutal, who herself symbolizes Judah, are used in a way that suggests a cultural bias against women. An underlying patriarchal attitude was a strong influence, whether conscious or unconscious, on the shaping of the thoughts and expressions of the authors and editors of this text. In any case, I argue that the pronoun "it" in v 12a refers to the vine: the mother lioness Hamutal who represents Judah. In v 12c, then, the stem is Zedekiah. Hence, v 12 speaks of the demise of Judah and the end of the Davidic line of kingship, a point further developed in vv 13-14.

Thus, vv 10-14 and vv 2-9 speak about the future of Judah's leadership in metaphorical language that is gender inclusive: the Queen mother and her sons will go into exile; the royal dynasty will come to an end; and the entire country of Judah—women and men—will collapse and suffer tragically. Clearly, then, while there are strong gender biases in the text that are brought to the forefront by the text's metaphors, this entire allegory is, essentially, about power that is ambitious, aggressive, hierarchical, and patriarchal; rests with the elite ruling class; but that also crosses the lines of gender in the struggle for domination of families and countries.

Ezekiel 34:1-10

"I will rescue my sheep from their mouths,
so that they may not be food for them." (34:10)

Another highly metaphorical passage in the book of Ezekiel that focuses on leadership and power is Ezek 34:1-10, a narrative about bad shepherds. In this passage, the shepherds are the political rulers of Judah who have used their power to oppress their sheep, the Judahites. The prophecy is spoken by God to the prophet Ezekiel who in turn delivers it to his audience; God takes the shepherds to task for their injustices and promises to do justice on behalf of the oppressed. The prophecy of judgment can be divided into two parts: an indictment (vv 2-6), and a judgment statement and message of hope (vv 7-10). A prophetic messenger formula introduces the passage (v 1).

In vv 2-6, God, angered by the shepherds' self-interest and lack of care for the sheep, launches a direct verbal attack on them: "You eat the fat, you clothe yourselves with the wool, you slaughter the fatlings, but you do not feed the sheep" (v 3). Furthermore, "You have not strengthened the weak, you have not healed the sick, you have not bound up the injured, you have not brought back the strayed, you have not sought the lost, but with force and harshness you have ruled them" (v 4). Judah's leaders are guilty of lack of care not only for the community as a whole but also for the most vulnerable within the community. Instead, the shepherds exercised forceful, harsh power over them.

Such abuse of power resulted in the sheep being scattered all over the face of the earth, where they wandered about without anyone knowing or caring about their whereabouts (vv 5-6). From a historical perspective, Judah's rulers are being blamed for the exile. The kings have cared for neither the strong nor the weak members of the Judahite populace.

Verses 7-10 describe further the condition of the sheep and what God intends to do to the shepherds. The sheep have become prey and food for all the wild animals (v 8); they have even become food for the shepherds (v 10). God promises to come to the sheep's rescue.

Possession of sheep in the ancient Near Eastern world denoted power and wealth. The shepherd's duty was to care for the sheep, providing food, water, shelter, and security. Sheep were easy prey for thieves and wild animals (1 Sam 17:34-35; Amos 3:12). This metaphor applied to Judah's leadership and the community, with the leadership being the shepherd and the community being the sheep, presents a potentially bucolic but hierarchical picture. The shepherd not only had to care for the sheep, but also had to lead them, and the sheep had to follow the shepherd if they wanted to be cared for. This metaphor was popular not only in Israel and Judah, but also in Mesopotamia, Egypt, and Greece, primarily because these cultures were patriarchal and hierarchical.

For Israel and Judah, this metaphor carried with it the weight of responsibility and a sense of accountability. Precisely because the political leaders neglected their responsibility, they were confronted by the prophet who informed them that they were accountable to God. Instead of exercising their power to uphold the common good while lending support to all who were struggling—both oppressed and oppressor—in the community, the leaders used their power to dominate and crush others with oppression and exploitation. Because of this egregious misuse of power and the failure to act and lend responsibly, God exerted power not to chastise as in previous accounts but to rescue the sheep—the Israelite community. Divine power was used for liberation, the effects of which are described in 34:11-31.

For some readers, the shepherd-sheep metaphor could be offensive because it favors a patriarchal-hierarchical mode of leadership whereby the shepherd is in control and the sheep must follow along. The metaphor allows for and models a style of leadership in which power is invested in the leader who has "power over" a people, with the people being essentially powerless and, like sheep, in a state of dependence.

Furthermore, while God uses divine power to liberate, God continues to be described in patriarchal and hierarchical images. Shepherd God (see v 15) will "rescue" the people from their miserable state, leaving the people dependent now on God. While the text speaks of power for the sake of liberation, it does not speak of interdependent relationships characterized by empowerment (see Part Three of this study).

Ezekiel 25

"Because Edom acted revengefully against the house of Judah . . .
I will stretch out my hand."(25:12-13)

Chapter 25 is part of a larger body of texts, Ezek 25:1—32:32, a series of prophecies against other countries. This chapter speaks of God taking Judah's part by confronting and chastising those countries who have mistreated Judah. Exiled and powerless, Israel stands ready to receive a word of hope, an expression of care. The chapter can be divided into four parts: a proclamation against Ammon (vv 1-7); a proclamation against Moab (vv 8-11); a proclamation against Edom (vv 12-14); and a proclamation against Philistia (vv 15-17).

In vv 1-7, Ezekiel's prophecy is directed toward Ammon.[21] Here, God is angry at the Ammonites because they rejoiced when both God's sanctuary was profaned and Judah was made to suffer at the hand of the Babylonians (vv 3, 6). Ammon celebrated Judah's downfall, interpreted as the result of God's chastisement on the country because of its wickedness. Following the confrontation between God and the Ammonites, God then outlines a series of chastisements that will come upon the Ammonites, the last of which is the promise that they will be "destroyed" (vv 4-7). God's power would be lethal. No one who mocks the Judahites in their downtrodden and exiled state would be shown mercy. God's final words to the Ammonites express the goal of God's behavior: "Then you shall know that I am the LORD" (v 7; see also v 5).

From this passage, readers see that one country, Ammon, had laughed at Judah and Israel when they were brought low; indirectly, the country was snickering at God when it gloated over the profanation of the sanctuary. Such inordinate behavior merited threats of strong corrective measures from God that, to the reader, may seem quite harsh. God is clearly defending Judah against a stronger country. Are the chastisements purely because Ammon rejoiced over another's misfortune, or might they be because God wants to assert who's "boss" over all countries? Also, might this passage serve to support the push toward monotheism on the part of the author and editors?

Finally, God defends the Judahites in their state of suffering. While this is noble, one must ask: Who ultimately was responsible for their condition? Granted, they may have transgressed, but the text portrays God as the cause of Judah's demise. Now God acts on behalf of the Judahites because they became victims of taunt. Is this divine justice and mercy? Ezekiel's next prophecy is directed toward Moab (vv 8-11).[22] God indicts Moab because it also has mocked Judah by boldly stating that "it too is like all the other peoples" (v 8). Moab denies Judah's special status as God's chosen. Verses 9-11 describe what God plans to do to Moab because of its arrogance. The prophecy predicts the fall of Moab to the "people of the East," the Kedarites, and its end as a politically independent country (v 10). The short pericope closes with the same divine statement that was made to Ammon: "Then they shall know that I am the LORD."

In this passage several points and related questions come to the fore. Many of the questions are similar to those that arise from the prophecy about Moab. God defends the house of Judah against a country that looks upon it as just any other country. Moab's stance toward Judah could be taken as an indirect attack on God because Judah was not like other countries; Judah was

God's chosen one. The text portrays God acting with mercy on behalf of Judah, the one being taunted, and with justice toward Moab, the one ridiculing Judah. Yet did not God use the Babylonians to level Judah in the first place because of its apostasy and transgressions? Was it not this that made the other countries see Judah as powerless, spurned, and defiled?[23]

From these two prophecies, readers see God's chosen people as the taunted of its neighbors because of its suffering. If God had brought Judah low and threatens to do the same to the other countries, is not Judah like the other countries—victims of God's raging anger that leads to fateful ends?

Finally, there is the statement that follows God's pledge of judgment on Moab: "Then they shall know I am the LORD." Readers are again faced with the perplexing question: What kind of Lord? the LORD who both defends countries after their divine judgment and then wipes out other countries because they have taunted the chastised country? Is God the LORD of justice and mercy on behalf of all people, or is God the LORD of volatile power whose method of control over the countries is through fear and punishment first and then mercy? Ezekiel's next prophecy is a word against Edom (vv 12-14).[24] In v 12 God indicts Edom for acting revengefully against Judah. The text here does not disclose Edom's crime against Judah;[25] but in Ezek 36:5, Edom is accused of taking land from the Judahites in a spirit of joy and utter contempt. In Ezek 25:13-14 Edom receives its message of impending doom from God: Edom will be completely laid waste, from humans to animals, as symbolized by the city Teman in the far north and Dedan in the south of the country. What was done to Judah will be done to Edom (v 14). The prophecy closes with a strong assertion: "and they shall know my vengeance, says the LORD."

In this passage, God is about to use divine power for the sake of Judah. Hence, in a manner similar to the prophecies against Ammon and Moab, God here also defends Judah against Edom's actions. The God who once asserted power against Judah now asserts power on behalf of Judah. While this seems to be positive for Judah, it is devastating for Edom. The text shows God using power for the benefit of one at the expense of another. Was such a deed meant as a tactic to strengthen the bonds between God and Judah after the exile?

Punishment includes creatures from the natural world. To what extent does the text portray a just God, a portrait that can be very different from a God of justice? Unlike the prophecies against Ammon and Moab, punishment in this prophecy is not seen as anthropocentric; it includes harm to the animals. In ancient Israelite society, human well-being or diminishment was connected to the well-being or diminishment of the natural world. Texts show that when the people sinned, the natural world suffered because God struck both (see, for example, Isa 4:6-13). Such a claim is made by this text and those who shaped the text into its present canonical form. Punishment extended to the animals was a way of cutting the people off from a food source. For those involved in socio-ecojustice, this text may cause some tension insofar as nonhuman life suffers because of the transgressions of human beings.

Ezekiel directs the final prophecy in this chapter against Philistia.[26] Verse 15 is the indictment; vv 16-17, the statement of divine retribution. The Philistines have acted in vengeance (v 15), and so God, in turn, will act with vengeance on them (v 17). Though no crime is stated that warrants divine rebuke and punishment, one could presume that it was because of the Philistines' biting hatred of Israel.

Here, God's power asserted on behalf of the Judahites is inferred and not overt as in the other prophecies in Ezekiel 25. Present are the strains of *lex talionis,* the law of reciprocal retaliation. The Philistines who acted with vengeance will also receive vengeance. God will retaliate against the Philistines on behalf of the Judahites.

In summary, these four prophecies pronounced against other countries share a common form—indictment and chastisement—as well as a common theme: God acts with power on behalf of devastated Judah. Readers see, however, that while these texts are favorable for the Judahites, they are not favorable for the other countries. God's use of power is intended for the destruction of other countries on behalf of "justice." Thus, the texts disclose an ethnocentric attitude that may have been embedded in the Jewish culture of which the writers and editors of the biblical text were a part.[27] Even though Judah was a country that had broken covenant and law, it was still the country most favored by God.

In these texts, readers are given a clear example of how violence begets violence. The message that vengeance is produced by divine favor and care needs to be addressed by readers globally because these texts could legitimate the use of aggression by some people to bring about justice for those who are powerless. History has shown that this strategy does not work even when it is well intentioned. For readers today, these texts, together with history, point to the need for a shift in how power is used so that a vision of well-being, justice, and care for all creation can be the goal and inspiration that fuels and empowers all praxis.

Ezekiel 36:1-15

"See now, I am for you; I will turn to you, and you shall be tilled and sown . . . and I will multiply human beings and animals upon you." (36:9-11a)

Lush with images from creation that speak of restoration and transformation, this prophecy is a marvelous proclamation of hope and a vision of renewed life for the people of Judah. For the surrounding countries, though, the picture is not as bright. As they have caused Judah to suffer insults, so shall they be made to suffer insults (v 7). The text celebrates the God of Israel/Judah, who acts with power on Israel's behalf. Also the text may imply a polemic against Baal, the fertility god. Throughout many prophetic texts, Israel and Judah are accused of apostasy and idolatry: Baal worship. The passage can be divided into three units: a diatribe against the other countries (vv 1-7), in particular Edom; promises to Judah (vv 8-12); and a prophecy of hope (vv 13-15).

In vv 1-7, the mountains, specifically, as well as other elements of the natural world—the hills, watercourses, valleys, desolate wastes, and deserted towns—are all recipients of divine favor; Edom and the other countries, divine scorn. This passage, with its specific reference, "aha!" harks back to Ezekiel 25, in which the country clapped and mocked and celebrated Judah's sad state of devastation and exile. Believed to have been caused by God, who supposedly sent in the Babylonians to destroy Judah because of that country's wickedness, Judah's demise prompted the other countries' mocking attitude, a direct attack on Judah and an indirect attack on God. The powerless and devastated condition of Judah would make countries question and doubt Israel's God now. Verses 1-7 respond to those taunts by presenting a picture of God using divine power to restore first the natural world of Judah, especially the land and its elements, which had become "a source of plunder and an object of derision to the rest of the peoples all around" (v 4). Edom and the countries will see that God, not themselves, will have the last word. The last word for Judah is not destruction; it is the promise of restoration (vv 8-13). For the other countries, however, there is still a word of rebuke.[28]

God's address to the mountains continues in vv 8-12, focusing on the restoration of Israel's land, its human beings, and its animals. The land will be tilled and sown (v 9); the population will increase; and the waste places will be rebuilt (v 10). Human beings and animals alike will "increase and be fruitful" (v 11).

Verses 13-15 speak of Israel's/Judah's transformation. Once a country of internal strife and wickedness—a condition that prompted scorn from other countries—Judah, through God's power, will be able to put an end to its own wickedness, which, in turn, will stop the wagging tongues of the other countries who by their mockery have caused the people of Judah to suffer insult and bear disgrace (vv 14-15). Later on in vv 33-36, readers learn that Judah will be cleansed by God of all its iniquities, and restoration will take place in the natural world.

Verses 1-15 as a whole present a wonderful picture of power and the interrelatedness between the restoration of the natural world and the redemption of humankind. This text suggests that the land and the natural world of Judah are promised restoration simultaneously as human beings are promised redemption from their own oppressive and wicked ways and liberation from the insults of others because of their wicked ways.

Israel's restoration, redemption, and liberation will come about through God's power used creatively. Verses 13-14 hint at a change of behavior among the Judahites that will happen only when God cleanses the people of Judah from their iniquities (Ezek 36:33). Thus, one can conclude that through God's power, the restoration of creation can happen, with humanity's transformation being an intricate and necessary part of the whole process.

Although this text was first intended to be a source of hope for exiled Judahites and their devastated land, it is revelatory for anyone who would read it in the context of the contemporary global climate that calls for socio-ecological justice. The planet and its inhabitants—both human and nonhuman—suffer not because of some divine judgment and chastisement as many of the Ezekiel texts would have readers believe. No, the planet and its inhabitants suffer because of what some people have done and continue to do that rapes all aspects of creation and devastates life as a whole.

Finally, Ezek 36:1-15 does provide a vision for its readers, yet this vision is imperfect. God is described as one who is ultimately responsible for accomplishing the task of restoration, redemption, and liberation independent of any human effort. The vision has hierarchical implications. It does not present a picture of God working through a person or persons to assist in the restorative, redemptive, liberative, and transformative process.

Furthermore, the condemnation of Edom and other kingdoms, and God's favoritism toward Israel do allow readers to see an ethnocentric attitude embedded in this text. Thus, the vision that the text describes is not an inclusive one and is incomplete. Ezekiel 36:1-15 suggests that there is still work to be done if restoration, redemption, and liberation are to be globally implemented for all peoples and all creation.

Ezekiel in Context

From the selected passages presented in this chapter, one can see that the book of Ezekiel is a provocative text with elegant metaphorical language. While the text includes some offensive elements, it also contains a valued liberative thrust. Even though there are inherent gender and ethnocentric biases in the text, coupled with hierarchical and patriarchal overtones, the book's cosmological dimension, which speaks of divine restoration, liberation, and redemption, offers a powerful and positive vision for readers today. It also challenges its readers to realize the texts' incompleteness and the need for ongoing work of interpretation and praxis.

Shifting from Power and Domination to Power and Liberation

Introduction

AFTER PART ONE'S EXAMINATION OF POWER and domination, Part Two focuses on power and liberation. The books of Daniel, Jonah, Haggai, Zechariah, Obadiah, Malachi, Nahum, and Joel all have as one of their central themes liberation from suffering and injustice.

Part Two focuses on how power can be exercised to empower a prophet to interpret dreams that assure life, how power can empower a king and a group of people to change their ways to prevent impending disaster, and how God will use divine power to liberate not only the the people of Judah but also other countries from injustices that are the result of the abuse of power. Embedded in the vision of social liberation is the vision of the restoration of the natural world. As people are freed from their pain and suffering, so is the natural world restored.

The texts presented in Part Two emphasize liberation instead of oppression. Nevertheless, even though this next group of texts was selected because of their emphasis on the exercise of power to liberate, several of the texts continue to evoke concerns in need of ongoing hermeneutical reflection and comment, particularly in relation to how they present God. Readers continue to be confronted, to some degree, with images of divine power being used aggressively and punitively. Although the emphasis has shifted from power used to dominate to power used to liberate, the texts are not totally free from expressions of punitive suffering and pain.

7

Daniel

Overview: A Historical, Literary, and Hermeneutical Interplay

PERHAPS ONE OF THE MOST DESCRIPTIVE NARRATIVES about what life was like for the people of Judah exiled in Babylon is the book of Daniel. More like a religious treatise than a historical document, the book encourages the Judahites to remain faithful to their way of life. At the same time, it presents a positive view of the Gentile world. The text's hypothetical historical setting spans the time of Jehoiakim, king of Judah in 606 B.C.E. up to the reign of Seleucid king Antiochus IV, a vicious tyrant who died in 164 B.C.E.

Like the book of Baruch, which also portrays the Judahites in exile, Daniel contains material that is part of the Roman Catholic canon but considered apocryphal by Protestants. Two prayers in Daniel 3 and the stories of Susanna and Bel and the Dragon, chapters 10 and 14, respectively, are not included in the Hebrew canon but are found in the Greek and Latin versions of the text. Furthermore, the book is written in Hebrew (1:1-2:4a; 8:1—12:13) and Aramaic (2:4b—7:28), with the three additions found in the Roman Catholic Canon Proper and the Protestant Apocrypha written in Greek. This chapter examines the book of Daniel incorporated into the one found in the Roman Catholic Canon of the NRSV, which, following the Septuagint, places Daniel among the prophets.

The book as a whole is comprised of three main parts: (1) stories about Daniel and his friends (1–6); (2) Daniel's visions and revelations (7–12); and (3) two short stories: Susanna and Daniel and Bel and the Dragon (13–14). The book contains extensive symbolism, dreams, prayers, visions, short vignettes, and a variety of character types. In general, the material is highly apocalyptic, especially with its end-time predictions and its use of both determined time periods and angels.

The book of Daniel demonstrates how power can become a helpful and liberating agent. Daniel is empowered by God to interpret dreams, to offer encouragement to his companions, and to withstand the trials and tribulations that threaten his and others' lives. The two prayers in chapter 3 dramatically portray how, through divine efforts, people are saved from having to experience fiery deaths. This chapter examines the liberative aspects of power embedded in selected texts from the book of Daniel, while also highlighting other points embedded in these passages that are in need of further hermeneutical consideration.

Daniel 2
*"Then the mystery was revealed to Daniel in a vision of the night,
and Daniel blessed the God of heaven." (2:19)*

Perhaps one of the most engaging narratives among the Prophets is the story of Daniel, the interpreter of dreams. The prophet finds favor with King Nebuchadnezzar because he is able to interpret the king's dreams on more than one occasion. This gift that Daniel has received from God, along with his faithfulness to God, saves his life. The first account of Daniel interpreting one of the king's dreams appears in chapter 2.

The chapter opens with the king being deeply disturbed by his dreams. He summons the magicians, enchanters, sorcerers, and other Chaldeans to come before him and interpret his dreams. He threatens that if they do not interpret his dreams, then he will have them torn limb from limb and will have their houses destroyed. If they do interpret the dreams, then he will give them gifts, rewards, and great honors. The magicians, enchanters, sorcerers, and Chaldeans were powerless, however, and could not perform the task, saying that it would have to be accomplished by the gods (vv 1-11).

Enraged, the king next commands that all the wise ones of Babylon be destroyed, including Daniel and his companions. When pressed, Daniel responds to Arioch, the king's royal official, with "prudence and discretion" (2:14): he raises a question concerning the king's decree that required the wise ones to interpret his dreams lest they be killed. Daniel requests time with the king to interpret the king's dreams, and the request is granted. Before Daniel meets with the king, he prays to God, and the "mystery of the night" is revealed to him. Daniel then praises God, acknowledges God's wisdom and power, and thanks God for having empowered him with these gifts also (vv 17-23).

After praying, Daniel then asks Arioch not to destroy all the wise ones in Babylon, but rather to bring him into the king. Arioch obliges and brings Daniel to meet with the king. Daniel reveals the dream to the king and proceeds to interpret it. The king falls on his face, worships Daniel, and has grain and incense offered to him. The king acknowledges to Daniel, "Truly, your God is God of gods and LORD of kings and a revealer of mysteries, for you have been able to reveal this mystery!" (2:47). The king then promotes Daniel, gives him gifts, assigns him leadership positions in Babylon, and grants him his request for his three friends, namely, that their lives be spared.

This story is about power and liberation. The king, the most powerful person in the land, cannot help himself, nor can any of his wise courtiers. Nebuchadnezzar struggles with dreams until Daniel arrives. Daniel's greatest power is his wisdom and faith in God. His prudence and discretion save him from death. His strong relationship with his God allows him to turn to God, who in turn empowers Daniel so that he can interpret the dream. Daniel's interpretation of the king's dream liberates the king from his concerns and fears and also frees him to acknowledge the Judahites' God. Finally, Daniel's gift also secures the lives of his three friends.

In summary, the text shows how divine power can empower others, who in turn can use their gifts and power to help liberate others from concerns and suffering and, in this case, even to help prevent unnecessary death.

Daniel 3

"But the angel of the LORD came down into the furnace to be with Azariah and his companions, and drove the fiery flame out of the furnace." (3:49)

Daniel's companions did not always enjoy a cordial relationship with Nebuchadnezzar. For example, when Hananiah (Shadrach), Mishael (Meshach), and Azariah (Abednego) were unwilling to serve or worship the golden statue that the king had set up (vv 1-18), they were thrown into a fiery furnace (vv 19-23). The three walked around in the midst of the flames while singing hymns to God (vv 24-45). The flames grew hotter and hotter (vv 46-48), "but the angel of the LORD came down into the furnace to be with Azariah and his companions, and drove the fiery flame out of the furnace as though a moist wind were whistling through it. The fire did not touch them at all and caused them no pain or distress" (vv 49-50).

Then Daniel's three companions sang a song of blessing and praised and glorified God (vv 51-90). The king was filled with amazement, and the text tells readers that ". . . the satraps, the prefects, the governors, and the king's counselors gathered together and saw that the fire had not had any power over the bodies of those men. . . ." (v 94). To such a wonder the king responded by issuing a decree that anyone who blasphemed against the God of the three would be "torn from limb to limb, and their houses laid in ruins; for there is no other god who is able to deliver in this way" (v 96). Then the king promoted the three companions (v 97).

Similar to Daniel 2, Daniel 3 talks about power and liberation. The king exercises his power over the three men and has them thrown into a fiery furnace, but the fire has no power over them, partly because of their prayer and mainly because of divine intervention—an angel who came and drove the fiery flame out of the furnace. Here, Divine power liberates the three men from a harrowing situation. This event also liberates the king to do three things: (1) to acknowledge Judah's God as the only god of salvation, (2) to issue a decree honoring this God, and (3) to promote the three men and thus free them from their immediate state of oppression. This story gives an insight into the dynamic faith of its authors, who represent the faith of the Judahite community, and celebrates the power of God that is at work trying to liberate people from those human and nonhuman powers that result in suffering. While the story is a polemic against the worship of idols, it does invite readers to grapple with the three companions' God, who, as the text shows, is known and believed in as a result of human experience.

Daniel 6

"For he has saved Daniel
from the power of the lions." (6:27)

Perhaps one of the best-known stories in the book of Daniel is the tale of Daniel in the lions' den. The story begins with King Darius, the Mede, planning to appoint Daniel over the whole kingdom. The presidents and satraps[1] become jealous and conspire against Daniel. They convince the king to decree and enforce an interdict stating that anyone who prayed to anyone—human or divine—other than the king, would be thrown into the lions' den. The king obliged, and the interdict went into effect (vv 1-9).

Meanwhile, Daniel continued living as usual and prayed three times a day to his God. The conspirators discovered him at prayer, reported him to the king, and forced the king to comply with the interdict, and thus Daniel was thrown to the lions to the distress of the king and despite the king's efforts. The king's last words to Daniel were: "May your God, whom you faithfully serve, deliver you!" (6:16) While Daniel was in the den, the king fasted all night and was sleepless (vv 10-18).

When morning arrived, the king went to the den and cried out to Daniel, "O Daniel, servant of the living God, has your God whom you faithfully serve been able to deliver you from the lions?" (v 20). Daniel responded: "O king, live forever! My God sent his angel and shut the lions' mouths so that they would not hurt me, because I was found blameless before him; and also before you, O king, I have done no wrong" (vv 21-22). Exceedingly glad, the king had Daniel taken out of the den and had the conspirators, along with their children and their wives, thrown to the lions (vv 19-24).

After these events, the king wrote another decree stipulating that all the people of his royal dominion should be filled with awe before the God of Daniel. In his decree, the king acknowledged that Daniel's God is "the living God" (v 26) and that this God "delivers and rescues" and "has saved Daniel from the power of the lions" (v 27). The story closes with a narrative comment about Daniel's prosperity during the reigns of Darius and Cyrus (v 28).

Daniel 6 shares a common theme with Daniel 2 and 3: power at the service of liberation. Daniel finds himself at the mercy of a group of conspirators because of an interdict written by the king at the persuasion of connivers. Because of the interdict, the king is forced, against his will, to send Daniel to the lions. But, as in Daniel 2, God comes to Daniel's rescue through an angel.[2] This divine intervention leads the king to write another decree and to acknowledge Daniel's God as the living God who saved and rescued Daniel. God is more powerful than the conspirators, the king, the interdict, and the lions all together. Thus, there is a hierarchy of power represented in the text, with God as the most powerful of all who use power. The divine power is used to liberate the righteous one from an unjust execution sentence.

One point that is disturbing in the story, though, is the gobbling up of the presidents' and satraps' children and wives by the lions. Women and children represent society's most vulnerable class. Presumably, they were innocent of the plottings since there is no mention of them except in relation to the presidents and satraps.[3] Their executions took place, however, at the order of the king, and it was not the result of a divine command. Furthermore, the text is androcentric in its depiction of God; the "savior" is envisioned as a male, a typical metaphor that emerges from the Judahite culture.

Daniel 2, 3, and 6 in Context

These three chapters of Daniel each have power and liberation as one of their themes. In chapter 2, Daniel's strong relationship with his God empowers him to interpret King Nebuchadnezzar's dream and to save the lives of his friends. In chapters 3 and 6, divine power intervenes in two harrowing situations to save the lives of Azariah and Daniel, respectively. God redeems from harm Daniel the "exile" and his companions again and again, and readers see a hint for Judah's future and hope for the rest of humankind.

8

Jonah

Overview: A Historical, Literary, and Hermeneutical Interplay

ITTLE IS KNOWN ABOUT JONAH BEN AMITTAI, the prophet in the book of Jonah, except that he prophesied during Jeroboam II's reign (around 786 to 746 B.C.E.) as indicated by 2 Kgs 14:25. This was a time when Assyria enjoyed a privileged position of power among the kingdoms of the ancient world.

Although the book is fiction, specific factual references give it a historical flavor. One of the central historical places mentioned is Nineveh, the capital of Assyria. According to the text, God commanded Jonah to go to Nineveh to declare to its inhabitants their wickedness so that the process of repentance could begin. The king of Nineveh initiated actions and a decree calling for repentance so that the city might be spared divine judgment. Unfortunately, though, historical evidence shows that the city did fall (cf. the books of Nahum and Zephaniah).

The book of Jonah was probably composed sometime during the fifth century B.C.E. when the people of Judah were recovering from the Babylonian exile. Thus, the story's setting was probably around the time of Obadiah and Joel. This period found people engaged in active questioning and reflection regarding God's justice and mercy as the prophets preached repentance.

Jonah contains three overall themes: (1) the power, inclusivity, and greatness of God; (2) the power of repentance; and (3) the power of divine compassion. Didactic in style, the book proclaims a theological message that celebrates the care of God for all creation. Comprised of four symmetrical chapters, the book can be divided into two parts: the first word of the LORD—Jonah's dilemma (1–2), and the second word of the LORD—Jonah's mission (3–4). Chapter 1 parallels chapter 3, and chapter 2 parallels chapter 4. Chapters 1 and 3 focus on Jonah's experiences with a group of sailors (chapter 1) and the Assyrians and their king (chapter 3). Chapters 2 and 4 focus on Jonah's conversations with God and God's response.

A variety of literary techniques enhance the book. Direct discourse allows the reader or listener to enter into the characters' lives and experiences. Questions and their answers serve to instruct the book's characters and readers alike. Repeated key words, such as "great" (1:2; 3:2; 4:11), add cohesion to the story, while irony weaves humor into it. Personification (for example, 1:4 and 1:15) and merisms (such as "days" and "nights" in 1:17; "great" and "small" in 3:5) contribute to the text's overall imagery and metaphorical quality. Phrases and ideas that echo other stories—for example, Jonah 4:2 harks back to Exod 34:6-7—tie this story to other biblical stories and traditions that often stress a similar point. As a whole, the book is an intricately crafted story whose artistic nature supports its striking and profound theological message.

The book of Jonah demonstrates how power can be both challenging and liberating. In the story the forces of the natural world pose dilemmas for human beings. Also, however, God's power has liberating effects for all creation. The text implies that God is, ultimately, the most powerful one who is in full control of creation.

Jonah 1

"Pick me up and throw me into the sea; then the sea
will quiet down for you; for I know it is because of me
that this great storm has come upon you." (1:12)

The author of the book of Jonah begins the tale with a focus on Jonah, who, fleeing away from God's presence, boards a ship headed for Tarshish. Jonah had received a word from God that told him to go to the city Nineveh[1] to deliver God's judgment against it because of its people's wickedness (vv 1-3)

Jonah's adventures begin after he goes to Joppa and boards the ship. Having set sail with his mariner companions, Jonah and crew are tossed and tumbled about by a violent storm at sea that threatens to destroy them. The text reveals that the storm has been created by God in response to Jonah's decision to flee from God's presence. Frightened, the mariners pray each to his god while Jonah lies fast asleep in the hold of the ship—but not for long. The captain calls Jonah to consciousness and orders him to pray to his (Jonah's) god (vv 3-6).

The sailors next cast lots to see what person among them is responsible for the calamity. When the lot falls to Jonah, the mariners confront him with all sorts of questions, and they hear from Jonah about his background and his god—"I worship the LORD, the God of heaven, who made the sea and the dry land" (v 9). Because the mariners knew that Jonah was fleeing from God, the revelation of the identity of Jonah's God makes them even more frightened (vv 7-10).

The mariners then discern with Jonah what they should do with him so that the sea will subside and the great storm quiet down. Jonah tells them that he is willing to sacrifice his life: "Pick me up and throw me into the sea; then the sea will quiet down for you; for I know it is because of me that this great storm has come upon you" (v 12). The mariners, reluctant to do such a thing, then pray to Jonah's God for pardon and mercy.[2] They do not want to perish themselves, nor do they wish to be made guilty by ending Jonah's life. But, with the prayer finished, they hurl Jonah into the sea, and then the sea stops raging. Seeing what has transpired, the mariners grow even more afraid of the power of God; they therefore offer a sacrifice and make vows to Jonah's God (vv 11-16). Yet God takes care of Jonah. God has made provisions for a big fish to swallow up Jonah, who stays in the fish's belly for three days and three nights (v 17).

Chapter 1 contains several examples of power that can be challenging and liberating. The sea as a character in the story adds a cosmological dimension that helps to show the relationship between the natural world, human beings, and God. With respect to power, God is the one who is in full control of Jonah and the elements of the natural world.[3] God challenges Jonah with a task, and when Jonah flees from God's presence, God causes havoc in Jonah's life by causing havoc in the natural world. God is also the one who, after indirectly saving the mariners from perishing at sea, indirectly saves Jonah from death by providing a fish that swallows Jonah. God gives Jonah a secure place for a brief time, even though Jonah probably does not think of it as secure.

God is the "Lord of Creation" who uses elements in the natural world to accomplish specific tasks: God uses the wind to create a storm that in turn enrages the sea, which, for its part, takes control over human beings. Only when God gets what God wants—Jonah—is the natural world restored to a sense of order.

The text implies the superiority of Jonah's God over other gods. When the mariners pray to their gods, nothing happens. When they pray to Jonah's God, after having heard Jonah's story, they fulfill Jonah's request and throw him overboard; they then experience the sea's subsiding, which makes them God-fearing/God-loving people. Thus, other gods are powerless in relation to Judah's God—Jonah's God—who through experiences, in concrete situations, moves them to turn from idols to worship "the one true God."

God has power over people: God has the power to create chaos and to create order, to make people's lives miserable, and then to free them from their misery (see also v 14). The text makes an argument for monotheism and asserts that God is Lord of all creation.

While Jonah is relatively powerless in relationship to his God, he does use his power of choice to produce liberating effects for others. Jonah chooses to allow the mariners to toss him overboard. This decision results in the calming of the sea, liberating the crew from their perilous state. When Jonah gives up his life, God gives back his life.

Jonah 2
"Deliverance belongs to the LORD!" (2:9)

From the belly of the great fish, Jonah prays to God (vv 1-8). Jonah's psalm of lament attests to his confidence in God and reveals his innermost thoughts and feelings. He acknowledges to God what God has done to him. God has cast him "into the deep," "into the heart of the seas"; there the flood surrounded him "and all God's waves and billows passed over him" (v 3). Jonah's experience makes him fear that he has been driven from God's sight (v 4). Then Jonah reiterates to God what has happened to him: the waters closed in over him; the deep surrounded him; weeds were wrapped around his head. Jonah was overpowered by the forces of nature (v 5). Yet when Jonah was on the threshold of death, Jonah's prayer reached God, and God rescued him (vv 6-7). Jonah's profession of faith signals that Jonah's original audience struggled with idolatry: "Those who worship vain idols / forsake their true loyalty" (v 8). Jonah closes his prayer with an expression of thanksgiving, a promise of sacrifice, and the proclamation, "Deliverance belongs to the LORD" (v 9). Following Jonah's prayer, the narrator comments that God spoke to the fish, and "it spewed Jonah out upon the dry land" (v 10).

Chapter 2 presents another side of Jonah. The one who tried to run away from God now surrenders to God. The character Jonah acknowledges that God uses power to save the one in distress. What is troublesome, however, is that the text portrays God manipulating situations, people, and creation in a less than positive way; God's power dominates to accomplish God's purpose, in this instance when the person commissioned for the task had refused. There is a difference between persuasion and control: here, the situation reflects God's control over the natural world, yet God also acts in a liberating way. Having created an oppressive situation for Jonah because Jonah did not do what God had in mind, God then liberates Jonah from it.

Jonah 3
"Get up, go to Nineveh, that great city, and proclaim to it the message that I tell you." (3:2)

Once Jonah is out of the belly of the great fish, he is commissioned by God again to go to Nineveh to proclaim God's message. This time, Jonah sets out without any reluctance, and upon arrival at the city pronounces to the community there a message of doom. Immediately the people proclaim a fast and begin to perform gestures of repentance (vv 1-5).

When the news reaches the king, he too begins to mourn. He proclaims a total fast and a time of mourning for both humans and animals. He decrees that all must turn from their evil ways and their violence in the hope that God would have a change of mind, turn from fierce anger, and spare them (vv 6-9).

In the final section, the narrator comments that God observed the people's actions, had a change of mind, and did not bring disaster upon them (v 10).

Jonah 3 illustrates how power can liberate. After surrendering to God's power, Jonah carried out his prophetic word and mission to Nineveh. The prophecy that Jonah proclaimed to the people was powerful. It empowered the people to fast and mourn. It helped them to take charge of their lives. When the king heard the word, he too was empowered by it to the degree that he decreed among the people a time of mourning, a fast, and a mandatory turning away from evil.

Chapter 3 presents a new vision of leadership. Here, leadership uses power to motivate and to mobilize the people for good so that their lives may be spared. And God does spare them. While God is still depicted as someone who can either cause or eliminate pain and suffering, human leadership is now seen in a new light. The king could have ignored the prophetic word; he could even have had the prophet bound up or put to death. Instead, he used his power to help liberate the people from their evil ways and "from the violence of their hands"(v 8). Furthermore, the hierarchy of power was transformed. Even though the king was considered to be the head of state, he deferred to the prophet and God's message. Thus, power was shared.

The text suggests that: (1) God's work of liberation comes through people and is associated with leadership, right judgment for all concerned, and cooperation on the part of all; (2) God's word is meant to liberate, even if it is a word of doom; and (3) God's overpowering of a person is not necessarily to make the person unfree but rather to set that person free to be a catalyst for others' liberation from evil and violence. When the perpetrators of evil turn from it, then those oppressed by it are liberated also. Of significance here is the fact that Nineveh is part of the non-Israelite/Judahite world. God's word and care are meant for those who would believe (v 5), regardless of ethnicity, class, or religious background.

Finally, the fact that both humans and nonhumans enter into a fast and postures of mourning underscores the relationship and solidarity that the ancient people shared with the natural world.[4] All creation—not just human beings—are to be redeemed and liberated. Would that all people could hear Jonah 3 with new ears.

Jonah 4

*"The L*ORD *God appointed a bush, and made it come up over Jonah,
to give shade over his head, to save him from his discomfort. . . ." (4:6).*

With the Ninevites on the right track with God and among themselves, one might think that Jonah would celebrate. Not so! Jonah is displeased with the outcome of events and becomes angry. In a heartwarming prayer to God, Jonah attests to his belief in God. He prays, "for I knew that you are a gracious God and merciful, slow to anger, and abounding in steadfast love, and ready to relent from punishing" (v 2). Jonah also admits to God that this is precisely the reason he was running to Tarshish in the first place. As Nowell puts it, "Jonah fears that he will be a successful prophet and convert the Ninevites. He is angry because he knows that God is not a judge who exacts retribution equal to the crime but rather a merciful God who repents of anger."[5] God responds to Jonah by asking him if it is right to be angry. Jonah then departs out of the city toward the east, makes a booth for himself to provide shade, and then watches to see what will happen to Nineveh (vv 1-5).

While Jonah is sitting in the shade, God causes a bush to come over Jonah to shade his head from the sun and to alleviate his discomfort. Jonah enjoys the bush until God causes a worm to attack the bush so that it withers. God then causes a hot east wind to intensify the sun so that Jonah becomes faint and asks God to let him die (vv 6-8; cf. v 3).

God responds to Jonah's complaint and request thus:

> "You are concerned about the bush, for which you did not labor and which you did not grow; it came into being in a night and perished in a night. And should I not be concerned about Nineveh, that great city, in which there are more than a hundred and twenty thousand persons who do not know their right hand from their left, and also many animals?" (vv 10-11)

This chapter depicts a marvelous relationship between Jonah and God. Jonah is so candid, so honest with God, and his prayer reflects those qualities. The fact that he "knew" God to be just and gracious presupposes experience. Jonah knows God not only from the tradition (see Exod 34:6-7 where words and ideas similar to Jonah 3:2 appear) but also from his personal encounters. Both Jonah's call and his candid personal prayer hint at a real relationship between God and Jonah that may have existed for some time. Jonah's ability to express his anger to God would also support the existence of such a relationship. Even though Jonah was reluctant to carry out God's directive the first time, God did not abandon Jonah. God continued to work with Jonah in all sorts of ways. When God reproved Jonah, it was never an experience that caused him harm; God's final reproof was verbal (4:9-11).

Jonah 4 proclaims a liberating God whose power is at the service of the Ninevites, Jonah, and even the cattle. Even though there are hints of God having "power over" creation—for example, the bush and the worm are both "appointed" by God—the predominate theme is God using divine power to empower Jonah to help transform the city Nineveh. By means of the bush and the worm, God teaches Jonah about divine care and compassion not only for people but also for animals. What is so liberating about this text is that it attests to the breadth of God's plan of salvation that includes non-Judahites and animals. This text helps to liberate God from a humanly constructed identity that is predominately if not exclusively androcentric in its concerns.

Jonah in Context

In summary, the book of Jonah is a fast-paced, heartwarming, and revelatory story about Jonah and his God and how that relationship affects other people, animals, and elements in the natural world. Jonah's genuine candor allows readers to appreciate the dynamics of his relationship with God. Cosmological in its focus, the book of Jonah breaks the boundaries of class and ethnicity to present a view of salvation and liberation that was prophetic for its day and remains so even now. The text affirms that God, the ways of God, and the power of God can be discovered in the midst of human life and all its experiences as well as in and through the natural world and the cosmos and that God uses all creation to bring about redemption and liberation for all. If the text reflects accurately God's care for human and nonhuman life even in the midst of humankind's sinfulness, then critical readers must ask: How can people use the insights from the book of Jonah to bring about liberation and transformation in a way that is nonviolent and inclusive? While the book includes only five Hebrew words of prophecy, its prophetic message runs deep.

9

Haggai and Zechariah

T HE BOOKS OF HAGGAI AND ZECHARIAH PORTRAY two prophets, Haggai and Zechariah, who are contemporaries of each other. Both texts have the reign of Darius I as their backdrop. Despite some foreboding news in each text, the books in general present a hopeful picture. Viewing the texts side by side, one notices that the message of Haggai begins with a specific time reference (1:1)—the second year of the reign of King Darius in the sixth month—that is picked up in Zech 1:1, where it is two months later. Significant in both books are the depictions of power, particularly with respect to God.

Haggai

Overview: Historical, Literary, and Hermeneutical Interplay

Next to the book of Obadiah, which consists of one chapter, Haggai is the shortest book in the Old Testament. The text's two chapters allude to the difficult times that the people of Judah endured during the reign of Darius I, who ruled around 521 to 486 B.C.E. One of the text's central figures is the prophet Haggai. Little is known about him, though scholars have argued for various identities.[1]

Haggai began preaching around 520 B.C.E., a time when the temple lay in ruins. This situation greatly concerned Haggai, so much so that much of his preaching revolved around the temple's reconstruction. Haggai directed his message to the Judahite community and to two leaders in particular: Joshua the high priest and the Davidic governor Zerubbabel. Both Joshua and Zerubbabel were recipients of Haggai's prophecies, but through Haggai, Zerubbabel received a divine promise: chosen by God, he would become like a signet ring (2:23). In the book of Haggai, prophecy and promise converge not only for the people addressed but also for the prophet (2:15-19).

The chapters of Haggai divide into two parts: a divine command to rebuild the temple (chapter 1) and a series of prophecies and promises pertaining to the temple, Zerubbabel, Joshua, the people of Judah, and Haggai (chapter 2). Time elements serve as both structural and literary devices. As time elapses, the narrative progresses (1:1, 15; 2:1, 10, 20). With the exception of the brief dialogues between God and Haggai, and Haggai and the priests, the text records God's addresses to Haggai without any verbal response from Haggai, and Haggai's addresses to the people without their verbal response. Haggai, Joshua, and the people obey God without comment (Hag 1:12).

Other literary techniques enhance the narrative's focus on either the temple or the people of Judah. These include rhetorical questions, imperatives, and in one instance, a simile. Although the narrative is tightly compact, it provides a sweeping view of God and God's intentions in postexilic times. Yet, like the other prophetic texts, this view is conditioned by history, time, and culture.

The book of Haggai offers a vision of how the use of power can have liberating and creative effects not only for the future of a heap of ruins but also for a community who once knew the pain of exile and the feeling of abandonment by a seemingly disinterested God.

Haggai 1

*"And the LORD stirred up the spirit of Zerubbabel son of Shealtiel,
governor of Judah, and the spirit of Joshua son of Jehozadak, the high
priest, and the spirit of all the remnant of the people; and they came and
worked on the house of the LORD of hosts, their God, on the twenty-fourth
day of the month, in the sixth month." (1:14-15)*

In Haggai 1, the prophet has the important task of convincing Zerubbabel, son of Shealtiel, governor of Judah; Joshua, son of Jehozadak, the high priest; and the remnant of the people of Judah to begin to rebuild the temple. Haggai inspires and empowers the leaders and the people with his prophetic words. They do listen to him, and then God stirs up the leaders' and the people's spirits, and they all begin work on the temple. The chapter can be divided into four sections: vv 2-6, vv 7-11, vv 12-13, and vv 14-15.

Following a superscription (v 1), Haggai begins his address to Judah's leaders, Zerubbabel and Joshua, and communicates God's word to them (vv 2-6). God, through the prophet, uses a rhetorical question (v 4) and a personal reflection on the social situation of the day (vv 5-6) to challenge the leadership. The economy is not good, and so God puts forth the argument that since the people are not faring well on their own, now is the time to rebuild the temple.

In vv 7-11, Haggai continues his prophecy. God again asks the people to reflect on their life situation. God directs the people to go and get wood to build the temple. God then informs them of their experience: when they looked for wood, they found only a little bit; when they brought the little bit home, God blew it away. God explains that the misfortunes they suffered were because they had not yet built the temple. In vv 10-11, God announces to the people that a drought will affect the land, hills, grain, new wine, oil, what the soil produces, human beings and animals, and all their labors. Again, the drought is because the people have not yet built the temple.

In both vv 2-6 and vv 7-11, God is depicted as being very persuasive: God points out that the people have not experienced divine blessing because the temple is not built. The text presents a very hierarchical view of God: the temple must be built so that God can take pleasure in it and be honored. Also, the title "Lord of hosts" suggests a hierarchical attitude.[2] God is clearly the one who rules over the people and their leadership. Additionally, God is Lord of all creation and controls creation according to the divine will. What can be troublesome to some readers is the fact that not only human beings suffer but also the land, produce, and animals suffer because of God's decision to send a drought because the people have not yet built the temple. Thus, the biblical text mirrors the interconnectedness and interdependent relationship that human and nonhuman life have with each other and with God.

In v 12 the leaders and the people all respond to God with obedience, which then elicits a further reassuring response from God to the people: "I am with you" (v 13). God finally wins control over the will of the people, and when that finally has happened, then God will grant the people the experience of divine presence. Here, obedience is not chosen freely; it is chosen while under divine judgment.

Verses 14-15 present God stirring up the spirit of Judah's leaders and the remnant of the people. When this happens, they all set out to work on building the temple. It is noteworthy that creating the temple begins not after the people have been convinced to do it, but after their spirits are stirred up by God. This section is the climax of Haggai 1; when the spirit is kindled and liberated within, then building is possible. The restoration of God's house by the community is intricately linked to the restoration of the people and the natural world. Hence, all of creation is meant for new life. Finally, in Haggai 1, the process of rebuilding gets underway when the prophet liberates the people by means of the prophetic word. His prophetic word is meant to be liberating, going forth with power to empower those who are able to receive it.

Zechariah

Overview: Historical, Literary, and Hermeneutical Interplay

The book of Zechariah features the prophet Zechariah who, like his contemporary Haggai, began preaching around 520 B.C.E. Similar to the book of Haggai, the Zechariah text reflects the historical times of Darius I, when the remnant of Judah was struggling against other kingdoms and cults. The remnant was also struggling to rebuild the temple. Very little is known about Zechariah; he may have been a priest.

The book of Zechariah combines both prose and poetry and can be divided into two parts: chapters 1–8 and 9–14. Scholars continue to debate the relationship of the two parts since they seem to reflect different authorship and dissimilar time periods. Chapters 1–8 contain four sections: (1) superscription and inaugural prophecy (1:1-6); (2) eight visions (1:7—6:8); (3) symbolic crowning of Joshua (6:9-15); and (4) a lesson on fasting and morality (7:1—8:23). Chapters 9–14 have two sections: (1) first prophecy—judgment against Judah's enemies (9:1-11:17), and (2) second prophecy—the future splendor and power of Jerusalem and Judah (12:1—14:21).

Zechariah contains a renewed respect for the monarchy and the priesthood, as well as an affirmation of ritual. The messianic prophecy in 9:9 and the allegory of the shepherds in Zech 11:4-17 are two of the better-known texts within the book. Christian Palm Sunday liturgies echo Zech 9:9, while the allegory of the shepherds was common in the ancient Near East. Zechariah contains many symbols and images that recall the pattern and content of Ezekiel. For example, both books feature a mysterious scroll (Ezek 2:1—3:3 and Zech 5:1-4). Some of the symbols and images in Zechariah show the influence of apocalypticism just as certain passages in Ezekiel do. Clearly, the book of Zechariah is an artistic work that contains a hopeful message celebrating the holiness and power of God (Zech 14:20-21), although parts of the book seem to border on the bizarre.

In the book of Zechariah, power, particularly divine power, is not always portrayed as a positive force for creation—for example, the plague that God intends to send upon those who wage war against Jerusalem. Unfortunately, the plague will have lethal consequences for the creatures of the natural world (see Zech 14:12-15). Yet events like this are understood under the guise of "justice." Although depictions of God using power destructively can raise hermeneutical questions, the focus of this chapter is the positive and liberating effects that power can have when used appropriately. Throughout Zechariah the power of the divine word becomes, for the prophet and his listeners alike, a source of hope and inspiration: the temple will be rebuilt and so forth (Zech 1:16-17). The following section of this chapter examines selected passages from Zechariah, with a view to highlighting the use of power in life-giving and life-sustaining ways.

Zechariah 9:9-10

"He will cut off the chariot from Ephraim
and the war horse from Jerusalem." (9:10)

Having experienced the perils and scars of war and exile and having lived through the destruction of the temple and the Holy City, Jerusalem, the Judahites probably rejoiced at the prophecy of hope that the prophet Zechariah announced to them. Set against the history of the Judahite kings, the new leader of the people will be quite different from all others. Verses 9-10 describe the coming of a new king to reign in Judah. This king will liberate the people and other countries from strife and war.

The vision of the new leader begins in v 9a with an exhortation to be jubilant: "Rejoice greatly, O daughter Zion! / Shout aloud, O daughter Jerusalem!" This opening line has the potential for engaging readers immediately because of its exuberance. Here, God speaks through Zechariah, and Jerusalem is personified as God's daughter. Although the line is bright in tone and brief in style, making it engaging, one must not overlook the metaphor "daughter Zion/daughter Jerusalem." Despite its familial tone, this phrase evokes the patriarchal and hierarchical world of ancient Israel and Judah. It presumes God to be male and a father, and Jerusalem to be female and subordinate. The metaphor does not convey a sense of equality and mutuality between God and Jerusalem. Rather, Jerusalem is in need of God's care, for which reason the king will come (v 9b-c).

Jerusalem's new king will be triumphant, victorious, and humble. He rides on a colt, the foal of a donkey. Nevertheless, this is quite a change from the kings that the Judahites had experienced. Jerusalem having a "king" reflects the hierarchy and patriarchy that existed in ancient Judah—the new leader would be a male and a king. Verse 10 describes the king's mission and his dominion. This new king will cut off the chariot from Ephraim, the war horse from Jerusalem, and the battle bow, and he will "command peace to the peoples." His dominion will be worldwide.

Together, these two verses suggest that the new leader of Judah will liberate Judah from violence and war and will establish peace among all kingdoms worldwide. This new king will assert his power with the goals of liberation and restoration, and not for the purpose of domination and oppression. With this new king, power associated negatively with patriarchy, hierarchy, and the male gender can be transformed.

This passage offers a vision to those in societies and cultures who would be leaders. While patriarchy and hierarchy are exclusive, leadership is not a vice unless it uses its power to abuse, dominate, control, and/or oppress creation. Power can be creative and life-giving if it is used for liberation and if the leader who possesses power also possesses humility.

Zechariah 10:6-12
"I will bring them home from the land of Egypt,
and gather them from Assyria." (10:10)

With passion and compassion, with tenderness and resolve, God promises to strengthen and liberate from captivity the people of Judah. These verses proclaim that restoration will take place after God has made the people victorious. The passage can be divided into two units: vv 6-7 and vv 8-12.

Verses 6-7 focus on what God is going to do with Israel and Judah. God promises to "save the house of Joseph" (Israel) and "to strengthen the house of Judah" (v 6a). Next God promises to bring the people back into the original relationship that they had with God (v 6b). When all this has taken place, "then the people of Ephraim shall become like warriors," and there will be rejoicing, especially in God (v 7). The text depicts God using divine power to strengthen the Israelites and Judahites and to restore them to covenant relationship. God uses power to empower, energize, and liberate the human person and spirit.

Verses 8-12 focus on God liberating the Judahites and restoring them to their lands. A people redeemed, they will be blessed with fruitfulness by God (v 8). Scattered among many countries, they shall remember God and return home (v 9). God will bring home the captives from Egypt and from Assyria and bring them in great numbers to Gilead and Lebanon (v 10). Nothing—no force in creation—will harm them (v 11). The oppression from Assyria and Egypt will come to an end. Strengthened by God, they will walk in God's name (vv 11-12).

In summary, this text highlights God's power that strengthens and liberates and does not overpower or dominate. God's power not only enables the exiles to return home but also restores Israel's and Judah's relationship with God.

Haggai and Zechariah in Context

These passages from the books of Haggai and Zechariah illustrate how power can be used to bring about liberation and restoration not only for the Israelite people, but for all peoples and all creation. The texts present a picture of God who passionately and compassionately cares for people and who wants to be with them and dwell among them. This God is actively involved with creation and works through all situations to bring about the best possible outcome, be it a new temple or a new piece of land to be resettled.

10

Obadiah and Malachi

EDOM, A COUNTRY DESPISED BY JUDAH, is the focus of the opening verses of the books of Obadiah and Malachi. In the prophetic text of Obadiah, God enumerates Edom's transgressions against Judah and declares what will be Edom's outcome because of its deeds. Edom will become rubble, but the exiles from Judah will be saved. The text attests to God using power to avenge the Judahites for the suffering they endured because of Edom's attitude and behavior. A people who had been dispossessed of land, the Judahites will be restored to the land, with boundaries clearly marked out. Divine power becomes a means to liberation (vv 17-18), restoration (vv 19-20), and deliverance (v 21).

The book of Malachi continues the focus on Edom (1:2-5) but then stresses God's love for the people of Judah and their responsibilities within the covenant relationship (1:6—4:6). In a series of disputation speeches, God disputes with Judah over a variety of transgressions. Some of these transgressions involve the corruption of the priesthood (1:6—2:9), the profanation of the covenant (2:10-17), false oaths, the oppression of not only hired workers but also the widow and the orphan, and the thrusting aside of the alien (3:5). Ironically, Judah remains silent and is heard only when God, in an address to Judah, quotes Judah's own words: "Will anyone rob God? Yet you are robbing me! But you say, 'How are we robbing you?' In your tithes and offerings!" (3:8). Furthermore, God's word and promised action overshadow the human word. All of Judah's arrogant and evildoers shall become stubble when the Day of the LORD comes, burning like an oven (Mal 4:1). God will liberate the faithful from the clutches of the unrighteous (Mal 4:3).

Both books attest to an understanding of power that has liberation as one of its goals. The way power is used in the texts to achieve liberation needs careful consideration, however, especially in light of the contemporary struggle between power used aggressively on the one hand and power used to liberate on the other. The latter enhances life; the former may not.

This chapter examines specific texts from the books of Obadiah and Malachi in the context of how power is used. The discussion highlights the potential role power can play in liberation and the impetus it can have to shift paradigms so that the weak may become strong and the strong may not dominate. But how is God's use of power portrayed in the text? If God is perceived as being the most powerful among the Judahites and among the gods of the other countries, a God who acts justly on behalf of the poor and oppressed, then what is one to make of the rubble that wicked Esau is to become (Obad 1:18)? Are the wicked ones not a dimension of the face of the poor and oppressed on another level?

Obadiah

Overview: A Historical, Literary, and Hermeneutical Interplay

The shortest of all the Old Testament books, Obadiah consists of twenty-one verses. Nothing is known about the prophet himself except what one may glean from the text. The prophecy of Obadiah reflects a time somewhere during the late sixth century B.C.E. or early fifth century B.C.E. The prophet directs his message primarily against Edom, a small state southeast of Judah. Historically, Obadiah's prophecy against Edom is part of a long tradition of prophecies against foreign countries. An invective against Edom appears in many prophetic texts (see, for example, Isa 34: 5-17; 63:1-6; Jer 49:7-22; Ezek 25:12-14; Amos 1:11-12; Mal 1:2-4). The Edomites are guilty of exploiting Judah's weaknesses, and when the Babylonians took Jerusalem, they watched the city crumble (1:11). Then they looted the city (1:14) and turned fleeing Judeans over to the Babylonians (1:11, 13-14). Consequently, Edom is the recipient of God's righteous anger.

As a literary work, the book of Obadiah consists of two parts: a prophecy against Edom (vv 1-14) and a prophecy about the Day of the LORD (vv 15-21). Following a brief prose introduction (v 1a), the standard prophetic messenger formula opens the first part of the book: "Thus says the Lord GOD" (v 1b). The second part begins with the phrase, "For the day of the LORD is near" (v 15a). The reference to "the day of the LORD" is a major theme in the book of Obadiah as a whole and elsewhere in other prophetic texts (see, for example, Isa 2:12-22; Amos 5:18-20; Zeph 1). Vivid images, along with contrasts between pride and humility and inheritance and dispossession, are all elements common to other earlier biblical texts. Hence, the writers of Obadiah had a rich heritage of poetic language at their disposal. The tone of the book is resolute: those who acted unjustly toward Judah would be the recipients of divine chastisement; however, God would empower the remnant of Judah to overcome its enemies (vv 20-21).

In the book of Obadiah, the assertion of power becomes a means of liberation. With respect to Edom and Judah, what Edom has sowed it shall reap: the strong and powerful become the powerless; Judah, the once powerless, becomes powerful; the house of Jacob will be a fire—the house of Joseph, the flame, and the house of Esau, stubble (v 18). Then Judah will be freed from foreign rule; its boundaries will be restored and the people will assume their role of leadership and exercise dominion (vv 17-21). While this is indeed a celebration for Judah, the new political position is gained through force. The metaphor of the house of Jacob as fire and the house of Joseph as a flame suggests destruction (v 18). From a hermeneutical perspective, the text suggests that the use of power can lead to liberation, but at what cost to others?

Obadiah 1:17-21

"But on Mount Zion there shall be those that escape,
and it shall be holy;
and the house of Jacob shall take possession
of those who dispossessed them." (1:17)

What a hopeful message Obad 1:17-21 gives to the Judahite community whose historical experience is marked by military invasion, deportations, the loss of land and temple, and exile. The prophet Obadiah proclaims a day when Judah will be free, strong, and restored to its land. The coming Day of the LORD (v 15) will be a disastrous one for countries other than Judah, but for Judah, it will be a day of jubilation and celebration. Verses 17-21 describe Judah's liberation from exile and its restoration to the land. No longer under foreign control, Judah will regain its power through its possession of land.

Verses 17-21 outline the various lands that the Judahites will take possession of: the house of Jacob will take possession of the lands of those who dispossessed them; the people of the Negeb[1] will possess Mount Esau (v 19); those of the Shephelah, the land of the Philistines,[2] Ephraim,[3] and Samaria (vv 19ab); Benjamin shall possess Gilead (v 19c);[4] the exiled Judahites in Halah[5] shall possess Phoenicia (v 20a);[6] and the exiles of Jerusalem in Sepharad[7] shall possess the towns of the Negeb (v 20b). The language of these verses resembles that of the books of Joshua and Judges, which describe the Israelites' entry into Canaan. The notion of "possessing" the land is also associated with covenantal promise (see, for example, Gen 12:7; Exod 3:8; 2 Sam 7:10). Judah's restoration to the land is thus linked to its renewal of covenant with God.

In the powerful metaphor, "the house of Jacob will be a fire, the house of Joseph a flame, and the house of Esau stubble" (v 18), Jacob and Joseph represent the Southern Kingdom Judah and the Northern Kingdom Israel, respectively.[8] Thus, the whole country of Judah will overtake the house of Esau (Edom) and all the other countries that Esau represents. The "fire" and the "stubble" symbolize God's judgment on Edom. Through Judah, God will bring Edom to its end.[9] Freed from Edom's hand, Judah will no longer experience this country's domination, power, or oppressive control. The image of liberation through violence, however, continues to be a hermeneutical concern.

Verses 17 and 21 together form an *inclusio* that frames the entire passage. At Mount Zion, the Judahites will become God's judges over Mount Esau, and sovereignty will be restored to God. A people once oppressed by its enemy will now, with God, govern that enemy, and never again will Judah have to experience oppression at the hands of Edom.

From a hermeneutical perspective, the image of power in vv 17-21 is multi-faceted. For Judah, regaining its power as a country is tied to its being restored to the land, and being restored to the land is related to the covenant renewal with God. For some contemporary readers, the notion of Judah "taking possession of land" can be troublesome because it conveys an imperialistic attitude. Judah, however, is going to reclaim what was given to it through divine blessing. A country dispossessed of its land is now going to free its gift from the hands of those who had taken it by force. Thus, the text suggests that through God's power on the Day of the LORD, Judah will exert its strength to liberate from enemy possession the land that was once given to Judah as a gift. Furthermore, Judah's reclamation of the land allows God's sovereignty in the land to be established once more. How Judah reclaims the gift is not certain from the text.

In summary, the restoration of Judah to its gift of land is tied to covenant renewal between Judah and God, and that covenant renewal reestablishes and presumes a right relationship with God and with one another, the fruit of which is justice and peace. Hence, Judah's "ruling" Mount Esau from Mount Zion hints at a vision of justice and peace for all countries that will come through Judah. God's favoritism toward Judah, viewed earlier as "ethnocentric," now serves a larger purpose: universal deliverance for all peoples and countries.

Malachi

Overview: A Historical, Literary, and Hermeneutical Interplay

Appearing as the last book of the prophets in both the Hebrew text and the Greek Septuagint and consequently in the various English editions, the book of Malachi is a rigorous address to the restored Judahite community during postexilic times. Historically, this was a time of great disillusionment for the people of Judah. These sentiments prompted Malachi, the prophetic messenger of the text, to speak out to his people to assure them that, indeed, God still loved them. The Judahites' covenant relationship, however, needed honor, respect, and care not only for God, but for others as well. The prophet Malachi points out the injustices and abuses of the Judahite community. Other than the simple reference to the prophet Malachi in 1:1, no other mention is made of him and nothing is known about him.

The text of the book of Malachi is composed of a series of six disputations woven together and followed by two appendices. The disputations and the themes are as follows: (1) God's love (1:2-5), (2) God's honor (1:6—2:9); (3) faithfulness (2:10-16), (4) God's justice (2:17—3:5), (5) repentance (3:6-12), and (6) speech against God (3:13—4:3). The two appendices recall the Mosaic teaching (4:4) and foretell restoration and harmony before the Day of the LORD (4:5-6). In the book the prophet confronts sin (for example, 2:17—3:7), including idolatry (2:10-12), faithlessness in marriage (2:13-16), and social injustice (3:5). The social elite classes are direct targets of Malachi's prophecies. A variety of literary techniques, including vocatives (2:1, 3:6), rhetorical questions (2:10, 17; 3:2), similes (3:3-4), quotations (3:13-14), and imagery (4:1-3), give the prophetic message a straightforward tone and thereby enrich it. One can hardly ignore Malachi's message.

In the book of Malachi, power plays a predominant role. God is depicted as having great power that is exercised to liberate the Judahite community from their sufferings, fears, and doubts. For example, in 3:1-6, God promises to act on behalf of those who have suffered at the hands of others. In vv 8-12, God asserts divine power over the elements in the natural world for the sake of human beings and for the sake of showing the other countries that Judah's God is LORD of creation. While God's power does have a liberating and restorative effect, it also seems to be used for other purposes. The following section explores the relationship between power and liberation.

Malachi 3:1-5

"The messenger of the covenant in whom you delight—
indeed, he is coming, says the LORD of hosts." (3:1)

To some members of the Judahite community in postexilic times, Mal 3:1-5 offers a word of hope and a message of consolation. Life is not going to continue as it has been. Life is about to be transformed through God's judgment that will establish justice and righteousness and liberate the exploited, the widows, the fatherless, the aliens, and others from their sufferings and oppressions.

In vv 1-5, a prophecy of hope, God speaks through the prophet Malachi.[10] God announces the coming of a messenger (v 1).[11] A rhetorical question then underscores the messenger's power: "But who can endure his coming, and who can stand when he appears?" (v 2). Verses 2b-4 provide a metaphorical description of what the messenger is like and what he will do: he is "like a refiner's fire and like fullers' soap."[12] The messenger will not destroy the descendants of Levi; he will purify them (v 4). The coming of God for judgment follows the purification of the people (v 5). Those whom God will bear witness against include sorcerers, adulterers, liars, exploiters, those who cast out the alien, and those who do not fear God.[13]

In vv 1-5, God asserts power for the purpose of liberation. God first sends a messenger "of the covenant" to refine and purify the people. What the people will be purified of is not made explicit, but one could suppose that they will be liberated from all that keeps them from being in right relationship with their God and others.

The image of God coming as a judge to indict those guilty of social injustices is good news for those who suffer the injustices, particularly for the widow, the fatherless, and the alien, who are the most vulnerable in Judah's society. Various people will be liberated from their sufferings through God's power—here, through the power of judgment.

Finally, the phrase "Lord of hosts" identifies God twice in the passage (3:1, 5). The term, which is hierarchical and patriarchal here, connotes benevolence. For the perpetuators of injustice and other evils, though, the phrase may incite fear. God is going to judge. Hermeneutically, the text proclaims the good news of justice and liberation, but it also portrays a hierarchical God. Justice and liberation will come from above—from God who will "draw near" (v 5). The text raises the questions: Where is room in the Judahite community for a person, with God, to judge community members fairly? Does power rest only with God?

Malachi 4:1-6
"You shall go out leaping like calves from the stall." (4:2)

Images of burning and stubble that appear in 4:1 echo Obad 1:18, in which the house of Esau will become stubble and will burn and be consumed. In Mal 4:1, the evildoers will become stubble and will also be burned. Like Obad 1:17-21, Mal 4:1-5[14] speaks of justice being meted out to the unjust so that the oppressed can be liberated. Verse 1 describes what will take place on the Day of the Lord. For evildoers, it will be a day of punitive judgment; for the righteous, a day of liberation. Imagery from the natural world concretizes the message and betrays Judah's agrarian culture (vv 1-3). God exhorts the people to remember Torah (v 4). In vv 5-6, God promises to send the prophet Elijah, who will enact a social transformation among the people so that God will not strike the land.

Malachi 4:1-6 gives readers a picture of the complex nature of power and a glimpse at the power of prophetic imagination. In v 1, "the Lord of hosts" will burn up all the evildoers. From the evildoers' perspective, the exertion of power on God's part is not a good thing; it brings their destruction. In v 2, however, power takes a turn. Because God acted against unrighteousness, the righteous will go free from bondage. Once freed, they will "tread down the wicked . . ." on the day when "the Lord of hosts" acts (v 3). Power associated with the evildoers' destruction is now associated with liberation. Furthermore, the idea of the righteous treading down the wicked on the day when God acts implies that the righteous have been divinely empowered to participate in the work of liberation.

Obadiah and Malachi in Context

The books of Obadiah and Malachi are both concerned with justice and righteousness for those who have been oppressed. The Day of the Lord, a feature in both texts, is a day of reckoning for the unrighteous and a day of liberation for the righteous. Readers see in selected passages how power can liberate when it is exercised assertively and not aggressively.

The powerful metaphors and images from life and the natural world that are used in both books indicate to readers the influence that culture can have on language and praxis and how language and praxis, in turn, can have an effect on culture. In sum, both works are rich in content and form and continue to offer challenges to contemporary readers.

11

Nahum and Joel

I N THE BOOKS OF NAHUM AND JOEL, the texts' central message comes to the fore through imagery. One image that occurs in the books of Nahum and Joel is that of the locust (see, for example, Nah 3:15-17 and Joel 1:4). A second image common to both is fire (see, for example, Nah 3:15 and Joel 2:3). Both images are associated with human and divine power—the main theme. Both texts are beautifully crafted so as to make one central theological assertion: power can be used to dominate, control, and oppress, but it can also be used to liberate and set free. The complex nature of power is not something new. It is present in the books of Nahum and Joel and in today's world.

This chapter focuses on how power can be a source of liberation for all creation. To this end, various passages from both biblical books are examined to uncover examples of how power can be used in a positive way to bring about a world of justice, compassion, and beauty for all of life. The texts of Nahum and Joel present a vision of how the Spirit of God is at work in the human and nonhuman world—in all of creation—trying to liberate creation from the power of domination, control, and oppression. While the vision is not perfect, the vision present in the texts challenges the readers to retrieve from it what will help them move forward in grace toward a greater deliberateness in the use of power for liberation rather than its abuse in domination and destruction. A vision of a world of harmonious and just relationships directs the focus of the final part of this work.

Nahum

Overview: A Historical, Literary, and Hermeneutical Interplay

With enthusiasm and eloquence, the prophet Nahum proclaims a hopeful message of liberation and restoration for the people of Judah. Historically, very little is known about the prophet except that he came from the town of Elkosh (1:1). However, the central focus of the prophecies is certain: Nineveh, the capital of Assyria, will be destroyed, and Judah will never again have to fear Assyria's invasion. But what neither prophet nor people realized was that Judah would suffer its final blow at the hands of the Babylonians. Nineveh was destroyed by a group of Babylonians, Medes, and Persians in 612 B.C.E.; this fact suggests that the setting of the text's events is a time prior to the exile.

The three chapters of the book of Nahum can be divided into six parts: (1) a theophany report (1:2-5), (2) a hymn to God's power (1:6-11), (3) a prophecy of hope (1:12—2:13), (4) a metaphorical denunciation (3:1-10), (5) a declaration of judgment against the Assyrians (3:11-17), and (6) a declaration of judgment against the king of Assyria (3:18-19). As a literary work, Nahum is, perhaps, unmatched in the prophetic corpus for its highly stylized images, metaphors, similes, personifications, and other artistic expressions. Many of these images and expressions admit, however, to a certain violence that was indeed a part of Nahum's culture and shared by later editors. Of significance is how the text portrays God as a storm god, a warrior, and a king. Perhaps the central image of God that likely was consoling for the text's original audience but that can be disturbing to later readers is the image of an all-powerful God who has power over creation (see, for example, 1:3b-6), over adversarial countries (see, for example, 1:7-11), and over Judah for both woe (see, for example, 1:12b) and fortune (see, for example, 1:13, 15). Common to all these metaphors is a God as a God of power who uses power in multiple ways. No element in creation, whether it be a mountain, a rock, an adversarial country, or even the country of Judah is left untouched or unaffected by God's power. Thus, the text's accent on God's power opens the door for a rich hermeneutical discussion.

The text testifies to the fact that the use of power by God can be both liberating and destructive simultaneously. Power can console some people, as in the case of the people of Judah, while at the same time setting others' teeth on edge, as in the case of the Assyrians. Hence, the image of God as a God of power needs to be examined because of its far-reaching hermeneutical implications that can affect theology and praxis.

The text seems to legitimate the use of destructive power for the sake of liberation in the face of oppression. While this may be understood as justice, is it really? And while power can have liberating effects, is there something further about power that needs to be grasped and executed if power is to be a truly liberating experience for all creation? These and other questions are considered in relation to a study of selected passages from the book of Nahum that highlight the use of power as a means for liberation.

Nahum 1:12-15

"Celebrate your festivals, O Judah,
fulfill your vows,
for never again shall the wicked invade you;
they are utterly cut off." (1:15)

With gusto, the prophet Nahum proclaims a prophecy of hope to his audience that announces the end of Judah's affliction by the Assyrians and the
breaking of their yoke bonds that have bound the country for years. Verses
12-13 picture Judah as a country harnessed and beaten by enemy forces
greater than itself. A country overpowered, it waits to be freed and healed.
God now promises Judah liberation from its suffering. Historically, these
verses refer to the conflict between Assyria and Judah (see 1:1). For more
than three hundred years, Assyria had controlled the Near Eastern world,
including Judah. Brutality, deportation of peoples from their native lands,
heavy tribute, and an unwillingness to reach compromises or make treaties
with the countries under its power characterized Assyria's reign of terror. The
Judahites had thought that God had sent the Assyrians against them as a way
to chastise them for their apostasy and wickedness. Hence, God makes a
promise to end such affliction (v 12). God will assert power for the sake of
liberation (vv 12-13). The God who once caused Judah to be overpowered
now promises to end their distress.

Verse 14, continuing the sentiments presented in vv 12-13, addresses the
king of Assyria. In order to carry out the promise of liberation for Judah, God
now promises to destroy the Assyrian ruler, his lineage, and his gods. Historically, Nineveh, the capital of Assyria, was destroyed in 612 B.C.E. When the
capital fell, the entire empire collapsed and never regained its strength.[1] The
text attributes this historical event to the power of God.

Verse 15 exhorts Judah to rejoice. No longer under Assyrian captivity,
Judah will now be able to celebrate its festivals and fulfill the pledges it has
made to God. Thus, the entire prophecy celebrates the end of Assyrian
oppression, an event that chapters 2 and 3 of Nahum describe in detail.

In summary, vv 12-15 is a pivotal text. Traditionally, the focus has always
been on how Assyria is crushed. The focus in these verses, however, is on liberation for Judah, the less represented perspective. Verses 12-15 portray God
using divine power to free others from grueling oppression. This is good
news. On the other hand, the freedom is effected through the use of military
force, aggression that, though inevitable historically and politically, is attributed to God. Divine power is thus depicted as being used aggressively and
destructively for the purpose of liberation. The text seems to legitimate the
use of violence for the sake of liberation from unjust oppression. While the
emphasis can shift from power and domination to power and liberation, it

has not shifted far enough. The text acts like a mirror to reflect images of past situations that present themselves in the here and now.

Joel

Overview: A Historical, Literary, and Hermeneutical Interplay

With gusto and directness, the prophet Joel addresses, with a series of commands, an inclusive and wide variety of people in Judah:

> Hear this, O elders, give ear, all inhabitants of the land! (1:2)
> Wake up, you drunkards and weep; and wail, all you wine-drinkers. . . . (1:5)
> Lament like a virgin dressed in sackcloth. . . . (1:8)
> Be dismayed, you farmers, wail, you vinedressers. . . . (1:11)
> Put on sackcloth, and lament, you priests; wail, you ministers of the altar. (1:13)
> Sanctify a fast, call a solemn assembly. (1:14)
> Blow the trumpet in Zion; sound the alarm on my holy mountain! (2:1)
> Proclaim this among the nations: Prepare for war . . . (3:9)
> Come quickly, all you nations all around. (3:11)
> Put in the sickle, for the harvest is ripe. Go in, tread, for the wine press
>   is full. (3:13)

Readers are plunged immediately into two worlds: present and future, as visions of the effects of a locust plague, the actual experience of it, and impending relief from God amid God's judgment upon enemy countries are described in language and imagery unparalleled in the prophetic corpus. The text describes an ecological disaster that may seem cosmic in scope because of the prophet's intense, descriptive language, but that, in reality, seems to have affected only Judah.

Beginning with Joel 3:9, the prophet's message assumes a more universal tone with a shift from the locust plague to divine judgment upon those countries that have caused tribulation to Israelites in the past. The plague and divine judgment are both attributed to God and God's ways of justice. The locust plague strikes all creation in Judah because of humanity's breach of covenant obligations and responsibilities. This plague was understood to be a form of divine chastisement, along with the demise of certain countries because of their unjust deeds against Israel and Judah.

The book of Joel portrays God interacting within creation, among human beings, and through a prophetic figure. Such interaction has as its goal justice, compassion, and liberation and involves the exercise of God's power, a point that needs further discussion.

The literary structure of the book baffles scholars. There is, however, a two-part division for the entire book: Part 1 (1:2—2:17) with 1:1 as a superscription; and Part 2 (2:18—3:21). The first part presents a vision of disaster; the second, a vision of hope. Both parts pertain primarily to the people of Judah and the natural world and make only brief reference to other countries. The two parts are intricately woven together. The text's verbs, speakers, time markers, and linguistic shifts suggest distinct units and the relationship that exists among them. For example, in 2:2-14, the prophet addresses and exhorts the Judahite community, relaying to them a prophetic vision articulated with a series of prophetic perfect tenses. The use of past tense verbs to relate a future event is a literary device meant to signal the prophet's and later audiences that, in fact, the vision will become a reality. Here the prophet Joel sees what the people have yet to experience: the devastation from the locust plague. Consequently, he rouses them to attention and action. In 1:15-20, the prophet proclaims the imminence of the Day of the Lord (v 15) and a vision of its consequences (vv 16-18), which is followed by the prophet's lament (vv 19-20).

In Joel 2:1-2a, the prophet again addresses members of the Judahite community and once more announces the imminent coming of the Day of the Lord. In 2:2b-17, the Day of the Lord has finally arrived and is symbolized by the arrival of the locust plague. The prophet next exhorts the people to repent and lament (vv 12-17).

Chapters 2:18—3:8 is a prophecy of hope for Judah, and 3:9-21, while it is a proclamation of impending disaster for the countries, is also a message of hope for Judah. In vv 9-10, 12, 17-21, God speaks through the prophet; in vv 11, 13, the prophet addresses God; in vv 14-16, Joel reflects on the situation at hand and the presence of God in the midst of it. This series of interlocking units, together with shifts in time and speaker, and the use of metaphorical language and personification, help to create a unified text of intricacy and artistic beauty.

The text portrays God as one who has power over all of creation. The text suggests that God uses certain elements in the natural world, and in this case, the locust, to teach people a painful lesson. Unfortunately, the locust affects the land, vegetation, water sources, and the animals. What kind of God uses creation for destruction? Or is this merely projection of what the author and editors thought about how God acts with and toward creation? The injustice done by other countries and the divine justice imposed as chastisement both involve using children as pawns (3:3-8). Does this sort of action done in the name of justice appease the original injustice?

This part of Joel 3 focuses on how power can be used as a means of liberation. It portrays God as truly caring for creation and thus exercising power to free creation from the divine chastisement earlier imposed. The prophet is empowered by God to mobilize the Judahite people and help them make choices that will liberate them from the locust disaster. Finally, the text shows that through divine power, the people of Judah will be liberated from the domination, control, and oppression of other countries.

In the context of the contemporary world with its environmental concerns, the book of Joel makes an important statement: power can be used to liberate the oppressed. What does the human community need to do to ensure that in the future the mountains shall drip sweet wine and the hills flow with milk (3:18)? This is a divine promise within a prophetic text. What sort of power must be exercised to bring the promise to fruition? The study examines selected passages in the book of Joel with emphasis on how power can be a liberating force for all of creation today.

Joel 2:18-27

*"O children of Zion, be glad
and rejoice in the* Lord *your God;
for he has given the early rain
for your vindication." (2:23)*

What a wondrous promise God gives to the people of Judah and their land: liberation from a locust swarm. This ecological disaster has plagued the land, its herbage, and its creatures for years (v 25) and has shamed a people (vv 26, 27), making them a mockery among countries (v 19). And to whom does the text attribute this disaster?—to God, who is said to have afflicted the people (2:25). God now promises in vv 18-27 to end this disaster because ". . . the Lord became jealous for his land, and had pity on his people" (v 18).

The text shows a shift in power when God has a change of heart. Power used for chastisement that results in oppression shifts to power directed toward liberation and restoration. What is significant to note is the intimate relationship between humanity and creation. The people of the ancient world knew and understood this relationship. What affected creation, affected people; and what affected people affected creation. This relationship, as suggested by the book of Joel, has hermeneutical implications for those who view life from a socio-ecological perspective.

The shift from power for chastisement that results in oppression to power for liberation that results in restoration begins in v 18, where the prophet describes what seems to be God's change of heart. In vv 19-27, God, through the prophet: (1) announces the divine plan for liberation and restoration for all creation (vv 19-20, 25-26), (2) offers a word of comfort to the natural world (vv 21-22) and to the "children of Zion" (vv 23-24), and (3) offers the people a word of assurance that, indeed, their God is with them and never again shall they be put to shame (v 27). The last verse foreshadows bright days ahead for the people of Judah. Since the writers and editors of the text seem to have understood that God had shamed the people in the first place, might there be embedded in the text the implication that God would no longer use power to cause harm and oppression?

In vv 19-20 and 25-26, divine power is both liberative and restorative. In v 19, God will give the people grain, wine, and oil to satisfy them. Hence, through God's power, the earth will become fertile again. In v 20, God declares that the "northern army," the locusts,[2] will be removed far from the people and driven into a "parched and desolate land," "its front into the eastern sea and its rear into the western sea." Then, "its stench and foul smell will rise up." The verse closes with the phrase, "Surely he has done great things!" Through God's power, the pestilence that has plagued people and creation (vv 18, 21-22) will be removed. This is a great thing indeed. Nevertheless, from an ecological perspective the text is troublesome because of what God will do with these pests. God intends to drive the pests into a parched and desolate land and push them into the sea.

The text suggests that when God liberates the people from the locust plague (v 20), the natural world will be liberated as well from the suffering caused by this plague. In vv 21-22, God talks directly and tenderly to the soil and animals: "Do not fear . . . do not fear." Just as the people will enjoy the fruits of the earth once more (v 19), so will the animals (v 22). As God liberates the people from their oppression (vv 20, 25), so is the land liberated from its oppression (v 21). And just as the land and the people are restored to each other (vv 19 and 23), so are the land and the animals restored to each other (v 22).

Hermeneutically, Joel 2:18-27 still poses problems with respect to the text's image of God; God uses elements in the natural world, that is, the locusts, to chastise people, and this action, in turn, causes oppression for the animals. Again, this image coincides with the ancient people's hierarchical belief that God was "Lord over creation" and their patriarchal understanding of power as a legitimate force used to dominate, control, and conquer. Joel 2:18-27 proclaims a vision, however, that affirms that sin and oppression do affect the natural world, and that as people are liberated from both, so is the natural world. Further, as people are restored to life, so also will creation be restored. A picture of harmony rooted in transformation emerges, springing from a change of heart. Today, this change of heart must take place in the human community that has made real what God is said to have done, metaphorically, in the biblical text.

Joel 2:28-29
"Then afterward I will pour out my spirit on all flesh." (2:28)

Following the liberation and restoration of the people and the natural world from the locust plague, God makes another marvelous promise:

> Then afterward
>> I will pour out my spirit on all flesh;
> your sons and your daughters shall prophesy,
>> your old men shall dream dreams,
> and your young men shall see visions.
> Even on the male and the female slaves,
>> in those days, I will pour out my spirit. (vv 28-29)

Liberated and restored, God's people will now experience God's blessing: God will gift creation with the divine Spirit. This spirit will empower sons and daughters to prophesy, old men to dream dreams, and young men to see visions. Even on male and female slaves God's Spirit will be poured out. Hierarchy and patriarchy have been diminished as well as the notion of power associated with both. God's Spirit will now "empower" all flesh—everything that has life and breath—and prophecy will become the gift for the many and not just for the few. Yet the full portrait remains gender-specific: males will dream dreams and will see visions.

For readers today, this text is anthropocentric and limited in its theological message because God's spirit has been poured out upon all creation (Ps 19:1-4; 104:1-30; Prov 12:7-10; 38—41). Yet the text is liberating, revelatory, and eschatological for ancient and contemporary readers because it affirms God's presence in all people, regardless of gender, race, class, or status. The vision is slowly unfolding but is not fully realized: human prejudice and discrimination continue to persist.

Nahum and Joel in Context

The books of Nahum and Joel, with their prophecies of approaching armies of Assyrian warriors on the one hand (Nahum) and swarms of locusts on the other (Joel), have the potential to catch the reader's attention. Images of power shift back and forth as people and land suffer together. Yet in the mix of these images and power shifts are those prophecies that speak of a time when, through God's power, both people and the natural world will be liberated from the forces that have long been oppressing them. With liberation comes the promise and vision of restoration. The prophecies selected for study in this chapter offered hope to the Judahites of an ancient time, and they continue to offer hope with vision for people today who live in a time of power struggles and power shifts that continue to have their effect on creation. Would that the bonds that bind all life be broken and the yokes be snapped as promised in the days of Nahum, and would that sons and daughters prophesy, old men and women dream dreams, and young men and women see visions of what God's great plan for all creation is: life lived freely in peace.

PART THREE

Shifting from "Power Over" to "Power With": Harmonious Relationships

Introduction

PARTS ONE AND TWO EXAMINED HOW POWER can be used both to dominate and liberate; Part Three now shifts to consider how power can be used to establish justice and righteousness that facilitate harmonious and interdependent relationships among God, humankind, and the natural world. This new paradigm is dialectical and grounded in mutuality. Its vision can be found throughout the prophetic texts, particularly in Hosea, Isaiah 1–39, and Isaiah 40–66.

The prophet Hosea envisions a new covenant: humankind will participate in a new relationship with the natural world and with God, a theme picked up in Isaiah 11. Selected texts suggest that there is an intricate connection between the redemption of humanity and the restoration of the natural world. This theme occurs also in Isaiah 1–39. Within the texts is embedded the message that all creation is meant to participate in the divine plan of transformation, renewal, and salvation. Within Isaiah 40–66, the vision of the glorious new creation breaks forth, a vision connected to God's power working through human beings to empower them to bring forth justice and righteousness in nonviolent yet assertive ways. The vision is embodied in "the servant."

Although these texts are not without their problems for modern readers, they do suggest a direction for living out a new vision that can lead to a powerful transformation for all creation. In this new model effected by the servant, divine justice and righteousness will be accomplished through assertive yet nonviolent means and through means that attest to the intrinsic goodness of all life and to the reverence and respect that is its due.

12

Hosea

Overview: Historical, Literary, and Hermeneutical Interplay

F OR THE NORTHERN KINGDOM OF ISRAEL , the eighth century B.C.E. was a time of prosperity and disaster. Guided by the leadership of Jeroboam II, Israel experienced great economic wealth and international political strength. Internally, however, religious conflict and infidelity contributed to all sorts of injustices that riddled the kingdom. The internal situation weakened the country enough to allow Assyria the opportunity to invade it. Under such force the Northern Kingdom was overtaken and eventually collapsed. The prophet Hosea disclosed this mixture of the country's assuredness, on the one hand, and social unrest and impending disaster on the other.

Little is known about the prophet Hosea. He lived during the eighth century B.C.E. and most likely began his prophetic career during the last years of Jeroboam II. Some of the proclamations contained in the book of Hosea are associated with the Syro-Ephraimite War and the ensuing events of Tiglath-pileser III. This complex historical and social situation is described through a plethora of images and metaphorical language.

The book of Hosea is comprised of two main parts: Hosea's marriage (1–3) and Hosea's prophecies (4–14). Hosea uses imagery and figurative language (1) to set up a polemic against Baalism, (2) to foreshadow the social and political devastation that is Israel's lot, and (3) to appeal to the audience's religious imagination and life experience in an effort to move some of them from infidelity to fidelity to Yahweh. In the Hosea text, God condemns Baal (see, for example, Hos 2:13, 17; 11:2) and then takes on many of Baal's characteristics. This establishes a polemic against Baal worship and declares to the Israelites that there is one God and one God alone who is to be held in esteem.

Perhaps no other text in the Old Testament uses as many images from the natural world as does the book of Hosea. For example, in addition to God being described as a physician (7:1; 11:3; 14:4), a shepherd (13:5), and a fowler (7:12), God is also like showers (6:3a), spring rains (6:3b), a lion (13:7a), a leopard (13:7b), a bear (13:8), dew (14:5), and an evergreen cypress (14:8). Natural world images describe Israel as well. Israel is like a dove (7:11; cf. 9:11), a luxurious vine (10:1), morning mist (13:3a), and dew (13:3b). The new covenant cut is not only between God and Israel but also between Israel and the natural world (2:16,18). Divine compassion restores the relationship between God and the people. The text uses images from the natural world (see, for example, 14:4-9) to describe this relationship.

The book of Hosea does contain some metaphorical language and imagery that is offensive, especially to women. For example, in chapters 1–3 the central metaphor depicts the relationship of Yahweh and Israel as that of a husband and wife. The prophet Hosea is commanded by God to take back Gomer, his wife of whoredom. The directive and its execution is symbolic of the relationship that God has with Israel and of the future of that relationship. Because in Israel males occupied a privileged position and females a subordinate one, the metaphor is problematic. In the marriage story of Hosea and Gomer, Hosea is the faithful male and Gomer is the unfaithful female. When the story becomes an allegory and metaphor, God is a male deity, the faithful husband, and Israel, his wife, is the unfaithful one. This type of metaphorical language is fraught with theological problems. The text gives a preference for and an affirmation of the male gender while offering a negative image of the female gender. The one who is faithful is male; the one who is unfaithful is female. When this type of metaphorical language is associated with the Divine, the question arises: Is the male to be preferred? The text's metaphorical language communicates an image that could legitimate and support misogyny, both ancient and modern.

Other images in the text can also be disconcerting for contemporary readers. For example, Israelite society was primarily an agrarian society, and so many metaphors reflect a life of agriculture and husbandry. But those metaphors that compare people to animal and plant life can be heard negatively, especially if the images are not positive ones, as in the case of Israel being compared to a "stubborn heifer" (4:16) or a "trained heifer" (10:11). Today, some people could take offense at such comparison, because if viewed hierarchically, it demotes the human being. To compare a person or group of people to an animal or a plant can give them a lower status. On the other hand, to those who understand life on the planet as a relationship among all forms of life—human and nonhuman alike—such comparisons would not be offensive. Perhaps as people move closer to this latter attitude, ecological interdependence will be rediscovered and give way to metaphors that are more reciprocal in nature. Then a person might not take offense at being compared to a heifer or at the comparison of a heifer to a person.

The book of Hosea also contains examples of the exercise of power. God, the victim of a relationship gone sour, behaves like a hunter, a warrior, and a lion going after the people of Israel, specifically, women and children (see, for example, 9:12; 13:16), the two most vulnerable groups in society, both then and now. Other depictions of God using power aggressively and violently are woven throughout the book.

Despite these disconcerting points that need to be assessed critically, there are in the book of Hosea those images that speak of a movement from having power over, whether to dominate or to liberate, to using power to create harmonious relationships between the Divine and all of creation and among human beings, the Divine, and the natural world. Specifically, the new covenant of 2:14-23, the message of divine compassion in 11:1-11, and the assurance of forgiveness in 14:4-9 all speak of a new paradigm in which power is no longer the dominant force. Rather, what comes to the fore is the emphasis upon a mutuality between all of creation and its Creator. Thus, even liberation is not the final word; rather, beyond liberation is reconciliation and restoration whereby God and all of creation are once again seen as integral. These ideas are explored in this chapter in relationship to Hos 2:14-23; 11:1-11; and 14:4-9. These passages continue to be prophetic insofar as they speak to a world that continues to struggle over issues of power—its use and abuse—and one that stands on the brink of ecological disaster that threatens the extinction of both human and nonhuman life forms, a world challenged to take to heart this message of Hosea.

Hosea 2:14-23

*"I will abolish the bow, the sword, and war from the land;
and I will make you lie down in safety." (Hos 2:18)*

One of the central themes of the Old Testament is covenant. God enters into a covenant with Noah, Abraham, Moses and the Israelites at Sinai, and David, and promises a new covenant to Jeremiah and Hosea.[1] Like the Noachic covenant, the covenant promised in Hosea involves God, people, and the natural world. It envisions a time when God will restore the land to Israel (v 15). God promises to make for the Israelites a covenant "with the wild animals, the birds of the air, and the creeping things of the ground" (v 18), a covenant similar to the covenant that God made with Noah, Noah's descendants, and every living creature that was with Noah (Gen 9:10). Although the Hosea covenant uses espousal imagery that can be disconcerting (see chapter 6, above, on Ezekiel 16), this new covenant envisions harmonious relationships that flow from the relationship with God. For the people of Hosea's time, this covenant offered tremendous hope; for readers today living in a time of socio-ecological crises, the covenant holds out a vision that is indispensable if the planet is to have a future.

Following a lengthy judgment speech (2:1-13), Hos 2:14-23 initiates a shift in tone and images. Having been presented with a picture of an angry God enraged with Israel, expressed through the metaphorical language and imagery of a husband-wife relationship, the section portrays a God who woos Israel with tender words and the promise of a renewed relationship with the land (v 15a) and with God (v 15b). Verses 16-17 envision Israel's turn from apostasy to faithfulness, a turn that God initiates.[2] Verses 18-20, which are perhaps the heart of the pericope, depict a renewed relationship between human beings and the natural world (v 18a), an end to violence. Peace and security for all creation (v 18b) are intricately linked to the renewal of relationship between God and human beings (vv 19-20). Through the redemption and restoration of the Israelite people to their God, the natural world is also redeemed and restored.

Verses 21-23 open with a stock phrase, "on that day" (v 21). The future holds a day of divine blessing and a time of cosmic salvation: heaven and earth will now answer each other, and the earth shall respond to its productivity, which, in turn, will respond to human beings as symbolized by the name of Hosea's child Jezreel (see 1:4), which means "God plants." Finally, the LORD will respond to Hosea's children, that is, the covenant people, in the land. B. C. Birch has seen in these verses "the reestablishment of the chain of interrelationships in God's harmonious creation."[3] He notes that "the chain of restored harmony is initiated from the heavens (the realm of God and the rain), and then to the earth (and land, the soil), then to the produce of the land (grain, wine, oil), and finally to the people (Israel, humanity)."[4] Following on Birch's point, R. A. Simkins broadens the picture further with his reading of vv 21-23: "God will reestablish the ecological web that unites God's own creative activities with both the natural world and humankind."[5]

In summary, Hos 2:14-23 is a visionary passage that speaks of a new covenant that will affect all creation. Hermeneutically, this passage depicts a new understanding of the relationship between human beings and the natural world, one that is mutual and interdependent, affirming that the redemption of humanity is connected with the restoration of creation. This divinely promised redemption and restoration lead to a vision of creation that embodies justice, righteousness, peace, and harmonious relationships. Hosea 2:14-23 challenges contemporary readers to a new ethic, a justice that is not anthropocentric in nature and construct, but rather one that speaks of justice for all creation. The biblical vision of covenant in Hosea is cosmic[6] and carries with it the potential for a new global ethic.

Hosea 11:1-11

*"I led them with cords of human kindness,
with bands of love." (Hos 11:4)*

Hosea 11:1-11 is a poem that might be described as the window to God's heart. The text discloses what could be termed the vacillation of God's heart. In vv 1-4 God remembers how, when Israel was a child, God loved Israel, but how Israel moved farther and farther away, choosing to sacrifice to the Baals and offer incense to idols (vv 1-2). The metaphor here compares God's relationship with Israel to that of parent with child. The text's allusion to being called out of Egypt (v 1) harks back to the Exodus story where the intimate relationship between God and the Israelites first began. Verses 3-4 describe God's nurturing and parental love for Israel and provide a contrast to Israel's rejection of God's tender love (v 2).

Verses 1-4 provide a glimpse into the heart-warming, heart-wrenching relationship that God has with Israel. God is the one who is "long-suffering" in the relationship, the one who faithfully cares for Israel despite Israel's lack of appreciation of the gift.

Verses 5-7 shift the poem's focus and tone. With love unreturned, God now vows to send Israel back to its days of oppression, which, paradoxically, may already have been occurring (v 6).[7] Verse 7 describes God's frustration with Israel: "My people are bent on turning away from me." Verse 8 expresses the folly associated with calling on false gods. Thus far, the text has portrayed God in a very personable and human way, as one who loves Israel deeply but is aggravated with the people's lack of responsiveness and apostasy.

Verses 8-9 initiate another shift in tone. God uses a series of rhetorical questions to engage in self-reflection. God wonders how Israel could ever be given up, how Israel could ever be handed over, how God could ever make or treat Israel like others. Verse 8c provides a glimpse of God's deepest feelings: "My heart recoils within me / my compassion grows warm and tender." Because of God's recoiling heart and warm and tender compassion, God will not execute fierce anger or take any other measures of chastisement (v 9a). The verse ends with a divine self-confession: "for I am God and no mortal / the Holy One in your midst / and I will not come in wrath" (v 9b).

The poem presents a human portrait of a loving God with intense feelings for Israel. Throughout many of the passages studied thus far, God has been depicted as possessing many human and culturally conditioned qualities. Verse 9 presents God not coming in wrath or violence but rather, in spite of Israel's unfaithfulness (v 7), coming with love and compassion. God here professes difference from humankind: the Holy One will not "come in wrath" (NRSV), "come against the cities" (NIV), or "let the flames consume you" (NAB).[8] Whatever the accurate Hebrew rendering, the thrust is clear: God will refrain from violence. A challenge to traditional deuteronomic theology, v 9 makes clear that the unfaithful will not receive the punishment their unfaithfulness has warranted; God, despite their offense, will not execute power against them.

The conclusion of the poem depicts God metaphorically as a lion who roars, whose "children" come trembling from the West "like birds from Egypt and like doves" from Assyria (vv 10-11). God will return the Israelites to their homes (v 11). With Israel's return from Egypt and Assyria, the exile (v 5) is reversed. Although vv 10-11 convey hope, they depict God as a ferocious father and the Israelites as children who shake at their father's beckoning. This father-child imagery recalls similar imagery that appeared earlier in the poem, but for modern readers, it suggests a patriarchal and paternalistic relationship, one that betrays religious and cultural attitudes present in Israelite society during the eighth century B.C.E. and later.

In summary, Hos 11:1-11 conveys a very human and divine image of God, but one that is not without its flaws. Central to the passage is the language of relationship—the language of a vacillating heart that moves back and forth from care to frustration to care and compassion with the promise of future restoration. The passage depicts a loving God whose love transcends human love and who will not harm the beloved.

Hosea 14:4-9

"I will be like the dew to Israel;
he shall blossom like the lily,
he shall strike root like the forests of Lebanon." (Hos 14:5)

The divine compassion expressed in Hos 11:1-9 continues in 14:4-9, a divine promise. In v 4, God promises to heal the Israelites' infidelity and to love them freely. In vv 5-7, God promises to be "like dew" to Israel; Israel in turn will blossom "like the lily," strike root "like the forests of Lebanon" (v 5), become beautiful "like the olive tree"(v 6), smell "like Lebanon," "live beneath [God's] shadow," "flourish as a garden," "blossom like the vine," and smell "like the wine of Lebanon" (v 7). God as depicted here resembles Baal, the rain god of fertility. God is about to water Israel to make the land flourish. Verse 8 describes God as an evergreen cypress from which Israel's faithfulness originates. God, not Baal, is responsible for Israel's future life. Verse 9 affirms the righteous ways of God in which the upright walk but transgressors stumble.

The verses depict God as the sustainer, nurturer, and transformer of life, who offers hope to all. Israel is portrayed by means of flourishing natural world imagery. There is a relationship between the restoration of human life and the restoration of the natural world. The text portrays a sense of beauty and peace, and speaks to the relationship that God and the Israelite people have with creation. For contemporary readers, the text offers a refreshing message that God desires reconciliation and the well-being and fruitfulness of all creation.

Hosea in Context

These three passages from the book of Hosea employ imagery and figurative language, mostly from the natural world, to communicate a multifaceted message: (1) God, not Baal, is the source and sustainer of life; (2) there is an intricate link between the redemption of humanity and the restoration of the natural world; (3) ultimately, God is a God of compassion; and (4) the divine plan and prophetic message speak of the love that God has for people and creation—a love that is transformative.

Overview: A Historical, Literary, and Hermeneutical Interplay

THE FIRST PART OF THE BOOK OF ISAIAH (chapters 1–39) has traditionally been understood as a text that, for the most part, reflected the life and times of the second half of the eighth century B.C.E., which is also the time when Amos, Micah, and Hosea are believed to have been active. Scholarship, however, has determined that several chapters of this first section were not from the prophet himself but come from a later date.[1] While most of chapters 1–39 are judgment and condemnation, there are interwoven into this material poetic pieces that contain a positive voice of hope. These texts are considered in this chapter.

Very little is known about Isaiah the prophet, except that he had relations with a prophetess (8:3) who was supposedly his wife, though the text makes no mention of this point specifically. Together, Isaiah and the prophetess had at least one son, Maher-shalal-hash-baz (8:3). Isaiah also had another son, Shear-jashub (7:3). There may have been other children, but they are not mentioned in the text.

The prophet of First Isaiah began his prophetic career sometime around 740 B.C.E. and continued until 687 B.C.E. During that time, the people of Judah and their kings rejected Isaiah's call to reform their ways and attitudes, especially their lack of concern for the poor. Three events in particular marked Isaiah's career: (1) the Syro-Ephraimite War between 735 and 733 B.C.E.; (2) the rebellion of the Northern Kingdom against Assyria, which ended in the fall of Samaria, the capital of the Northern Kingdom in 722 B.C.E.; and (3) Sennacherib's campaign in 701 B.C.E. that was prompted by King Hezekiah's revolt and that resulted in the almost complete ravaging of the Southern Kingdom of Judah. These checkered historical events, as well as the injustices that characterized Judah's social, religious, and political spheres, form the background of the First Isaiah text. Nevertheless, the text contains the vision of a new day and a new paradigm, to which justice, peace, righteousness, and harmonious relationships are integral.

First Isaiah contains of a variety of literary units and forms: (1) an address to the heavens and the earth in which God expresses dissatisfaction with Judah's present state (1); (2) a prophecy of hope (2:1-4); (3) a prophecy of judgment (2:5—4:1); (4) a prophecy of hope (4:2-6); (5) a parable (5:1-7); (6) six woe prophecies that denounce social injustice (5:8-30); (7) a call narrative and the poetic commission of the prophet (6); (8) the book of Immanuel (7–12); (9) prophecies against the countries (chapters 13–23); (10) an apocalypse (24–27); (11) a series of later additions that are comprised of prophecies of judgment, prophecies of hope, warnings, and promises (chapters 28-35); and (12) a historical appendix (chapters 36–39). The variety of literary techniques used throughout the thirty-nine chapters (rhetorical questions, metaphors, personifications, and so forth) add to the book's distinctive tapestry and to the ebb and flow of the prophetic message, which speaks both to injustice and to a new paradigm characterized by harmonious and interdependent relationships.

Isaiah 1–39 contains certain elements that need further hermeneutical consideration (for example, the gender-specific imagery of "Jerusalem" / "Zion" personified as a female apostate). Moreover, the chapters contain expressions of divine anger and the assertion of power that have as their goal the chastisement of all those people who have acted unjustly and who refuse to reform their ways.

Isaiah 1–39 contains several passages that herald a vision of peace and prosperity for all of creation. Swords are beaten into plowshares, and spears are turned into pruning hooks (2:4). The wolf one day will live with the lamb, and the nursing child will play over the hole of the asp (see, for example, 11:6-9). The images speak of a new creation that is ordered by harmonious relationships. Prophetic and eschatological visions in Isaiah 11 can support a new ethical paradigm and lead to a praxis that attests to the holiness and interrelatedness of all of life.

This chapter focuses on those passages in Isaiah 1–39 that offer a vision of a new created order that has as its strength the interconnectedness of all of creation. It is this vision that is most compelling for life on the planet today; this vision can enable the human community to see that the redemption of humanity is indeed tied to the restoration of creation. Thus, the need for a new ethical paradigm that includes care for all creation becomes as compelling as the vision itself.

Isaiah 2:1-4

"They shall beat their swords into plowshares,
and their spears into pruning hooks." (2:4)

Isaiah 2:1-4 provides a vision of weapons of destruction being transformed into tools of production. Moreover, this is done by the choice of the people. Potential death is rejected in favor of potential life. What a hopeful, life-affirming vision.

Following a brief superscription (v 1), the prophecy opens with a promise for the future (v 2). In days to come, the Lord's mountain will be reestablished. Mount Zion, in its day, was considered to be a sacred mountain that held importance for the entire world.[2] The image of all countries streaming toward it suggests a sense of unity (v 2), and the emphasis upon going "to the mountain of the Lord" and "to the house of the God of Jacob" to learn God's ways and instruction suggests a certain religious solidarity that the countries will have with Judah (v 3). Verse 4 depicts God as a judge but not as a human judge, rather an arbitrator for many peoples whose goal is the establishment of universal peace.

For the Judahites, religion and politics were intertwined, and abiding by Torah was paramount to establishing peace. Here, the Judahites are to set an example for other countries through their worship that will attract other countries to join them. J. J. Collins points out that "this recognition and the acceptance of Yahweh's instruction are seen as the keys to world peace, when swords will be beaten into ploughshares."[3] Although the text portrays God as a male deity, Isa 2:1-4 speaks of a time when countries will no longer use power to dominate, control, overpower, or oppress one another. Rather, there will be peace—a harmonious coexistence—among them. The peace that can exist among all countries and the unity of all peoples with the Divine continues to be the goal for world politics and world religions.

Isaiah 9:1-7

"His authority shall grow continually,
and there shall be endless peace
for the throne of David and his kingdom." (9:7)

Perhaps one of the most famous prophecies of the book of Isaiah, Isa 9:1-7, is a messianic prophecy that describes an ideal king whose coming reign is assured but still in the future. Historically, the new king to be born is probably Hezekiah, Ahaz's successor, who began his reign in either 725 or 715 B.C.E. Although this prophecy has a definite historical referent, it continues to offer vision insofar as it begins to outline the characteristics needed for effective leadership. The ideal leader, portrayed as a male figure, emerges from Judah's patriarchal culture.

Following a brief narrative comment (v 1), the poetic prophecy opens in the past tense and describes a new way of life for northern Israelites who live under Assyrian oppression. This new way of life, this new hope, will not come through God directly but through a person characterized by goodness and holiness. The use of the past tense is a literary device used to communicate to audiences that what is envisioned will indeed happen. This new time will be a time of freedom and peace for the Israelites that will dawn through just and righteous leadership (v 7). The phrase "from this time onward and forevermore" gives an eschatological dimension to the prophecy. Finally, the one to initiate this great work is God (v 7).

The prophecy claims that the establishment of justice and righteousness can come through effective leaders whose power lies in "transparent vulnerability which makes defiance pointless."[4] This task is being accomplished through "the zeal of the LORD of hosts," not solely through human effort (v 7). It will come to pass through God's passionate involvement with people in history.

Finally, the prophecy describes a time of freedom and peace. This part of the divine plan for life will be accomplished when human leaders choose the way of justice and righteousness for the well-being and liberation of all creation. The androcentric and anthropocentric assumptions in this prophecy are, however, themselves in need of transformation. Thus, Isa 9:9-17 offers a wonderful, though limited, vision to be both embraced and expanded. The prophecy illustrates both how a biblical text can have a positive impact on contemporary culture and how contemporary culture can inform the biblical text.

Isaiah 11:1-9

"Righteousness shall be the belt around his waist,
and faithfulness the belt around his loins." (11:5)

Images and themes employed in Isa 9:1-7 continue in Isa 11:1-9. This poem of "extraordinary generative power"[5] presents a magnificent vision of a new creation that comes to birth through the exercise of justice and righteousness. The text can be divided into two sections: vv 1-5 and 6-9. Historically, this poem became a source of comfort for those in the midst of the tension and turmoil of the Assyrian crisis; for contemporary readers, the poem offers a vision of life's possibilities when order and integrity are restored.

In vv 1-5, the prophet combines metaphorical language and imagery from the natural world with historical and religious allusions to describe the attributes of a new type of leader. This leader will be connected to a tradition that is already in place but will not be the same as what has always been (v 1).[6] The new leader will be empowered by God's Spirit—a spirit of wisdom, understanding, counsel, might, knowledge, and love of God (vv 2-3a). Verses 3b-4 describe how this new leader will exercise power. The person will not judge by appearances or hearsay but with righteousness and equity; decisions will be carried out with power but without physical violence (v 4);[7] and all this will be possible since the leader is personally espoused to justice and faithfulness (v 5).

Verses 6-9 describe a lovely pastoral picture in which domestic animals— the "lamb" (v 6), the "kid" (v 6), the "calf" (v 6), the "fatling" (v 6), the "cow" (v 7), and the "ox" (v 7)—together with the wild animals—the "wolf" (v 6), the "leopard" (v 6), the "lion" (v 6), and the "bear" (v 6)—and human beings—symbolized by "a little child" (v 6), a "nursing child" (v 8), and the "weaned child" (v 8)—all live together peacefully and securely on God's holy mountain (v 9a). This peace will come to be when "the earth [is] full of the knowledge of the LORD as the waters cover the sea" (v 9b). Apparently, knowing the LORD is meant to produce behavior that does "not hurt" or "destroy," behavior dependent upon harmonious relationships.

Isaiah 11:1-9 presents an idyllic picture that has often seemed unrealistic to the ecologically informed. As R. A. Simkins points out, "Is not the natural world *inherently violent?* The balance of nature is dependent on one species' preying off another. Nature is 'red in tooth and claw,' yet without violence it would cease to sustain itself."[8] Yet, for the Israelites and Judahites, all creation belonged to God; and therefore, all of life was to be treated with reverence and respect by humans. This does not cancel out "laws of nature" whereby species prey off others. Rather, it envisions an eschatological time of life-enhancing interdependence.

In vv 1-5 and vv 6-9 as a whole, the vision of a new order characterized by human beings having reverence and respect for creation is directly associated with and contingent upon the carrying out of justice and righteousness by human beings, especially those in leadership positions who themselves must embody the qualities of justice, equity, nonviolence, and faithfulness. All of these qualities flow from being in right relationship with God, who is the author of and power behind the vision.

In summary, Isa 11:1-9 envisions an ethical way of life that insists upon responsible living and responsible stewardship grounded in a holy reverence for all of life.

Isaiah 32:1-8, 16-20

"The effect of righteousness will be peace,
and the result of righteousness, quietness and trust forever." (32:17)

Isaiah 32:1-8 and 16-20, visions that focus on just and righteous leadership and its effects on all creation, echo themes and ideas from Isa 9:1-7 and 11:1-9. Isaiah 32:1-8 uses language from the wisdom tradition to contrast sense and nonsense (vv 3-8). Verses 1-2 speak of a day when a king will reign with righteousness and princes with justice (v 1), a day when they become sources of protection and support for people. Verses 3-8 contrast life under good leadership (open eyes, listening ears, ordinarily rash minds using good judgment, stammering tongues speaking distinctly, the fool and villain unmasked) with the social disarray and injustice existent among the Judahites because of poor leadership (fools speaking folly, plotting iniquity, protecting ungodliness, uttering error, disregarding the hungry and the thirsty, devising wickedness, ruining the poor).

Verses 16-20 describe the effects that good leadership will have. Those who govern with justice and righteousness (v 1) will bring about justice and righteousness (v 16) that, in turn, will cause peace, serenity, and security to flourish. Not only people will enjoy these benefits but also the natural world. Verse 20 implies agrarian well-being: "Happy will you be who sow beside every stream / who let the ox and donkey range freely." The growth will be so abundant that the animals can be let loose to graze.

Although vv 1-8 are androcentric and monarchic in tone, representing a leadership structure that was in place in ancient Judah, vv 1-8 and vv 16-20 do suggest that when leaders of countries act justly and righteously with integrity, a full quality of life for all creation is possible. As leadership is transformed (vv 1-2), so shall the society be transformed (vv 3-8), and as the society is transformed (vv 3-8), so shall creation be transformed when it is nurtured and allowed to heal (vv 16-20). Isaiah 32:1-8 and 16-20, like Isa 9:1-7 and 11:1-9, present a vision that is culturally and historically conditioned but one that depicts a world in which all of life can thrive in peace.

Isaiah 30:18-26

"He will give rain for the seed with which you sow the ground, and grain,
the produce of the ground, which will be rich and plenteous." (30:23)

Having glimpsed a vision of peace among peoples and the quality of leader needed to facilitate peaceful and secure habitats and relationships for the benefit of all creation, Isa 30:18-26 describes a time when people are restored to their God and to the natural world.

Verse 18 offers words of comfort to the Judahites in the wake of the imminent destruction of Jerusalem. Here the people are encouraged to wait for God who will be gracious and merciful to them, for "the LORD is a God of justice." Verses 19-20 reiterate that God will be gracious, merciful, and just. In v 19 the people are assured that God will indeed hear and answer their cry. Verse 20 describes a change of heart that God is supposed to have. The LORD, who may give adversity and affliction, will not, however, remain hidden; rather, the Teacher, that is, God, will guide the people in the way they should walk (v 21). This will result in the people forsaking their idolatrous and pagan ways (v 22).

With images of fertility and prosperity, vv 23-26 describe the future happiness of the people. God will water the earth, and the land will become rich and plenteous, especially for the work animals (vv 23-24). Brooks will flow with running water on every mountain and hill—"on a day of the great slaughter, when the towers fall" (v 25).[9] Even the light of the moon and the sun will be brighter than usual when God heals the people of the wounds "inflicted by his blow" (v 26). Here, again God is depicted as behaving much like the fertility god, Baal. God, not Baal, is the source and sustainer of life.

These verses give readers a benevolent view of God, who cares for people, animals, and the rest of the natural world. The image of God as a male deity, who "gives the bread of adversity and the water of affliction" (v 20) and who "heals wounds inflicted by his blow" (v 26), has been shaped by the theology and culture of the day. Above all, this text affirms the relationship that exists between the redemption of humanity and the renewal and restoration of the cosmos. Divine power is asserted for the purpose of bringing humankind and the cosmos to a fuller, richer life. For contemporary readers, Isa 30:18-26 offers both a vision and a challenge, to see the relationship that exists among all elements of creation, and to work toward the restoration of this relationship on a planet that is suffering, broken, and in need of healing.

Isaiah 35:1-10

"The wilderness and the dry land shall be glad,
the desert shall rejoice and blossom." (35:1)

Images of renewal, restoration, and liberation continue in Isa 35:1-10. This vision celebrates Judah's liberation, with imagery closely connected to second Isaiah (see, for example, Isa 40:3; 42:7; 43:19; 51:11). It contains a timeless message of comfort and hope.

The passage is comprised of three units: vv 1-4, vv 5-7, and vv 8-10. In vv 1-4, there are two images: the natural world (vv 1-2) and people with weak hands, feeble knees, and fearful hearts—people who are vulnerable (vv 3-4).

In the coming age, the natural world will be transformed into a place of great beauty, dignity, and fertility.[10] To whom the commands are addressed in vv 3-4 is uncertain, but their recipients, those who are vulnerable, are given words of great encouragement and comfort: God will come and save them. The advent of God will bring beauty, transformation, encouragement, and liberation for the natural world and humanity (vv 2, 4).

This transformation and liberation will have far-reaching effects: the healing of infirmities (vv 5-6a) and the gushing forth of water on thirsty ground and parched land to create wetlands and cause grass to flourish (vv 6b-7). People and the natural world will come to the fullness of life.

In this new transformed order, there will be a highway called "the Holy Way," which will be for God's people (vv 8-10).[11] It will be a way that is safe, and on it the redeemed shall walk as they make their return to Zion. No one unclean will walk on this road. Finally, in the future there will be no more sorrow or sighing. Historically, this passage promises a time when the Judahites, freed from exile, will be resettled in their land and experience new growth.

Isaiah 35:1-10 presents a glorious picture of a future when the natural world and humanity have been transformed, liberated, and graced into the abundance of life. The outcasts will be welcomed home, and joy will be the prevailing sentiment. As in the other Isaian texts studied in this chapter, the message is clear: the divine plan for renewal and restoration is meant for both human and nonhuman life forms. To this extent, Isa 35:1-10 has the potential to challenge an anthropocentric paradigm of salvation and to open eyes to one that is creation-centered. Only vv 8-9 are troublesome, with their reference to those who will be excluded from traveling the highway. The unclean, whether human or animal, will be excluded; fiercely predatory animals will also be excluded. Unclean persons were not suitable to enter Zion, the central place of worship, and participate in the Yahweh cult; unclean animals were not suitable for sacrifice. Creatures of violence were also excluded from traveling the Holy Way; those inhabiting the restored land would not be endangered by these predatory animals. Yet are these not discriminatory exclusions that result from the cultural and religious beliefs of the day that might cloud this harmonious vision? In the fullness of the predicted future, might not the unclean be cleansed? Might not the ravenous beasts be tamed?

Isaiah 1–39: Selected Passages in Context

All the passages discussed in this chapter speak of a relationship that exists between God and people, God and the natural world, and God and all creation. Isaiah 2:1-4 proclaims the harmonious and peaceful relationship that all countries are meant to enjoy when weapons of war are turned into tools for tilling. Isaiah 9:1-7; 11:1-9; and 32:1-8, 16-20 all focus on a new type of leader who asserts power to ensure peace, justice, and righteousness for all creation. Isaiah 30:18-26 and 35:1-10 depict the new life that will unfold for people and the natural world in the future age. All of these texts describe deep transformations that lead to peace, security, and joy. With the exception of Isa 2:14, all of these passages suggest that the redemption of humanity is intricately linked to the restoration of the natural world, and that all creation is meant to participate in the divine plan of transformation, renewal, and salvation. The passages promote a world that is characterized by relationships that are respectful of life where the Divine is at work in the midst of all.

From an ancient world and an ancient people has emerged a vision for life for which they hoped and to which they looked forward. Today, all creation groans and awaits the coming age of which the prophets spoke. The ancient prophetic word speaks to a world that totters between life and death as people search for ways to repair broken relationships that have left the present in social and ecological turmoil. Despite the texts' flaws from historical and cultural influences and conditioning, they contain a liberative and transformative power to help usher in "the coming day," which still remains but a vision.

14

Isaiah 40–66

Overview: A Historical, Literary, and Hermeneutical Interplay

ERHAPS SOME OF THE MOST EXTRAORDINARY PASSAGES found in the entire prophetic corpus occur in Isaiah 40–66, texts that challenge the human community and provide a vision for all creation. While the challenge and the vision were directed first toward the Judahite community—the faithful remnant, the exiled, and those being reestablished in the land—the message remains ever new and calls forth a response from all those who are responsible for the quality of life of and on the planet.

Traditionally, Isaiah 40–55 has been labeled Second Isaiah and 56–66, Third Isaiah. The authors of both parts of the book are unknown but believed to be different from the author of Isaiah 1–39. The original addresses of Second Isaiah are the Judahite exiles in Babylon; those being addressed by Third Isaiah are the Judahite people resettled in their own land. Unlike the confident, prosperous, and optimistic people assumed by First Isaiah, the community in Second Isaiah is discouraged, destitute, and on the brink of religious despair; all of their important symbols have been destroyed or overturned, that is, the temple and the Davidic line. The servant songs contained in Second Isaiah offer a message of comfort and hope that speaks of divine empowerment for the sake of liberation. In Third Isaiah, the now resettled Judahite community continues to struggle, frustrated and disillusioned. There are bitter strifes among community members and circumstances that alienate them from one another. The new visions of life in the future offer a renewed sense of hope. These visions of a new heaven and a new earth have been typically labeled "apocalyptic" or "eschatological." And yet the servant songs and the visions of a new creation can constitute both a mission and a goal for the human community today.

From a literary perspective, Second and Third Isaiah can be viewed as a single unit with two main subdivisions: (1) a message of comfort and assurance of redemption (40:1—55:13), and (2) a message of hope, judgment, lament, and vision (56:10—66:24). Both parts make use of a wide variety of literary techniques, including rhetorical questions, personifications, metaphors and similes, and imperatives, all of which enhance the beauty and intricacy of the poetry interspersed with a few narrative prose sections. Among the major theological themes that pervade the material are: (1) the centrality of Jerusalem, (2) the power of the divine work, (3) the justice of God, and (4) the comfort to be derived from divine care and a renewed life for all creation.

Both Second Isaiah and Third Isaiah contain gender-specific images that diverge completely from those found in First Isaiah. Specifically, in First Isaiah, Jerusalem/Zion is depicted with a negative image—as a woman who is a harlot and an apostate (see, for example, Isa 1:21-23 and 3:18-26). In Second Isaiah and Third Isaiah, Jerusalem/Zion is again portrayed as a woman, but this time the imagery has positive connotations for the female gender (see, for example, Isa 52:1-2 and 66: 5-13). However, amid such positive imagery, there remains a strain of the negative (see, for example, Isa 57:3, 6-13; see also the description of virgin daughter Babylon in Isa 47:1-15).

Thus, while Second and Third Isaiah present a more positive view of women, the metaphor of God as a divine husband/lover/maker and Jerusalem/Zion as God's wife/beloved/daughter is inherently hierarchical/ patriarchal and troublesome theologically. Such metaphors on the one hand affirm the goodness of women, but, on the other hand, allow for the presumption that women, not men, are faithless. In fact, the social situation of Judah would most likely be a testimony against such a metaphor, since those guilty of religious apostasy and political scandal were, for the most part, males; they held the positions of power and privilege within the society.

In Second Isaiah and Third Isaiah, the positive feminine imagery associated with God is striking. In Isa 42:14, God is compared to a woman in labor. Isaiah 49:15 is a rhetorical question that serves as an affirming response to Zion's statement in 49:14. Zion claims that God has forgotten her (v 14); in Isa 49:15, God responds, "Can a woman forget her nursing child, or show contempt for the child of her womb? Even if these may forget, yet I will not forget you" (v 15). The metaphorical language presumes that God is like the mother who does not forget her child. Thus, God has not and will not forget Zion. A similar image found in Isa 66:13 speaks of divine comfort for Jerusalem. As a mother comforts her child, God promises to comfort the inhabitants of Jerusalem. Such metaphors, then, hint at a renewed and tender relationship that God will have with the Judahite people. Furthermore, the fact that feminine imagery is used is an explicit affirmation of the nurturing, tender qualities often associated with the "feminine" that inheres in both females and males.

Isaiah 40–66 speak of mission and the divine vision that God has for all of creation. The text of Second Isaiah presents a composite picture of a servant whose mission is to bring about justice, mercy, and liberation from oppression. Some of the imagery is reminiscent of First Isaiah, specifically Isa 11:1-5 (see above). For the Judahite community in exile, this was indeed a hopeful message. Second Isaiah, especially those passages that describe the character and identity of God's servant, offer direction to those who take seriously the understanding of leadership in relationship to service; this model of leadership differs from a hierarchical and patriarchal one associated with domination and control.

Third Isaiah heralds a message of restoration and renewal while presenting a glorious vision of cosmic transformation (Isa 65:17-25). Again, this message or vision was good news for the postexilic Judahite community that struggled among its members. Often labeled "apocalyptic" or "eschatological," this vision echoes ideas presented in Second and First Isaiah (see, for example, 43:18-19 and 11:6-90, respectively). The vision depicted here does not, however, speak of some ideal life to be lived in the hereafter; it is a vision to be embraced in the present. Hence, life was to be lived free from unnecessary suffering and pain, free from lack of care or discrimination, free from exploitation and oppression, and free from power, domination, and violence.

This chapter focuses on selected passages from poems that depict Yahweh's servant (Isaiah 42; 49; 52–53; 61) and the vision of the glorious new creation (Isa 65:17-25) in order to highlight four points in particular: (1) the redemption of humankind is connected to the restoration of creation; (2) the human community has a responsibility toward all of creation; (3) the vision of Isa 65:17-25 can no longer remain apocalyptic or eschatological but must become a reality for the planet and life on the planet; and (4) the divine vision for all creation is one that speaks of respect for all of life and life lived in balance and in relationship.

The challenge to turn swords into pruning hooks and then to use the pruning hooks to cultivate the potentially beautiful and lush garden is the task at hand. The focus must shift from the use of power to dominate, control, and oppress to the use of power to empower oneself and others and liberate all of creation from its groaning and oppression. Hierarchical, patriarchal, sexist, classist, and racist paradigms must shift from exclusion to inclusion if the human community is to establish mutual, harmonious relationships among its members, and if its members, in turn, are to establish balanced, respectful relationships with the natural world. Second and Third Isaiah provide the vision.

Isaiah 42:1-9

"I have put my spirit upon him;
he will bring forth justice to the nations." (42:1)

One of the themes introduced in Isaiah 1–39 was the righteous reign of the coming king, who would establish justice and righteousness for all of creation. This theme of leadership, justice, and righteousness continues in Isaiah 40–66 through the person of the servant. In Isa 42:1-9, God is the speaker who, through the prophet Isaiah, first introduces the servant and then goes on to describe the servant's mission. God empowers the servant to help bring about the restoration of Judah and to be a light to the peoples so that deliverance can reach to the ends of the earth.

Isaiah 42:1-9 opens with a description of the servant. God's servant, upheld by God, is God's chosen one in whom God's soul delights (v 1). The servant, imbued with God's Spirit, is to bring forth justice to all peoples. This verse suggests that the servant has a special relationship with God who has empowered him; God is "with" the servant.

Verses 2-4 develop how the servant will bring forth justice. He will do it quietly, gently, faithfully, and steadfastly. With regard to the servant's use of power, J. N. Oswalt offers a striking interpretation and comment on v 3 that links this passage to Isaiah 9 and 11:

> . . . whereas all the other royal figures who have claimed to set up justice on the earth have done so through a gleeful use of their power to smash and rebuild, this one will be radically different. He is so far from smashing the mighty that he will not even break off the reed that is bent over and cracked. Rather, he will support it and straighten it. Nor will the blast of his mighty proclamations tear up the cedars by their roots. He will not even puff out the most dimly glittering lamp wick (smoldering wick). Rather, he will trim it and rest it more deeply in the oil. It is not necessary to press these figures so far as to define who the reed and the flax are intended to represent. The point is plain: like the child of chap. 9 and the branch of chap. 11, God's answer to the oppressors of the world is not more oppression, nor is his answer to arrogance more arrogance; rather in quietness, humility, and simplicity, he will take all of the evil into himself and return only grace. That is power.[1]

Verse 4 states that the servant is to establish justice "in the earth." This phrase reflects the universal scope of the servant's mission, certainly with respect to the countries, but perhaps also for all creation.

Verses 5-7 describe the servant's commission. God, the author and sustainer of creation, establishes a relationship between God and the servant (vv 5-6a). God, "the LORD of life, of creation," has called to the servant in righteousness and has taken the servant "by the hand." The divine purpose that underlies the relationship becomes clear in vv 6b-7. The servant is to be a covenant to the people and a light to other countries (v 6b). The tasks associated with God's servant are the following: making the blind see and the prisoners free (v 7). The servant will show that the covenant is not abrogated and that a blessed relationship with the transcendent God is still possible.[2]

Finally, in vv 8-9, God distinguishes God's self from idols. Judah's God, not idols, has the power to bring about what has been promised and will, through the servant, accomplish it. The servant, a prophetic figure, heralds God's transforming power at work in the midst of all creation to bring about a glorious new creation (see Isa 65:17-25).

The dominant male attitudes of ancient Israelite and Judahite society envisioned God as a male deity and God's servant as a male; nevertheless, this passage contains a vision that transcends its initial historical intent. Although the servant is not named,[3] the fact remains that the servant is entrusted with a mission that although begun has yet to come to completion. New Testament writers saw Jesus as the embodiment of this servant, whose mission has continued to the present. Justice had yet to be established on the earth, and the paradigm of power that the servant models had yet to be established among people and countries. Furthermore, the threads of covenant waited to be woven together to bring all peoples and all of creation into a relationship grounded in justice and righteousness that brings dignity, respect, and peace.

This text suggests a model of leadership style that is nonhierarchical; that is, the text does not associate the servant specifically with royalty or monarchy. Empowered by God, the servant's power rests in the ability to work with all people—to establish a relationship, a covenant—among all people that becomes the framework for liberation and the groundwork for cosmic transformation (Isa 42:9; 65:17-25). The historical and theocentric implications of this passage, together with its prophetic and visionary nature, suggest that the divine mission of the servant has yet to be accomplished.

Thus, Isa 42:1-9 offers a vision of how all of life can continue to be restored to its intended fullness and beauty. Furthermore, while this text poses a challenge to the leadership style of all world leaders, if its vision is to be accomplished, then all peoples must participate in right relationships with one another and with all of creation.

Isaiah 49:1-7

"I will give you as a light to the nations,
that my salvation may reach to the end of the earth." (49:6)

The theme of the servant and the servant's mission begun in Isa 42:1-9 continues in Isa 49:1-7. The servant addresses what could be considered today a "global" audience. Verses 1–7 publicly proclaim the servant's call even before birth (vv 1-4) and the divine task assigned to the servant at birth (vv 5-6). Verse 7, a prophecy of hope, is intended to encourage, comfort, and affirm the servant as the servant fulfills God's mission.

This passage differs from Isa 42:1-9 in that the servant is named: Israel. God will be glorified in Israel (49:3). Also, the mission of the servant is more clearly defined here than in Isaiah 42. In addition to bringing forth justice to other countries (Isa 42:1) and being a "light to the peoples" (Isa 42:6; 49:6), the servant is to restore Jacob, to gather Israel (Isa 49:5). The servant's power to do these things rests in God, who is the servant's strength (v 5). Verse 7 makes clear that deliverance will be accomplished by the power of God working faithfully through the servant, not through the royal power of kings and princes.

Isaiah 49:1-7 suggests that (1) the divine plan of deliverance is universal; (2) God's plan will be accomplished by divine power working through a person(s); (3) local and international leadership will not be able to accomplish the divine plan on its own (nor will the mission and power be divinely entrusted to the leaders directly); and (4) restoration implies not just the restoration of a people to its land or a people to one another, but restoration of an estranged country, an "estranged world," to God.[4] This text serves as a challenge. If God's deliverance is universal, then there is no place for prejudice or discrimination of any sort. Nor is there any room for religious triumphalism or political nationalism. While Israel became a great kingdom, in earliest times it was a multicultural group of people. This dimension of Israel, as servant, provides tremendous hope for the peoples of the world. Isaiah 49:1-7 can further challenge because it invites to a deeper search into the mystery and understanding of who this God is who works through people to bring about deliverance.

Historical and cultural influences and perspective embedded in this text have provided a servant model that is gender-specific, a God-image that is somewhat ethno-specific, and a vision of deliverance that is anthropocentric. Nevertheless, the text goes beyond these elements to involve a profound and universal vision. God is greater than human interpretation and imaginings; God's servant is to be found in the midst of the human race; and God's plan of deliverance is for all creation that waits and groans for redemption and restoration.

Isaiah 61:1-4

*"He has sent me to bring good news to the oppressed,
to bind up the brokenhearted." (61:1)*

A third passage that focuses on the servant is Isa 61:1-4. In tone, function, and language, this passage is similar to Isa 42:1-9 and 49:1-7.[5] In this pericope, the speaker focuses on a mission to be accomplished. As in 42:1-9 and 49:1-7, the speaker is empowered by the Spirit of God; hence, God is "with" a human being. But different from the other two servant passages, this person's mission here is focused on the oppressed and those in need. This servant has an active role in the ongoing plan of deliverance. The servant not only preaches deliverance but also applies the message, working concretely toward the goal. The servant brings good news by proclaiming liberty to captives and release to prisoners, the year of the Lord's favor and the day of God's vengeance (vv 1-2). The servant also provides empowerment for the people so that they can "build up the ancient ruins . . . , raise up the former devastations, . . . repair the ruined cities, the devastations of many generations" (vv 3-4). Once helped and liberated, those who were suffering become strong and righteous themselves, ready to continue the work of restoration and transformation.

Historically, this passage reflects the exile of the Judahites to Babylon. The "captives" and "prisoners" are likely these exiles; the "year of the Lord's favor" is the sabbatical year (see Deuteronomy 15), when all debts are canceled and Hebrew slaves are set free. But, as J. J. Collins so aptly points out, "the importance of the passage transcends its historical context. . . . It presents a concise summary of the mission of a servant of God in any age. It is a mission to raise up the lower strata of society. The Gospel of Luke has Jesus read this text, with minor variations, at the outset of his career (Luke 4:17-19)."[6]

Thus, this passage serves as a challenge to readers in many of the same ways as Isa 42:1-9 and 49:1-7 do. Again, the power of God rests in humanity, and now the servant becomes not only an advocate of deliverance but also actively involved in making the vision become a reality for those members on the "lowest rung of the social ladder," who, when assisted, can continue the work of restoration. God's plan of deliverance will come to fruition when people not only talk about the plan and embrace its vision, but do something to make the talk and vision a lived experience.

Isaiah 52:13—53:12
"Upon him was the punishment that made us whole;
and by his bruises we are healed." (53:5)

Another passage that features the servant is Isa 52:13—53:12.[7] Here the servant is presented as someone who stands in solidarity with the community. God has acted through the servant to empower the servant to be a direct means of deliverance for the community. Hence, the servant is "the suffering servant," the "righteous one" (v 11), who shall make many "righteous" (v 11)— the broken one who through the strength of his person brings others to wholeness. Although people have despised and rejected the servant, the servant receives a portion with the great in the company of the strong. Perhaps no other person is so representative of a paradigm shift in power as the suffering servant who stands in solidarity with humanity, one with God, and who, through metaphorical language, is seen as connected to the natural world.

The main speaker in Isa 52:13—53:12 is God, speaking through the prophet Isaiah in order to teach a lesson (52:13-15; 53:11b-12) by means of an example and reflection (53:1-11a). The lesson is meant to assure the righteous, the sinners, and all in exile that God's plan is for all to be saved. In Isa 52:13-15, God describes the servant and the effect the servant will have on others. These verses serve as an introduction to the larger poem insofar as they describe the anticipated good fortune of the servant, a theme that resonates in Isa 53:12.

In Isa 53:1-6, God quotes a report that describes a person deemed absolutely repulsive by society. This repulsive one is the servant (52:14; 53:3). Two rhetorical questions open the report: "Who has believed what we have heard?" and "To whom has the arm of the LORD been revealed?" (v 1). The speakers seem to be a group of Judahites living in exile.[8] Verse 2 describes the servant. Metaphorical language selected from the natural world (a young plant, a root out of dry ground) vivifies the description. Verse 3 depicts the servant's suffering specifically: he was (1) despised and rejected by others; (2) a man of suffering acquainted with infirmity; (3) shunned; and (4) held of no account. This servant was society's "outcast," who suffered social abuse and isolation.

In vv 4-5 the speakers come to understand, in retrospect, why the "servant" has suffered so severely. To them, it seemed as though the "servant" had been a wicked person chastised by God (v 4b). This perception reflects a religious belief commonly held in the ancient world. The speakers, however, now acknowledge with understanding that the "servant" had suffered because of their sicknesses and pains—their "wickedness" (vv 4a-5). The servant "was wounded" on account of the people's transgressions. "He" bore the pain and suffering of the people's sins in his own person, and through his suffering, he enabled the people to be restored to their God, whom they had abandoned. Returning to images from the natural world, the speakers compare themselves to sheep that have gone astray. Having abandoned God, they abandoned God's ways as well (v 6). Thus, the text describes how the suffering of one became a source of healing and restoration for others.

In vv 7-11a God recounts the painful experience of the servant, its final outcome, and the reason for it (vv 7-10a), specifically so that those who had sinned could be restored to God and God's ways through the servant.[9] In vv 10b-11a, God describes the rewards of the one who did not deserve to suffer such pain. Here the servant and the sacrifice will not go unrewarded or unrecognized; such suffering as the servant experienced leads to life, not death (v 10b).

In vv 11b-12, God continues to comment on the servant and the suffering endured. The despised and rejected one was "the righteous one," God's servant, through whom many would be made righteous (v 11b) and whose self-sacrifice on behalf of transgressors God will reward (v 12).

A critical reading of this text leads to the question, What kind of God asks people to suffer because of others' wrongdoings? On the other hand, if the Spirit of God is within the human person, then whenever the human person suffers, God suffers, whether it be from the knowledge of the pain that an injustice is causing or because of the direct effects of pain that the injustice has caused.[10] Whenever the choice is made to act justly and to love tenderly (cf. Mic 6:8b), it indeed may lead to painful experiences in the face of injustice and iniquity.

Thus, Isa 52:13—53:12 provides the insight that to be God's servant is perhaps to be God's prophet and to be God's prophet is to be one who may have to suffer "with God," suffer the effects of the brokenness of the human condition, suffer the pain of the natural world because of the injustices done to it also, and suffer because of the choice to act justly and love tenderly. Suffering can lead to a positive sense of advocacy on the part of the one who has experienced such suffering and on the part of those who choose to work toward the alleviation of such suffering. Then justice and righteousness may have the chance to become the foundation for restoration and the seeds for transformation. Because Isa 52:13—53:12 is anthropocentric and gender-specific with respect to the servant's image, the text presents the same challenges laid out in the discussion of Isa 49:1-7. Socio-ecological suffering exists today, and anyone who lives in relationship with God, the human community, and the natural world cannot escape the pain of injustice or shy away from the pain that may be involved in working to bring about justice and righteousness for all creation.

Isaiah 65:17-25

*"For I am about to create new heavens and a new earth;
the former things shall not be remembered or come to mind." (65:17)*

What has been foreshadowed in Isa 11:6-9, what has been foretold in Isa 42:9, and what has been announced in Isa 43:18-19 is revealed in Isa 65:17-25, the vision of the glorious new creation. Isaiah 65:17-25 proclaims a splendid vision of earthly life, of what the "coming day"—the transformed order—will look like when the servant's work of justice and righteousness is brought to completion. This is an ancient vision that an ancient prophet has made known to guide our feet into the way of peace.

¹⁷For I am about to create new heavens
   and a new earth;
the former things shall not be remembered
   or come to mind.
¹⁸But be glad and rejoice forever
   in what I am creating;
for I am about to create Jerusalem as a joy,
   and its people as a delight.
¹⁹I will rejoice in Jerusalem,
   and delight in my people;
no more shall the sound of weeping be heard in it,
   or the cry of distress.
²⁰No more shall there be in it
   an infant that lives but a few days,
or an old person who does not
   live out a lifetime;
for one who dies at a hundred years will be considered a youth,
   and one who falls short of a hundred will be considered accursed.
²¹They shall build houses and inhabit them;
   they shall plant vineyards and eat their fruit.
²²They shall not build and another inhabit;
   they shall not plant and another eat;
for like the days of the tree shall the days of my people be,
   and my chosen shall long enjoy the work of their hands.
²³They shall not labor in vain,
   or bear children for calamity;
for they shall be offspring blessed by the LORD—
   and their descendants as well.
²⁴Before they call I will answer,
   while they are yet speaking I will hear.
²⁵The wolf and the lamb shall feed together,
   the lion shall eat straw like the ox;
   but the serpent—its food shall be dust!
They shall not hurt or destroy
   on all my holy mountain,
            says the LORD.

Eschatological and cosmological, it is already unfolding in our midst, but it needs to be nurtured and hastened, for the cry of the poor—homeless, hungry, abused, forgotten, uncared-for men, women, and children—and the groan of creation—the blue heron in search of the wetlands, migrating deer looking for woodlands, all endangered species hoping to live, the land depleted of its minerals and nutrients—can still be heard from dawn till dusk and long into the silence of the night.

This new creation will be free from distress, free from premature death (vv 19b-20); and people will enjoy the fruits of their labors (vv 21-22). It will be a time of great blessing—prosperous and fertile (v 23). God and people will be in a mutual relationship (v 24), and there will be peace in the natural world as well. The wolf, a carnivore that preys on smaller animals, will not feed *on* the lamb but will feed *with* the lamb; the lion, also a carnivore, will eat straw like the ox. The destructive impulse of the serpent (cf. Gen 3:14) is forever tamed (v 25). Finally, in this new creation, there will be no violence, no "natural" or "legitimated" structures of destruction (see the discussion on Isa 11:9 in chapter 13, above).

Thus, the new creation bespeaks a transformed order. Life will be lived not hierarchically or under the power, control, or domination of others. Life will be lived with joy and delight, with health and longevity, with meaningful and successful labor, with fruitfulness, with intimate covenant relationships, and with peace. The passage implies an intimacy between God and the people, harmonious relationships among people, and peaceful relationships among the animals. All creation will be in peace with reverence and respect.

Although Isa 65:17-25 may be a vision of an ideal situation, Collins insists that "the ideal presented must also be taken seriously, however, as a portrayal of the goal toward which we strive, even if we cannot fully attain it."[11] Would that readers ponder the vision, understand its message, and join with the servant to help bring about this new creation—this transformed order—which is the vision and plan of the Divine for all creation.

Isaiah 40–66: Selected Passages in Context

The passages describing the servant (Isa 42:1-9; 49:1-7; 52:13—53:12), a person like the servant (Isa 61:1-4), and the glorious new creation (Isa 65:17-25) present a new paradigm whereby all of creation is seen as interrelated and all of life is lived in relationship. Justice and righteousness, as exemplified through the model and work of the servant, become the new ethic and the foundation for lasting peace.

These passages disturb, challenge, inspire, and evoke a response. Despite their sometimes limited scope, they contain a transcendent vision. It is this vision that has the potential to awaken a new awareness, a new consciousness, and a deeper sense of responsibility. Once that transformation occurs, then the journey toward the new creation can either begin or be hastened. Finally, the servant texts and the new creation text together suggest that God's plan is going to be accomplished through the efforts of human beings whom God empowers. Potentially the vision of this new creation can be embraced by all.

Conclusion

P ART ONE PROVIDED A GLIMPSE INTO THE EXPERIENCE of the Israelite people who were no strangers to pain and suffering. As a country, they were overpowered by vast empires and experienced devastation after devastation, leaving their land ravaged, their temple destroyed, their holy city decimated, and their people deported and exiled. As communities, the Israelites and Judahites struggled among themselves. Apostasy and idolatry on the part of some eroded a commitment to covenant and Torah that led to spiritual depravity and social unrest. Those who had social and economic power abused it by taking advantage of their own people to gain more power through exploitation, domination, and control. Many corrupt political and religious leaders contributed to injustice either by direct involvement or by their lack of ethical praxis.

In the midst of this climate of unrest resounded the voices of the prophets who confronted the people with the message that God does not tolerate injustice. The prophets portray God as someone who uses power aggressively and punitively to chastise those causing injustice. This aggressive and punitive use of power is seen as being sometimes destructive to people and the natural world.

This multidimensional picture of Israel and Judah in relationship to other countries, its own people, and its God, and the manner in which the text presents this picture have evoked several hermeneutical concerns. These concerns have been discussed at length and lead to the conclusion that power used aggressively, whether to dominate, control, oppress, or chastise, causes more violence and does not present a long-term, life-giving solution.

The theme of God's intolerance of injustice continued in Part Two. This section looked at how power can be used to free people from domination, oppression, and injustice. Leadership figures are empowered to call people to reform to avert further disaster; others' lives are spared through the power of divine intervention, and other countries' acts of aggression toward Israel and

Judah are finally put to rest when God asserts aggressive power over these countries that have long overpowered these peoples. Power used for liberation has both positive and negative aspects. Hermeneutical concerns were raised over instances in which power had been used to free some at the cost of others' lives.

Finally, Part Three focused on a new paradigm and a new vision that could lead to the transformation of all of creation. This new paradigm is characterized by a shift in power from domination to liberation to mutuality. Power is used in a nonviolent way to establish relationships between God, people, and the natural world that reflect harmony and interrelatedness. Power can be a positive force when it has as its goal the ultimate well-being of all.

In a world that struggles with injustices that are social and ecological, power used for domination is unacceptable; power used aggressively for liberation is inadequate; power placed at the service of restoration and transformation for all of creation is the only way to establish lasting peace. Thus, the message of Hosea and Isaiah can be a light to the nations but a stumbling block to those who use power aggressively and to dominate, because it calls for a radical shift in values. Furthermore, it calls for a new ethic that is creation-centered and not andro-anthropocentric.

All creation is groaning from oppression as it labors untiringly to give birth to new life. Would that we become people of compassion for whom power is a gift to be used to nurture and cherish life and transform the world.

Notes

Chapter 1

1. N. K. Gottwald, *The Hebrew Bible: A Socio-Literary Introduction* (Philadelphia: Fortress Press, 1985), 356; cf. S. M. Paul, *Amos* (Hermeneia; Minneapolis: Fortress Press, 1991), 2.

2. W. J. Doorly, *Prophet and Justice: Understanding the Book of Amos* (Mahwah, N.J.: Paulist, 1989), 24–25.

3. D. J. A. Clines, "The Ideology of Writers and Readers of the Hebrew Bible," in *Interested Parties: The Ideology of Writers and Readers of the Hebrew Bible* (JSOTSupp 205; Sheffield: Sheffield Academic Press, 1995), 19.

4. J. E. Sanderson, "Amos," in *The Women's Bible Commentary*, eds. C. A. Newsom and S. H. Ringe (expanded edition with Apocrypha; Louisville: Westminster John Knox, 1998), 218–19.

5. Ibid., 219.

6. In his recent book, F. Watson includes a chapter titled "The Rhetoric of Oppression" (60–77), in which he advocates studying biblical texts in their final forms and encourages readers to engage in serious critical analysis of the rhetoric of oppression, especially where such rhetoric has an impact on religious and theological ideas (*Text, Church, and World* [Grand Rapids: Eerdmans, 1994]). The issues and points raised in this particular chapter generate many ideas and insights that relate to the study of Amos in particular and the prophetic texts in general.

7. H. W. Wolff, *Joel and Amos* (Hermeneia; Philadelphia: Fortress Press, 1977), 154.

8. For further study on the use of agricultural metaphors, their connection to Israel as an agrarian society, and their historical, social, political, and literary function within prophetic texts, see S. Talmon, "Prophetic Rhetoric and Agricultural Metaphora," in *Storia E Tradizioni Di Israele*, eds. D. Garrone and F. Israel (Brescia: Paideia, 1991), 267–79.

9. It is assumed that Hazael was the name of an Aramean ruler, but here the reference is to the kingdom of Aram and not to the specific ruler. For further discussion, see Paul, *Amos*, 50.

10. Ben-hadad is also the name of an Aramean ruler. Here it seems that the reference is to a dynasty or a ruler. For further discussion, see Paul, *Amos*, 50; F. I. Andersen and D. N. Freedman, *Amos* (AB 24A; New York: Doubleday, 1989), 245–50.

11. The exact identity and site of the Valley of Aven (lit., "the valley of sin") is unknown. One suggestion by Andersen and Freedman is that it is probably "the Biq'ah Valley in present-day Lebanon" (*Amos*, 255).

12. Beth-eden (lit., "house of pleasure") seems to be Bit-Adini, an Aramaean state situated between two rivers: the upper Euphrates and the Balih (see Andersen and Freedman, *Amos*, 255).

13. The exact location of Kir is unknown. One suggestion is that it may be in Mesopotamia (M. L. Barre, "Amos," in *NJBC*, eds. R: E. Brown, J. A. Fitzmyer, and R. E. Murphy [Englewood Cliffs, N.J.: Prentice Hall, 1990], 211); cf. H. McKeating, *The Books of Amos, Hosea, and Micah* (Cambridge: Cambridge Univ. Press, 1971), 16; Andersen and Freedman, *Amos*, 257.

14. For a comprehensive view of God in the ancient biblical world and texts, see E. S. Gerstenberger, *Yahweh the Patriarch: Ancient Images of God and Feminist Theology* (Minneapolis: Fortress Press, 1996). See also, e.g., Exodus 1–15.

15. See, e.g., Deut 7:7-11.

16. For a detailed study on conflict in Israel and the ancient Near East, see S. Niditch's work, *War in the Hebrew Bible: A Study in the Ethics of Violence* (New York: Oxford Univ. Press, 1993). Wolff (*Amos*, 154–55) adds that "the imagery of devouring fire in our text carries with it the further connotation of Yahweh as a military leader and conqueror. The use of fire in conquering enemy cities, and espe- cially in destroying residential palaces, was an accepted military practice in the ancient Near Eastern world."

17. See, e.g., Gen 1:1-31.

18. McKeating, *The Books of Amos, Hosea, and Micah*, 16.

19. For further study on corporate punishment and corporate responsibility, see J. Kaminsky, *Corporate Responsibility in the Hebrew Bible* (JSOTSupp. 196; Sheffield: Sheffield Academic Press, 1995).

20. Paul (*Amos*, 56) notes that "the wholesale deportation of the population was for the economic gain that occurred through slave traffic (compare Ezek 27:13; Joel 4:6-7). The sale of human booty on the slave market was a well-known practice that became a profitable by-product for the victors in war." See also Wolff, *Amos*, 157–58.

21. Ibid., 48–49. See also Deut 9:3. The use of fire to destroy an enemy city first occurs in Num 21:27-30. Paul notes that the motif of divine fire is common in ancient Near Eastern mythology and is usually associated with military assaults (*Amos*, 49).

22. Wolff, *Joel and Amos*, 159.

23. Paul, *Amos*, 63. See also J. L. Mays, *Amos* (OTL; Philadelphia: Westminster Press, 1969), 35.

24. Sanderson, "Amos," in *Women's Bible Commentary*, 220. See also Wolff, *Amos*, 161, who traces this heartless crime back to the Near East and to Homer.

25. See, e.g., Gen 38:24; Lev 20:14; 21:9.

26. B. Birch, *Hosea, Joel, and Amos* (Westminster Bible Companion; Louisville: Westminster John Knox, 1997), 186. See also Isa 3:15 and Prov 22:22 for the abuse of the poor and deprivation of their rights.

27. Law codes restricted the taking of certain items for collateral and also set limits on how long something could be kept. For example, a widow's garment could not be taken from her (Deut 24:17), nor could a poor person's cloak be kept overnight (Exod 22:25-27; Deut 24:12-13).

28. Birch, *Hosea, Joel, and Amos*, 187.

29. For further discussion on the namelessness of the poor, see P. A. Bird, "Poor Man or Poor Woman? Gendering the Poor in Prophetic Texts," in *Missing Persons and Mistaken Identities: Women and Gender in Ancient Israel* (OBT; Minneapolis: Fortress Press, 1997), 67–78.

30. Clines (*Interested Parties*, 91) notes that most commentators agree with Amos that both Israel and the surrounding countries should be punished for their crimes and that punishment should be capital. Clines also points out that most commentators do not note "the conflict between the apparent injustice of punishing those who deserve it and the obvious injustice of punishing those who do not." He insists that metacommentators have to ask scholars if they are aware of what they are doing when they comment on a text. In my opinion, Clines is right on the mark with his insistence that scholars need to tease out the ideologies underlying biblical texts while examining their own assumptions, which also enter into the interpretative process.

31. Clines asserts that "to be sure, the future *was* very much as the prophecy says—whether it predicted it or wrote it up in hindsight. Things *were* awful, for rich and poor alike. But it is even more awful to ascribe the destruction of a state and the forcible deportation of its citizens to an avenging God. If that is how a believer finds himself or herself impelled to conclude that it is a terrible thing to fall into the hands of the living God, the metacommentator can respect that. But to affirm it casually, to pretend that it is unproblematic—*that* is not scholarly, it is not even human."

32. The majority-held scholarly view is that the "cows of Bashan" is a reference to the upper-class women of Samaria. See, e.g., Paul, *Amos*, 128–29; Mays, *Amos*, 71; Sanderson, "Amos," 218–19. Other scholars, i.e., Wolff (*Joel and Amos*, 204–5) and Andersen and Freedman (*Amos*, 421), are not as definitive. Andersen and Freedman suggest that the metaphor refers to men and serves as a parody.

33. Paul, *Amos*, 129. See also Deut 32:14; Ezek 39:18; Ps 22:12-13; Jer 50:19; Mic 7:14.

34. For further discussion on the issue of wealth and oppression with respect to the upper-class women of Samaria, see Sanderson, "Amos," 209, and Paul, *Amos*, 128–29.

35. Wolff, *Joel and Amos*, 207.

36. See, e.g., Cant 1:9; 2:9; 4:5; 7:3; Ps 68:30; Nah 2:13; et al. For an extensive study on Israelite metaphors from the natural world, see H. Eilberg-Schwartz, *The Savage in Judaism: An Anthropology of Israelite Religion and Ancient Judaism* (Indianapolis: Indiana University Press, 1990); and Talmon, "Prophetic Rhetoric and Agricultural Metaphora," 267–79.

37. B. Lang ("Peasant Poverty in Biblical Israel," *JSOT* 24 [1982]: 54) comments that "comparing women to the well-fed cows of the Bashan region seems impolite as it violates our notion of female beauty, but in fact, even in the contemporary Near East some well-to-do women do not care much for a slim body." Wolff (*Joel and Amos*, 206) comments that ". . . for Amos the point of the simile is not fullness of bodily features, but abusive social attitudes and behavior."

38. Sanderson, "Amos," 208.

39. J. Dunayer, "Sexist Words, Speciesist Roots," in *Animals and Women: Feminist Theoretical Explorations*, eds. C. J. Adams and J. Donovan (Durham, N.C.: Duke Univ. Press, 1995), 11.

40. Ibid., 12.

41. See, e.g., Deut 7:12-26; 28:1-68.

42. See Gen 1:1—2:4a.

43. In v 8 the prophet's message is directed against the pride of Jacob, and in v 14, the house of Israel is to be the recipient of God's wrath. It seems, then, that in vv 8-14 the audience being addressed is the same: members of the house of Jacob/Israel.

44. Within the biblical world, there were laws that governed honest scales, weights, and balances; see, e.g., Lev 19:35-36; Deut 25:13-15; Prov 16:11;and Ezek 45:10-11.

45. Amos 8:14 features two oaths related to the impending divine chastisement upon certain Israelites on account of their apostasy. These oaths have been the subject of much scholarly debate. For a comprehensive discussion, see S. M. Olyan, "The Oaths of Amos 8:14," in *Priesthood and Cult in Ancient Israel*, eds. G. A. Anderson and S. M. Olyan (JSOTSupp 125; Sheffield: Sheffield Academic Press, 1991), 121–49.

46. Paul (*Amos*, 260) notes that "an earthquake is a familiar portent of the anger of the LORD (Hab 3:6; Zech 14:4, 5) and often is expressed by the verb *rgz* (1 Sam 14:15; Joel 2:10; Ps 77:19; Prov 30:21). This terrestrial upheaval with all its concomitant destruction and tragedy shall result in the mourning of the entire population." See also Mays, *Amos*, 145.

Chapter 2

1. N. K. Gottwald, *The Hebrew Bible: A Socio-Literary Introduction* (Philadelphia: Fortress Press, 1985), 375. See also J. I. Alfaro, *Justice and Loyalty: A Commentary on the Book of Micah* (International Theological Commentary; Grand Rapids: Eerdmans, 1989).

2. There is no scholarly consensus on how the book of Micah should be divided. For further discussion on this threefold division, see T. K. Cheyne, *Micah* (Cambridge Bible for Schools and Colleges, vol. 27; Cambridge: Cambridge Univ. Press, 1902 [original, 1882]), 10; J. M. P. Smith, et al., *Micah, Zephaniah, Nahum, Habakkuk, Obadiah and Joel* (ICC 24; Edinburgh: T. & T. Clark, 1911 [reprint 1985]), 8. Other scholars argue for other divisions. See, e.g., D. E. Miller, *Micah and Its Literary Environment: Rhetorical Critical Studies*, Ph.D. Diss., Univ. of Arizona (Ann Arbor: University Microfilms, 1991), 8; J. L. Mays, *Micah* (OTL; Philadelphia: Westminster Press, 1976) 3, among others.

3. For a detailed study of Micah 1:2-7, see C. J. Dempsey, *The Interplay between Literary Form and Technique and Ethics in Micah 1-3*, Ph.D. Diss., Catholic Univ. of America (Ann Arbor: University Microfilms, 1994), 90–103.

4. On the literary form of the woe oracle, see R. J. Clifford, "The Use of *Hoy* in the Prophets," *CBQ* 28 (1966): 458–64; E. Gerstenberger, "The Woe Oracles of the Prophets," *JBL* 81 (1962): 249–63; G. Wanke, "'*wy* und *hwy*," *ZAW* 78 (1966): 215–18; K. C. Hanson, "How Honorable! How Shameful! A Cultural Analysis of Matthew's Makarisms and Reproaches," *Semeia* 68 (1995): 83-114, among others.

5. On the "disputation," see R. M. Hals, *Ezekiel* (FOTL 19; Grand Rapids: Eerdmans, 1989), 349.

6. See, e.g., Gen 50:20; 1 Sam 18:25; 2 Sam 14:13; Ps 21:12; Jer 18:18; Zech 7:10; and 8:17. Sometimes the verb is used positively (e.g., Mal 3:16).

7. Humankind has the power to choose to do good or harm. Those who choose to

use their power to do harm often make others powerless. See Gen 31:29 and Deut 28:32. The Hebrew vocabulary in these references is similar to Mic 2:1.

8. H. W. Wolff, *Micah: A Commentary* (Continental Commentaries; Minneapolis: Fortress Press, 1990), 77–78.

9. Mays, *Micah,* 63.

10. Some scholars think that Micah is speaking and citing his opponents, e.g., C. Westermann, *Basic Forms of Prophetic Speech* (Louisville: Westminster John Knox, 1991), 104–6; E. A. Neiderhiser, "Micah 2:6-11: Considerations on the Nature of the Discourse," *BTB* 11 (1981): 104–7; A. S. van der Woude, "Micah in Dispute with the Pseudo-Prophets," *VT* 19 (1969): 244–60; B. K. Waltke, et al., *Obadiah, Jonah, and Micah* (Tyndale Old Testament Commentaries; Downers Grove, Ill.: InterVarsity, 1988), 159; and Mays, *Micah,* 67–69.

11. For further discussion on this point, see Wolff, *Micah,* 99.

12. W. J. Wessels, "Conflicting Powers: Reflections from the Book of Micah," *Old Testament Essays* 10/3 (1997): 540.

13. Ibid., 539. Wessels' article nuances many issues of power in Micah 2:3. He provides an exposition of 2:1-13 and then deals with chap. 3 in a thematic way, i.e., "the power of position," "the power of ideology," and the "power of conviction."

14. L. C. Allen, *The Books of Joel, Obadiah, Jonah and Micah* (NICOT; Grand Rapids: Eerdmans, 1976), 377.

15. Ibid., 388.

Chapter 3

1. W. L. Holladay provides the historical data behind the lion metaphor:

"Lions" here, like Assyria in vv 18 and 36, refer to Babylon, which had taken Nineveh in 612 and defeated the remainder of the Assyrian army again at Haran in 610. Egypt marched through Palestine in 609 to help what was left of the Assyrians against the Babylonians; Josiah was killed at Meggido, and the Egyptians had de facto control of Palestine—they deposed Jehoahaz after three months of rule and placed Jehoiakim on the throne as an Egyptian vassal. Thereupon the Babylonians defeated the Egyptians at Carchemish in 605 and routed them southward, defeating them again near Hamath, so that Jehoiakim transferred his vassalage to Babylon. The Babylonians have "roared" against Judah. (*Jeremiah 1* [Hermeneia; Philadelphia: Fortress Press, 1986], 93–94)

2. P. Bird asserts that "the metaphorical use of ZNH invokes two familiar and linguistically identified images of dishonor in Israelite culture, the common prostitute and the promiscuous daughter or wife. As a sexual metaphor, it points to the sexual nature of the activity it represents. Its female orientation does not single out women for condemnation; it is used rather as a rhetorical device to expose men's sins" (*Missing Persons and Mistaken Identities: Women and Gender in Ancient Israel,* OBT [Minneapolis: Fortress Press, 1997], 236). While I agree with Bird in general, I disagree with her point that the image of a harlot, prostitute, or whore "does not single out women for condemnation." While the condemnation may not be specific, it is implied. Any reference that has derogatory overtones to it, whether direct or implied, is denigrating and can negatively affect the creative and religious imaginations of readers. Such an image serves to reinforce certain attitudes that some people have toward a gender. Not to address such images or metaphors could be viewed as participating in the silence of consensus.

3. W. Brueggemann adds further that "the end of these cities means the end of organized life and the exposure of urban life to a variety of threats that the walls currently stave off. Urban life is under assault and is sure to end, bringing down with it all institutionalized and structural supports for public life. With the destruction of the walls, the coming of social chaos is not far behind" (*A Commentary on Jeremiah: Exile and Homecoming* [Grand Rapids: Eerdmans, 1998], 66).

4. Ibid., 72.

5. R. P. Carroll, *Jeremiah*, OTL (Philadelphia: Westminster Press, 1986), 198.

6. See, e.g., ibid., 197–99; Brueggemann, *Jeremiah*, 71–73, specifically, 73; and D. R. Jones (*Jeremiah* [Grand Rapids: Eerdmans, 1992], 134–36) who offers no comment on justice and violence in his interpretation of Jer 6:13-15.

7. Brueggemann, *Jeremiah*, 91.

8. Holladay, *Jeremiah 1*, 431.

9. Jehoiakim, a vassal king enthroned by the Egyptians, was known for his despicable deed of taxing Judah to raise tribute for Pharaoh (2 Kgs 23:35). His reign was characterized by extensive social injustice.

10. Carroll, *Jeremiah*, 202.

11. Damascus, located near Mount Hermon, was the capital city of three Syrian states. Hamath and Arpad (Jer 40:23-24) were two other main cities of Syria. All three cities were in northern Syria. Hamath and Arpad were Assyrian vassals; Damascus fell to the Assyrians in 732 B.C.E. (see 2 Kgs 16:9). Sometime later, Damascus became a Babylonian vassal and joined forces with the Babylonians to overtake Judah.

12. Ben-hadad was a dynasty in Syria during the ninth and eighth centuries B.C.E. It is also the name of several Syrian rulers (see, e.g., 1 Kgs 15:18; 20:1-34; 2 Kgs 13:3, 24).

13. Kedar is mentioned in Gen 25:13; Isa 21:16; and Jer 2:10.

14. F. B. Huey Jr., *Jeremiah–Lamentations*. NAC 16. (Nashville: Broadman, 1993), 405.

Chapter 4

1. See Deut 28:53; Lam 2:20; 4:10.

2. See Isa 2:4 and Mic 4:3.

3. For other references in which children are associated with cannibalism, see Lam 2:20; 4:4, 10. For an example of children as victims of the society's powerful ones, see Mic 2:4.

4. The Decalogue specifically demands that one should honor one's parents (Exod 20:12). Children's duties toward their parents are clearly outlined throughout Wisdom literature (e.g., Sir 3:1-16). With the exception of Jewish law that forbade the sacrificing of children to the pagan god Molech (see, e.g., Lev 18:21; 20:3, 4; 2 Kgs 23:10), very few other laws, if any, within the Old Testament safeguard children. Nor are there any ethical codes within the Israelite culture that address cannibalism as it affects children. The fact that prophets like Baruch make note of it indicates that it is an outrageous deed.

5. The command to listen and be attentive is common in Wisdom literature; see, e.g., Prov 1:8; 4:1, 10; 5:7; and 8:32-33.

6. C. A. Moore notes that "although these men had the wealth and leisure to own

sporting birds ..., the wealthy have not learned from the creatures the wisdom they should have: 'But ask the beasts, and they will teach you; the birds of the air, and they will tell you. ... Who among all these does not know that the hand of the LORD has done this?' (Job 12:7, 9); cf. also Job 35:11" (Moore, Carey A., *Daniel, Esther, and Jeremiah: The Additions* [AB 44; Garden City, N.Y.: Doubleday, 1977, 298]). It is no surprise that those addressed in the passage do not learn wisdom from the natural world. How could they when they perceive themselves as lords over the animals on earth?

7. For a balanced discussion on the gender-specific references and metaphors as they relate to cities and nations, Israel in particular, see J. J. Schmitt, "The Gender of Ancient Israel," *JSOT* 26 (1983): 115–25.

8. See, e.g., F. B. Huey Jr., *Jeremiah–Lamentations*. NAC 16. (Nashville: Broadman, 1993), 447.

9. For further study on the literary forms and types in the book of Lamentations, see O. Kaiser, *Introduction to the Old Testament* (Minneapolis: Augsburg, 1975), 356–58.

10. For further discussion on the understanding, purpose, and artistry of the book of Lamentations, see D. Hillers, *Lamentations* (AB 7A; New York: Doubleday, 1972), xv–xxxix; and N. K. Gottwald, *The Hebrew Bible in Its Social World and Ours* (Atlanta: Scholars, 1993), 166–67. For an extensive study on the history of interpretation, see C. Westermann, *Lamentations: Issues and Interpretation* (Minneapolis: Fortress Press, 1994), 24–85. For a concise introduction and commentary on Lamentations from a feminist perspective, see K. M. O'Connor, "Lamentations," in *The Women's Bible Commentary,* eds. C. A. Newsom and S. H. Ringe (Louisville: Westminster John Knox, 1998), 187–91.

11. Hillers (*Lamentations,* 18–19) notes that Jerusalem is compared to a widow because widows, together with orphans, were the most defenseless people in ancient society (cf. 5:3; Isa 49:20-21; 51:18; 54:4-6) and the most pitiable.

12. "Lovers" and "friends" refer to Jerusalem's former political allies who have now become her enemies; see also v 9; Jer 27:3; and 30:14.

13. The phrase "precious things" refers to the temple treasures that the Babylonians took; see 2 Kgs 25:13-17.

14. Zion and Jerusalem are used interchangeably and refer to each other; see, e.g., Mic 3:10.

15. The "treasures" that Israelites traded in order to get food were probably their children. Hillers also cites Theodoret (died ca. 460 C.E.) and argues that "the picture of the Israelites giving up mere possessions to stay alive lacks poignancy. That they gave up children to buy food is both more striking and better paralleled in ancient descriptions of famine ..." (Hillers, *Lamentations,* 25–26).

16. The image of the roads to Zion mourning may have had its origin in Canaanite myth; see Hillers, *Lamentations,* 44–45.

17. Hillers (*Lamentations,* 23–24) points out that "nakedness" can be understood on three levels, one of which is related to the stripping experience that is part of the treatment meted out to a prostitute (Ezek 16:35-39; 23:29; cf. Isa 3:17); when used metaphorically, it refers to the punishment of countries (Isa 47:2-3; Lam 4:21; Nah 3:5). Hillers comments further that "... 'whoredom' with idols or other nations makes the land (pictured as a woman) unclean, ritually impure; thus Hosea 5:3; 6:10; Jer

2:23; Ezek 23:7, 13" (24). See also O'Connor ("Lamentations," in *Women's Bible Commentary*, 189) for further discussion on "nakedness" and "uncleanness." O'Connor also argues that Daughter Zion's uncleanness arises from her adultery.

18. C. Westermann (*Lamentations*, 224) comments that God's wrath and anger are but "moods." While this may be accurate, it is important to note that in Lam 1:12, God's wrath and anger are named as the cause of the people's suffering. For those living in the ancient biblical world, God's wrath and anger, according to the text, were much more than merely a "mood"; they persisted, contra Westermann.

19. Unlike O'Connor ("Lamentations," in *Women's Bible Commentary*, 189), who suggests that "Lamentations 1:2 . . . transforms the innocent widow into a loose woman whose 'lovers have abandoned her,'" I suggest that the "widow" of Lamentations 1 and 2 is a widow precisely because she was a "loose woman." Abandoned by her lovers, she ultimately feels abandoned by her God, the one with whom she shares a covenant relationship.

20. For a provocative discussion on God and metaphors, see E. S. Gerstenberger, *Yahweh the Patriarch: Ancient Images of God and Feminist Theology* (Minneapolis: Fortress Press, 1996), 156–58. Gerstenberger suggests that one move beyond gender-specific metaphors to genderless ones. The problem in vv 1-22, however, would not be solved because the central gender-specific metaphor of God as lover and husband is related theologically to the ancient notion of covenant and covenant relationship understood as a marriage-type relationship between God and God's people. See, e.g., Hos 1:2—2:20.

21. See, e.g., Ps 110:1, which states: "The LORD says to my lord, 'Sit at my right hand until I make your enemies your footstool.'"

22. See, e.g., Pss 18:35; 60:5; 73:23; 89:5; 98:1; 121:5; and 137:5.

23. See, e.g., Ps 110:1.

24. Hillers provides additional comment on the traditional Jewish mourning ritual and links it to other biblical and Near Eastern texts. The image of old men and young girls in mourning may be derived from an old literary tradition involving the myth of the mourning virgin goddess. See Hillers, *Lamentations*, 44–45.

25. See ibid., 45.

26. By human commodification and a utilitarian attitude, I am referring to a mindset that does not respect the intrinsic goodness of all of creation, but rather sees people, natural resources, and so forth as commodities to be used for one's personal profit and gain.

27. In a paper delivered at the Pacific Northwest Region of the Society of Biblical Literature (May 1998), I argued that there is a difference between "false prophets" and "corrupted prophets." A "corrupted prophet" is one who is chosen by God, hence, a true prophet, but who, for whatever reason, delivers a false prophecy. A false prophecy is not grounds for labeling one a "false prophet."

28. Here, the reference to "children" may refer to the actual Israelite children who suffered during the demise of Jerusalem and the Southern Kingdom Judah; it may also refer to the suffering and slaughtered citizens of the personified Jerusalem. For further discussion, see Hillers, *Lamentations*, 47.

29. See, e.g., Exod 2:23-24; 3:9-10.

30. The NRSV translates 3:1 as "I am the one . . . ," but the Hebrew of the MT reads, "I am the man . . . ." The NRSV has translated the Hebrew masculine pronoun into a

gender-inclusive one, potentially causing confusion. Since the speaker is not identified, there are several possibilities, but without a doubt the masculine noun, "the
man," does not refer to Jerusalem. "She" could have been a possible choice for the reference "one."

31. See the reference to "us" in vv 43, 45, 46, and 47.

32. See, e.g., Pss 10:9; 22:13. In Isa 38:13, God is compared to a lion, and in Hos
13:7, to a lion and a bear. Hillers (*Lamentations*, 68) notes that in the Isaiah and
Hosea texts, God in his anger is often compared to a lion and/or a bear. Similes and
metaphors from the natural world are commonly ascribed to be both God and God's
people (see also Ezek 34:11-22; Hos 14:5; Ps 125:1, and so forth).

33. For further discussion and evaluation of hunting for sport (in the United
States), the environment, and the relationship between the two, see M. Kheel,
"License to Kill: An Ecofeminist Critique of Hunters' Discourse," in *Animals and
Women*, eds. C. J. Adams and J. Donovan (Durham, N.C.: Duke Univ. Press, 1995),
85–125.

34. See note 36.

35. Verse 52 reads: "Those who were my enemies without cause. . . ." This statement
suggests that the speaker is an "innocent victim."

36. R. M. Berger and J. Polter quote Sister Dianna's account:

> Many of you know my story. I was in San Miguel Acatan, teaching Mayan children to
> read and write and to understand the Bible in respect to their culture. For a long time I
> received death threats. Then on November 2, 1989, I was abducted from the back yard
> of the Posada de Belen retreat center in Antigua by members of the Guatemalan security
> forces. They took me to a clandestine prison where I was tortured and raped repeatedly.
> My back and chest were burned more than 111 times with cigarettes. I was lowered into
> an open pit packed with human bodies—bodies of children, women, and men, some
> decapitated, some lying face up and caked with blood, some dead, some alive—and all
> swarming with rats. . . . The memories of what I experienced that November day haunt
> me even now. I can smell the decomposing bodies, disposed of in an open pit. I can see
> the blood gushing out of a woman's body as I thrust a small machete into her. For you
> see, I was handed a machete. Thinking it would be used against me, and at that point in
> my torture wanting to die, I did not resist. But my torturers put their hands onto the
> handle, on top of mine. And I had no choice. I was forced to use it against another
> human being. What I remember is blood gushing—spurting like a water fountain—and
> my screams lost in the cries of the woman. (18)

See "Death's Dance Broken," *Sojourners* 25.4 (July–August 1996): 16–20.

Chapter 5

1. J. J. M. Roberts (*Nahum, Habakkuk, and Zephaniah* [OTL; Louisville: Westminster John Knox, 1991], 95) notes that "even though Hab. 1:6 does not explicitly state
that the purpose for God's raising up the Chaldean empire is to punish Judah, the
numerous parallels to the motif make that obvious (Amos 6:14; Isa. 5:26-30; 9:9-
10[10-11]; 10:5-6)." Roberts adds further that this idea of God raising up other countries to punish the Israelites occurs in the Deuteronomistic History (see, e.g., 1 Kgs
11:14, 23).

2. Roberts (ibid., 89) points out that during the reign of Jehoiakim, when the

prophet Habakkuk was actively preaching, both the king and his officials were guilty of acts of oppression, some of which involved forced labor and physical violence. See also Jer 22:13, 17.

3. The Chaldeans are the same as the Babylonians.

4. Roberts points out that "the concept of enemy nations as agents that Yahweh could raise up to punish his own people was incorporated into the Deuteronomistic History (e.g., 1 Kgs 11:14, 23) . . ." (ibid., 95).

5. R. L. Smith (*Micah–Malachi,* WBC (Waco, Tex.: Word, 1984], 110) suggests that the speaker of Hab 2:6-20 "seems to be the nations." I have suggested otherwise. For examples in which God refers to God's self as in vv 12, 14, 16, and 20, see Isa 49:7; Mic 2:7, 12-13; 4:6-7.

6. Smith (ibid., 111) claims that here the injustice is debauchery: "the guilty ones here are those who ruin their fellow men by strong drink in order to gaze on their shame." On the contrary, Roberts (*Nahum, Habakkuk, and Zephaniah,* 124) argues that the language is metaphorical. Drawn from a "particularly shocking abuse," it illustrates the "brutality of imperialistic conquest, which, after rendering the conquered peoples helpless, systematically strips away their dignity and honor for the conqueror's own selfish, shameful, and insatiable gratification." I agree with Roberts, especially given the historical times of Habakkuk when conquest of peoples and countries was frequent.

7. See Roberts, *Nahum, Habakkuk, and Zephaniah,* 122.

8. For extensive discussion on God's cup of wrath, see P. Raabe, *Obadiah* (AB 24D; New York: Doubleday, 1996), 206–12.

9. Habakkuk 3 does not appear in the Qumran commentary of Habakkuk and has thus led some scholars to think that it was an independent composition added secondarily to the book.

10. In his discussion of God as warrior, Brueggemann points out that God is a warrior "in the service of Israel" but that this image can also be one "mobilized against Israel" (Brueggemann, *Theology of the Old Testament,* 243).

11. Ibid.

12. The Zion tradition is associated with Zion/Jerusalem and protection. The Judahites thought that because God was in the holy city of Jerusalem, it could not be shaken by chaos, internally or externally.

13. The prophecies against the Moabites and the Ammonites will be discussed in detail in chapter 6.

Chapter 6

1. For the background to Jerusalem's status of special election and privilege, see the book of Deuteronomy, particularly Deut 12:11.

2. E. S. Gerstenberger (*Yahweh the Patriarch: Ancient Images of God and Feminist Theology* [Minneapolis: Fortress Press, 1996], 87) sheds light on the ancient origins of male imagery for God: "The concentration on the one and only God Yahweh was not sexist in origin, but because of the patriarchal theocratic social structure, its effects inevitably were. Given the unconscious desires of the male minds that articulated and informed the notion of God, that notion inevitably succumbed to male interests, tasks, and anxieties, even though, from the outset, God was consciously understood

to be transcendent (Deut 4; 1 Kgs 8:27; Ps 90:2)." He adds further that "though God was essentially transcendent and beyond human sexuality, the image of God was in reality strongly tied to the male world—and since there was no female counterweight, this fact resulted increasingly in discrimination against women."

3. On the topic of cannibalism, D. I. Block (*The Book of Ezekiel: Chapters 1–24* [NICOT; Grand Rapids: Eerdmans, 1997], 204) comments that "while the motif of cannibalism figures prominently in ancient Near Eastern treaty curses, the present statement finds its inspiration in Yahweh's own covenant curse, an abbreviated form of which is preserved in Lev 26:29. . . ." Cannibalism is also mentioned in Deut 28:53-57.

4. For a fuller treatment of Ezekiel 16, see C. J. Dempsey, "The 'Whore' of Ezekiel 16: The Impact and Ramifications of Gender-Specific Metaphors in Light of Biblical Law and Divine Judgment," in *Gender and Law in the Hebrew Bible and the Ancient Near East,* eds. V. H. Matthews, B. M. Levinson, and T. Frymer-Kensky (JSOTSupp 262; Sheffield: Sheffield Academic Press, 1998), 57–78.

5. L. Allen (*Ezekiel 1–19* [WBC 28; Dallas: Word, 1994], 247) offers a personal reflection on the chapter's content while doing a critical analysis of it. He states that "in the present climate of thought its [Ezekiel 16's] disparaging depiction of the female as victim of social violence is particularly upsetting (cf. K. P. Darr, "Ezekiel's Justifications of God: Teaching Troubling Texts," *JSOT* 55 [1992]: 97–117 [114–16]). To appreciate the prophetic agenda, we must distinguish between ancient norms of handling marital infidelity and the shocking use to which Ezekiel put them. It was a vehement play to communicate the necessity of the fall of Jerusalem, dragging Judah down with it." To some extent, I agree with Allen's comments; but whether or not one can "appreciate the prophetic agenda" with its "disparaging depiction of the female" remains uncertain. M. G. Swanepoel ("Ezekiel 16: Abandoned Child, Bride Adorned or Unfaithful Wife?" in *Among the Prophets: Language, Image and Structure in the Prophetic Writings,* eds. P. R. Davies and D. J. A. Clines [JSOTSupp 144; Sheffield: JSOT Press, 1993], 84–104) examines the metaphorical language of Ezekiel 16, but her analysis is for the purpose of "a new understanding and appreciation of Yahweh" (85). On the other hand, R. J. Weems ("The Lady Is a Tramp: Rhetoric and Audience in Ezekiel," *Battered Love: Marriage, Sex, and Violence in the Hebrew Prophets,* OBT [Minneapolis: Fortress Press, 1995], 58–67) points out the offensiveness of Ezekiel's gender-specific metaphors. See also M. Shields, "Multiple Exposures: Body Rhetoric and Gender Characterization in Ezekiel 16," *JFSR* 14 (1998): 5–18, in which she exposes "the relational and political implications of the marriage metaphor and of God's character in Ezekiel 16" (18).

6. T. Craven ("Ezekiel," in *Collegeville Bible Commentary* [Collegeville, Minn.: Liturgical, 1986], 545) discusses in detail vv 43bb-58 as a diatribe. Craven begins the unit at v 44 and not at 43bb.

7. J. Blenkinsopp (*Ezekiel* [Interpretation; Louisville: John Knox, 1990], 77) points out that "exposure of unwanted children, especially female children, was the alternative to birth control or abortion in several ancient societies. . . ." See also K. W. Carley, *Ezekiel* (Cambridge: Cambridge Univ. Press, 1994), 96, and L. E. Cooper, *Ezekiel* (NAC 17; Nashville: Broadman and Holman, 1994), 169.

8. For additional discussion on foundling children and legal rights in the ancient world, see M. Malul, "Adoption of Foundlings in the Bible and Mesopotamian Documents: A Study of Some Legal Metaphors in Ezekiel 16:1-7," *JSOT* 46 (1990): 96–126.

9. For further discussion on child sacrifice, see Swanepoel, "Ezekiel 16," 97, and Cooper, *Ezekiel*, 172. In the ancient Near East, children were sacrificed to pagan gods such as Molech. This practice was widespread by the time of Josiah's rule (2 Kgs 23:10). W. H. Brownlee (*Ezekiel 1-19* [WBC 28; Waco: Word, 1986], 231) notes that "the special place of this evil cult [child sacrifice] was not in the temple, but on a special altar in the valley of Hinnom (2 Kgs 23:10; 2 Chron 28:3; 33:6; Jer 7:31-32; 19:5-6; 32:35)."

10. Carley (*Ezekiel*, 101) notes that "the metaphor of Jerusalem as a young maiden is sustained by the reference to the Philistine cities as women."

11. The identity of the second "cub"/king could be either Jehoiachin or Zedekiah. The text gives no specific hints, and since both Jehoiachin and Zedekiah were dethroned and exiled to Babylon in 597 B.C.E. and 586 B.C.E., respectively, it is difficult to know for certain to which king the text refers. Scholarly opinion vacillates between the two. See, e.g., R. E. Clements, *Ezekiel* (Westminster Bible Companion; Louisville: Westminster John Knox, 1996), 3; Blenkinsopp, *Ezekiel*, 85; and especially Block (*Ezekiel 1–24*, 604–6), who gives a detailed discussion on the topic.

12. There is no scholarly consensus on the identity of the second male reference in vv 5-9. Some identify him as Jehoiachin; others, as Zedekiah. See, e.g., the divergent views represented in the studies by Block, *Ezekiel*, 604–7; Blenkinsopp, *Ezekiel*, 85; Clements, *Ezekiel*, 83; and A. Cody, *Ezekiel* (OTM 11; Wilmington, Del.: Michael Glazier, 1984), 91–92.

13. Genesis 49:8-9, where the lion imagery first appears in relation to Judah, may have influenced the writers and editors of Ezekiel 19.

14. See Clements, *Ezekiel*, 83.

15. Clements (ibid., 85) states that "clearly powerful families, strong administrators, and, not least, ambitious royal women all carried weight and influence that spread over into royal policy and patronage, as Ezekiel's singling out of the influence of one eminent Queen Mother illustrates."

16. Clements (ibid.) notes that "while [the mother] herself comes in for no specific criticism, the prophet remarkably shows clearly that her ambitious plans for her sons brought both of them to an untimely death. Personal ambition is all very well, and maternal ambition can be fundamental to the strength of a family, yet, if pressed too far and too ruthlessly, it can lead to great grief." While I agree with Clements, I would argue that the point needs to be pressed further. Most likely a mother's ambition for her sons was shaped by underlying patriarchal and cultural attitudes.

17. Blenkinsopp (*Ezekiel*, 85) argues that the "strongest shoot" was Zedekiah; Block (*Ezekiel*, 610) argues that it could be two kings, Jehoiachin and Zedekiah. Block thinks that v 12 refers specifically to Jehoiachin, with vv 13-14 referring to Zedekiah. While Block's argument is certainly possible because of the obscure pronoun reference in vv 11-14, I agree with Blenkinsopp's suggestion, shared by Clements (*Ezekiel*, 84) because it fits the overall theme of the unit, a story about the end of Judah and the end of the Davidic line of kingship. Zedekiah was, in fact, the last king.

18. Blenkinsopp, *Ezekiel*, 85.

19. Clements, *Ezekiel*, 84.

20. If vv 10-14 of the poem are not solely about Zedekiah's death, as Clements

(*Ezekiel*, 84) claims they are not, then his interpretation of the verses as a lament for the death of Hamutal would suggest that the statement infers a condemnation on how mothers, particularly royal ones, raised their sons in ancient Israel. With respect to Hamutal, Clements writes: "She had had the remarkable and probably unprecedented experience of seeing two of her sons elevated to the royal throne in Jerusalem. Since the poem opens by referring to her august and powerful reputation, we can conclude that Ezekiel's allegory was intended as an obituary of excessive human ambitions" (84). I agree with Clements' argument but wish to point out that his final statement about "excessive human ambitions" neutralizes the gender bias that is inherent in the text and that must not be allegorized.

21. Ammon was an Aramean state that was formed around 1200 b.c.e., the beginning of the Iron Age. Rabbah in v 5 was Ammon's principal city. Blenkinsopp (*Ezekiel*, 113) notes that "hostility between Ammonites and Israelites goes back to the settlement of Israelite tribes in the Transjordanian region" and that the "Ammonites took part in the Babylonian-sponsored raids on Judean territory during Jehoiakim's reign (2 Kings 24:2)." According to Ezek 21:18-23, 28-32, Ammon did not experience the devastation that Judah did, a devastation that was attributed to "divine retribution." The events described in this prophecy reflect the destruction of Judah and the exile of its inhabitants.

22. Moab was also formed around 1200 b.c.e. Once conquered by David (2 Sam 8:2) and Omri (2 Kgs 3:4), the state eventually was freed from Ahab, Omri's son. Beth-jeshimoth, Baal-meon, and Kiriathaim in v 9 are Transjordanian sites.

23. Cf. Jer 33:5.

24. Edom was located to the south of the Dead Sea and attained its statehood around the beginning of the Iron Age. The country shared a special kinship with Israel (see Deut 23:7-8).

25. Given the nebulousness of the text, scholars have speculated about Edom's crime. For example, Block (*Ezekiel 1–24, 25–48*) suggests that Edom's crime against Judah "undoubtedly relates to Edom's abandonment of his brother in the critical hour, and Edom's glee at the razing of Jerusalem (cf. Ps. 137:7)" (23). On the contrary, Blenkinsopp (*Ezekiel*, 114) argues that "the Edomites were especially reviled for having taken advantage of the Babylonian conquest to occupy the southern part of Judah." In view of Ezek 36:5, I agree with Blenkinsopp. Cf. Joel 3:19.

26. Philistia was a neighboring country of Judah and was known for being one of Judah's main rivals, even though it was once defeated by David.

27. For a provocative historical and contemporary discussion on the theme of God and the nations, see D. J. Hall and R. R. Ruether, *God and the Nations* (Minneapolis: Fortress Press, 1995).

28. To be noted is that countries other than Israel are offered a positive word in Isa 2:2-4 and Mic 4:1-5. This word will come through Israel.

Chapter 7

1. In his comments on the satraps, A. A. Di Lella (*Daniel* [AB 23; Garden City, N.Y.: Doubleday, 1977], 198) takes note of the hierarchical structure of power: "despite the story's legendary features in other respects, it correctly reflects the bureaucratic organization of the Persian Empire."

2. In Daniel 3 and 6, an angel of God rescues Amaziah and Daniel. This is significant because postexilic Judaism had a transcendent notion of God and therefore did not feature God as directly intervening. See ibid., 200, for further comment.

3. That wives and children are put to death does not speak of "justice" but of "family solidarity," a popular belief in Judaism and the ancient Israelite world. Therefore, if the head of a household committed a crime, his entire family would suffer (cf. Num 16:27-33; 2 Sam 21:5-9; Esth 9:13-14).

Chapter 8

1. Nineveh was an ancient city on the left bank of the Tigris River. It was occupied from the fourth millennium B.C.E. to around 612 B.C.E., when it was invaded and fell to the Babylonians and Medes.

2. Israel's legal codes as well as its wisdom tradition warned against killing innocent people (see, e.g., Deut 19:10, 13; 27:25; Prov 6:17). A procedure for purging a community's guilt when an unknown person took another innocent person's life is prescribed in Deut 21:1-9.

3. Both the sea and the sea creatures are mythological images in creation. See Job 40:25; Pss 74:12-14; 89:10-11; 104:25-26; Isa 27:1.

4. J. Limburg (*Jonah*, OTL [Louisville: Westminster John Knox, 1993], 83) remarks that "this [Jonah 3:7-8] is one of many biblical illustrations of the solidarity between humans and animals," and "since both humans and animals are creatures of the sixth day (Gen 1:24-25 . . .), the relationship between them is close."

5. I. Nowell, "Jonah," in *The Collegeville Bible Commentary,* ed. D. Bergant (Collegeville, Minn.: Liturgical, 1992), 831.

Chapter 9

1. R. Smith (*Micah–Malachi* [WBC; Waco, Tex.: Word, 1984], 146–47) outlines the various scholarly hypotheses that pertain to Haggai's identity, although no definitive identity has been recovered.

2. Ibid., 153. Smith notes that "Haggai believed that there was an authority greater than that of the Persian king. That was 'Yahweh of hosts.' This term 'Yahweh of hosts' is used fourteen times in this short book." Furthermore, the phrase was meant "to emphasize God's greatness and might."

Chapter 10

1. The Negeb was an area to the south of Judah that the Edomites occupied when they were associated with the Babylonians. This area is mentioned twice in the text (vv 19a and 20b) to underscore Judah's restoration after many years of suffering caused by the Edomites.

2. The Philistines were a long-standing enemy of Israel and Judah. The book of Judges describes vividly the clashes between the two countries.

3. Ephraim was a region to the north of Jerusalem and Judah. Its name is synonymous with the Northern Kingdom. Samaria was its capital.

4. Benjamin was a territory also to the north of Jerusalem; Gilead was a region to the northeast of Ephraim. Mentioned for the first time in Gen 31:23, Gilead is associated with Jacob's settlement with Laban. One of the goals of the Northern Kingdom's kings was to take control of Gilead for political reasons.

5. Halah was a city northwest of Nineveh (2 Kgs 17:6). The exact location of Halah is debated. 2 Kgs 18:11 mentions that the king of Assyria transported the Israelites from Assyria and put them in Halah.

6. Phoenicia was not a single country but a group of city-states along the Mediterranean coast. It included the city of Zarephath, which was about fourteen miles north of Tyre and eight miles south of Sidon.

7. The identity of Sepharad is not known. Possibilities include Babylon, Sardis in Asia Minor (see Rev 3:1), Spain, or Hesperides on Africa's northern coast.

8. See Ps 77:15 and Zech 10:6.

9. Cf. Exod 45:7 and Ezek 25:14.

10. M. M. Pazdan ("Malachi," in *Collegeville Bible Commentary* [Collegeville, Minn.: Liturgical, 1992], 630) argues that in vv 1a and 5 God speaks, and vv 2-4 are the prophet's narration. I disagree on the grounds of context and suggest that God is the speaker throughout the prophecy. In v 1 God announces the messenger's coming; in v 2 God describes the awesomeness of coming and what will be done by way of purifying the people. To a people purified, God will then draw near (v 5). See also D. L. Petersen, *Malachi* (OTL; Louisville: Westminster John Knox, 1995), 210–11.

11. The identity of the messenger is unclear. It may have been a Levitical figure.

12. These two metaphorical images appear often in prophetic literature; see, e.g., Isa 1:25; Jer 6:29-30; Ezek 22:17-22; et al.

13. "Fear" here is synonymous with "awe." Note also that in Ben Sira's theology, "fear of the LORD" is synonymous with "love of the LORD" (2:15-16). See A. A. Di Lella, *The Wisdom of Ben Sira* (AB 39; Garden City, N.Y.: Doubleday, 1987), 78–80.

14. Malachi 4:1-6 is 3:19-24 in the Hebrew text.

Chapter 11

1. For a detailed discussion of the conflict between Judah and Assyria, see J. J. M. Roberts, *Nahum, Habakkuk, and Zephaniah* (OTL; Louisville: Westminster John Knox, 1991), 53–54.

2. L. Allen (*The Books of Joel, Obadiah, Jonah, and Micah* [NICOT; Grand Rapids: Eerdmans, 1976], 89) notes that "the insects normally attack Judah from the south or southwest, borne by the prevailing winds, but cases are known of approach from the north. The plague that hit Jerusalem in 1915 came from the northeast."

Chapter 12

1. See, e.g., Gen 9:1-17; 15, 17; Exod 6:2-8; and Jer 31:31-34; cf. Isa 24:4-6.

2. For a detailed discussion on Baal, see M. S. Smith, *The Early History of God: Yahweh and the Other Deities in Ancient Israel* (San Francisco: Harper & Row, 1987), 44–48; see also G. I. Davies, *Hosea* (NCBC; Grand Rapids: Eerdmans, 1992), 75–77. H. McKeating (*Amos, Hosea, Micah* [CBC; Cambridge: Cambridge Univ. Press, 1971])

notes that "Baal was the god of rain and the giver of fertility" and that "Baal is spoken of as the husband of the land, and his people are spoken of in sexual terms" (71). For examples of God portrayed as one having Baal-like characteristics, see Hos 5:10; 6:3; 10:12; and 14:6.

3. B. C. Birch, *Hosea, Joel, and Amos* (Westminster Bible Companion; Louisville: Westminster John Knox, 1997), 39.

4. Ibid.

5. R. A. Simkins, *Creator and Creation* (Peabody, Mass.: Hendrickson, 1994), 220.

6. For further study of the notion of cosmic covenant, see R. Murray, *The Cosmic Covenant* (Heythrop Monographs; London: Sheed & Ward, 1992).

7. The editors of the NRSV translate verbs in the present; in this context, it may indicate that the Assyrian invasion of 733 B.C.E. had already begun. During this invasion many Israelite refugees fled to Egypt as others were being forced to surrender to Assyrian power.

8. The Hebrew of Hos 11:9 is uncertain; therefore, there are diverse English translations.

Chapter 13

1. See, for example, H. Wildberger, *Isaiah 13–27*, (Minneapolis: Fortress Press, 1997); J. N. Oswalt, *Isaiah 1–30* (Grand Rapids: Eerdmans, 1986), 3–28; J. Jensen, *Isaiah 1–39* (OTM 8; Wilmington, Del.: Glazier, 1984); and Roland E. Clements, *Isaiah 1–39* (NCBC; Grand Rapids: Eerdmans, 1980), 2–8.

2. This prophecy makes clear that Jerusalem will be redeemed; cf. Mic 4:1-4.

3. J. J. Collins, "Isaiah," in *Collegeville Bible Commentary* (Collegeville, Minn.: Liturgical, 1992), 418.

4. J. N. Oswalt, *The Book of Isaiah 1–39* (NICOT; Grand Rapids: Eerdmans, 1986), 248.

5. R. Murray, *The Cosmic Covenant: Biblical Themes of Justice and Peace, and the Integrity of Creation* (Heythrop Monographs; London: Sheed & Ward, 1992), 108.

6. In Isa 11:1, Jesse is David's father; the "branch" refers to a Davidic king.

7. The phrase "and he shall strike the earth with the rod of his mouth" in v 4b is metaphorical and symbolizes the universal power and appeal of the leader and does not imply the actual cursing of the land (see G. B. Gray, *The Book of Isaiah* [ICC; Edinburgh: T. & T. Clark, 1912], 218).

8. R. A. Simkins, *Creator and Creation* (Peabody, Mass.: Hendrickson, 1994), 226.

9. The reference to the slaughter and fall of towers in Isa. 30:25 is unclear. Oswalt (*Isaiah 1-39*, 562) suggests that it refers to "Judah's pride" (2:12-17; 32:14, 15; 57:15). On the other hand, Jensen (*Isaiah 1-39* [OTM; Wilmington, Del.: Glazier, 1984], 241) argues that it is an allusion to "the bloody destruction of Yahweh's (and Israel's) foes" (Isa 66:15-16; Joel 3:11-15). Either suggestion is possible; neither is conclusive from textual evidence.

10. The areas of Lebanon, Carmel, and Sharon are famous for their rich and abundant vegetation.

11. It is not certain whether there was an actual constructed highway between the countries of exile, whether there was a festal way that pilgrims used to go up to Zion, or whether the "highway" as a literary image exists only in the text.

Chapter 14

1. J. N. Oswalt, *The Book of Isaiah 40–66* (NICOT; Grand Rapids: Eerdmans, 1998), 111; see also M. Lind, "Monotheism, Power, and Justice: A Study in Isaiah 40–55," *CBQ* 46 (1984): 432–46.

2. Ibid., 119.

3. Speculation continues regarding the identity of the servant, e.g., Cyrus, Zerubbabel, Israel, etc.

4. Ibid., 294.

5. Isaiah 61:1-4 contains imagery and allusions that echo the specific Servant Songs (Isa 42:1-9; 49:1-7; 50:4-9; and 52:13—53:12) but is usually not considered a Servant Song.

6. J. J. Collins, "Isaiah," in *Collegeville Bible Commentary* (Collegeville, Minn.: Liturgical, 1992), 449.

7. Isaiah 50:4-9, also part of the cycle of Servant Songs, has not been included in this study.

8. For a detailed discussion on who the speakers are in Isa 53:1-6, see C. R. North, *The Second Isaiah* (Oxford: Clarendon, 1964), 235.

9. The text features God speaking of the divine self in the third person. For similar examples of this style, see Isa 49:7; Mic 2:12-13; and 4:6-7.

10. For further discussion of the suffering of God, see T. E. Fretheim, *The Suffering of God: An Old Testament Perspective* (OBT; Philadelphia: Fortress Press, 1984).

11. Collins, "Isaiah," 451.

Bibliography

Achtemeier, Elizabeth. 1986. *Nahum—Malachi*. Interpretation. Atlanta: John Knox.

———. 1996. *Minor Prophets I*. New International Biblical Commentary. Peabody, Mass.: Hendrickson.

Adams, Carol J. and Josephine Donovan, eds. 1995. *Animals and Women*. Durham, N.C.: Duke Univ. Press.

Alfaro, J. I. 1989. *Justice and Loyalty: A Commentary on the Book of Micah*. International Theological Commentary. Grand Rapids: Eerdmans.

Allen, Leslie. 1976. *The Books of Joel, Obadiah, Jonah, and Micah*. Grand Rapids: Eerdmans.

———. 1994. *Ezekiel 1–19*. Word Biblical Commentary 28. Dallas: Word.

Alter, Robert. 1985. *The Art of Biblical Poetry*. New York: Basic Books.

———. 1992. *The World of Biblical Literature*. New York: Basic Books.

Andersen, Francis I. and David Noel Freedman. 1980. *Hosea*. Anchor Bible 24. New York: Doubleday.

———. 1989. *Amos*. Anchor Bible 24A. New York: Doubleday.

Anderson, Bernhard W. 1994. *From Creation to New Creation: Old Testament Perspectives*. Minneapolis: Fortress Press.

Bailie, Gil. 1997. *Violence Unveiled: Humanity at the Crossroads*. New York: Crossroad.

Baron, Robert A. and Deborah R. Richardson. 1977. *Human Aggression*. New York: Plenum.

Barre, Michael L. 1990. "Amos." In *New Jerome Biblical Commentary*. Ed. R. E. Brown, J. A. Fitzmyer, and R. E. Murphy. Englewood Cliffs, N.J.: Prentice Hall.

Barstad, Hans M. 1984. *The Religious Polemics of Amos*. Leiden: Brill.

Barton, John. 1980. *Amos's Oracles against the Nations*. New York: Cambridge Univ. Press.

Bellis, Alice Ogden. 1994. *Helpmates, Harlots, and Heroes: Women's Stories in the Hebrew Bible*. Louisville: Westminster John Knox.

Ben Zvi, Ehud. 1996. *A Historical-Critical Study of the Book of Obadiah*. New York: Walter de Gruyter.

Bergant, Dianne, ed. 1992. *The Collegeville Bible Commentary: Old Testament*. Collegeville, Minn.: Liturgical.

———. 1997. *Israel's Wisdom Literature*. Minneapolis: Fortress Press

Berger, R. M. and J. Polter. 1996. "Death's Dance Broken." *Sojourners* 25.4:16–20.

Berlin, Adele. 1994. *Zephaniah*. Anchor Bible 25A. New York: Doubleday.

Berquist, Jon. 1992. *Reclaiming Her Story: The Witness of Women in the Old Testament*. St. Louis: Chalice.

Birch, Bruce C. 1997. *Hosea, Joel, and Amos*. Westminster Bible Companion. Louisville: Westminster John Knox.

Bird, Phyllis A. 1997. *Missing Persons and Mistaken Identities: Women and Gender in Ancient Israel*. Overtures to Biblical Theology. Minneapolis: Fortress Press.

Blenkinsopp, Joseph. 1990. *Ezekiel*. Interpretation. Louisville: John Knox.

———. 1995. *Sage, Priest, Prophet: Religious and Intellectual Leadership in Ancient Israel*. Library of Ancient Israel. Louisville: Westminster John Knox.

———. 1996. *A History of Prophecy in Israel*. Louisville: Westminster John Knox.

Block, Daniel I. 1997. *The Book of Ezekiel 1–24*. New International Commentary on the Old Testament. Grand Rapids: Eerdmans.

———. 1998. *The Book of Ezekiel 25–48*. New International Commentary on the Old Testament. Grand Rapids: Eerdmans.

Boff, Leonardo and Clodovis Boff. 1989. *Introducing Liberation Theology*. Trans. P. Burns. Maryknoll, N.Y.: Orbis.

Brenner, Athalya. 1985. *The Israelite Woman: Social Role and Literary Type in Biblical Narrative*. Sheffield: JSOT Press.

———. 1995. *A Feminist Companion to the Latter Prophets*. Feminist Companion to the Bible 8. Sheffield: Sheffield Academic Press.

Brensinger, Terry L. 1996. *Simile and Prophetic Language in the Old Testament*. Mellen Biblical Press Series 43. Lewiston: Mellen Biblical Press.

Bright, John. 1965. *Jeremiah*. Anchor Bible 21. New York: Doubleday.

Brock, Rita Nakashima, Claudia Camp, and Serene Jones, eds. 1995. *Setting the Table: Women in Theological Conversation*. St. Louis: Chalice.

Brown, Robert McAfee. 1984. *Unexpected News: Reading the Bible with Third World Eyes*. Philadelphia: Westminster.

Brown, William. 1996. *Obadiah through Malachi*. Westminster Bible Companion. Louisville: Westminster John Knox.

Brownlee, William H. 1986. *Ezekiel 1–19*. Word Biblical Commentary 28. Waco, Tex.: Word.

Brueggemann, Walter. 1994. *A Social Reading of the Old Testament: Prophetic Approaches to Israel's Communal Life*. Ed. P. D. Miller. Minneapolis: Fortress Press.

———. 1997. *Theology of the Old Testament: Testimony, Dispute, Advocacy*. Minneapolis: Fortress Press.

———. 1998. *A Commentary on Jeremiah: Exile and Homecoming*. Grand Rapids: Eerdmans.

Caird, G. B. 1980. *The Language and Imagery of the Bible*. Philadelphia: Westminster.

Camp, Claudia V. and Carole Fontaine. 1993. *Women, War, and Metaphor: Language and Society in the Study of the Hebrew Bible*. Semeia 61. Atlanta: Scholars.

Carley, Keith W. 1974. *Ezekiel*. Cambridge: Cambridge Univ. Press.

Carroll, R. Mark Daniel. 1992. *Contexts for Amos: Prophetic Poetics in Latin American Perspective*. JSOT Supplement Series 132. Sheffield: JSOT Press.

Carroll, Robert P. 1986. *Jeremiah*. Old Testament Library. Philadelphia: Westminster.

Cheyne, T. K. 1902 [original, 1882]. *Micah.* Cambridge Bible for Schools and Colleges, 27. Cambridge: Cambridge Univ. Press.

Clements, Ronald E. 1996. *Ezekiel.* Westminster Bible Companion. Louisville: Westminster.

Clifford, Richard J. 1966. "The Use of *Hoy* in the Prophets." *Catholic Biblical Quarterly* 28:458–64.

———. 1988. *Jeremiah.* Interpretation. Atlanta: John Knox.

Clines, David J. A. 1995. *Interested Parties: The Ideology of Writers and Readers of the Hebrew Bible.* JSOT Supplement Series 205; Gender, Culture, Theory 1. Sheffield: Sheffield Academic Press.

Cody, Aelred. 1984. *Ezekiel with an Excursus on Old Testament Priesthood.* Old Testament Message 11. Wilmington, Del.: Michael Glazier.

Collins, John J. 1992. "Isaiah." In *Collegeville Bible Commentary.* Ed. D. Bergant. Collegeville, Minn.: Liturgical.

———. 1993. *Daniel.* Hermeneia. Minneapolis: Fortress Press.

Conrad, Edgar W. 1991. *Reading Isaiah.* Overtures to Biblical Theology. Minneapolis: Fortress Press.

Cooper, Lamar Eugene. 1994. *Ezekiel.* The New American Commentary 17. Nashville: Broadman & Holman.

Cooke, G. A. 1985. *The Book of Ezekiel.* International Critical Commentary. Edinburgh: T. & T. Clark.

Craig, Kenneth M. Jr. 1993. *A Poetics of Jonah: Art in the Service of Ideology.* Columbia: Univ. of South Carolina Press.

Craven, Toni. 1986. "Ezekiel." In *Collegeville Bible Commentary.* Ed. D. Bergant. Collegeville, Minn.: Liturgical.

Crenshaw, James L. 1964. *Joel.* Anchor Bible 24C. New York: Doubleday.

Darr, Katheryn Pfisterer 1994. *Isaiah's Vision and the Family of God.* Louisville: Westminster John Knox.

Davies, G. I. 1992. *Hosea.* New Century Bible Commentary. Grand Rapids: Eerdmans.

Davies, Philip R. 1996. *The Prophets: A Sheffield Reader.* The Biblical Seminar 42. Sheffield: Sheffield Academic Press.

Davies, Philip R. and David J. A. Clines, eds. 1993. *Among the Prophets: Language, Image, and Structure in the Prophetic Writings.* JSOT Supplement Series 144. Sheffield: JSOT Press.

Day, Peggy L., ed. 1989. *Gender and Difference in Ancient Israel.* Minneapolis: Fortress Press.

Dempsey, Carol J. 1994. *The Interplay between Literary Form and Technique and Ethics in Micah 1–3.* Ph.D. Diss., The Catholic Univ. of America. Ann Arbor: University Microfilms.

———. 1998. "The 'Whore' of Ezekiel 16: The Impact and Ramifications of Gender-Specific Metaphors in Light of Biblical Law and Divine Judgment." In *Gender and Law in the Hebrew Bible and the Ancient Near East.* Ed. V. H. Matthews, B. M. Levinson, and T. Frymer-Kensky. JSOT Supplement Series 262. Sheffield: Sheffield Academic Press.

———. 1999. "Micah 2–3: Literary Artistry, Ethical Message, and Some Considerations about the Image of Yahweh and Micah." *JSOT* 85:117–28.

Di Lella, Alexander A. 1977. *The Book of Daniel*. Anchor Bible 23. Garden City, N.Y.: Doubleday.

Doorly, William J. 1989. *Prophet of Justice: Understanding the Book of Amos*. Mahwah, N.J.: Paulist.

Eichrodt, Walther. 1970. *Ezekiel*. Trans. C. Quin. Old Testament Library. Philadelphia: Westminster.

Eideval, Goran. 1996. *Grapes in the Desert: Metaphors, Models, and Themes in Hosea 4–14*. Stockholm, Sweden: Almqvist & Wiksell.

Eilberg-Schwartz, Howard. 1990. *The Savage in Judaism: An Anthropology of Israelite Religion and Ancient Judaism*. Indianapolis: Indiana Univ. Press.

Emmerson, Grace I. 1992. *Isaiah 56–66*. Old Testament Guides. Sheffield: JSOT Press.

Fisch, Harold. 1988. *Poetry with a Purpose: Biblical Poetics and Interpretation*. Indianapolis: Indiana Univ. Press.

Follis, Elaine R., ed. 1987. *Directions in Biblical Hebrew Poetry*. JSOT Supplement Series 40. Sheffield: JSOT Press.

Franke, Chris. 1994. *Isaiah 46, 47, and 48: A New Literary-Critical Reading*. Biblical and Judaic Studies 3. Winona Lake, Ind.: Eisenbrauns.

Fretheim, Terence E. 1984. *The Suffering of God: An Old Testament Perspective*. Overtures to Biblical Theology. Philadelphia: Fortress Press.

Gadamer, Hans-Georg. 1995. *Truth and Method*. Trans. G. Barden and J. Cumming. New York: Seabury.

Gerstenberger, Erhard S. 1996. *Yahweh the Patriarch: Ancient Images of God and Feminist Theology*. Trans. F. J. Gaiser. Minneapolis: Fortress Press.

Girard, René. 1977. *Violence and the Sacred*. Trans. P. Gregory. Baltimore: John Hopkins Univ. Press.

Gitay, Yehoshua. 1991. *Isaiah and His Audience: The Structure and Meaning of Isaiah 1–12*. Studia Semitica Neerlandica. Assen: Van Gorcum.

Gordon, Robert P., ed. 1995. *The Place Is Too Small for Us: The Israelite Prophets in Recent Scholarship*. Sources for Biblical and Theological Study 5. Winona Lake, Ind.: Eisenbrauns.

Gottwald, Norman K. 1979. *The Tribes of Yahweh: A Sociology of the Religion of Liberated Israel, 1250-1050 BCE*. Maryknoll, N.Y.: Orbis.

———, ed. 1989. *The Bible and Liberation*. Maryknoll, N.Y.: Orbis.

———. 1993. *The Hebrew Bible in Its Social World and in Ours*. SBL Semeia Studies. Atlanta: Scholars.

Gray, G. B. 1912. *The Book of Isaiah*. International Critical Commentary. Edinburgh: T. & T. Clark.

Greenberg, Moshe. 1983. *Ezekiel 1–20*. Anchor Bible 22. Garden City, N.Y.: Doubleday.

Griffin, William Paul. 1997. *The God of the Prophets: An Analysis of Divine Action*. JSOT Supplement Series 249. Sheffield: Sheffield Academic Press.

Gustavo Gutiérrez. 1987. *On Job: God-Talk and the Suffering of the Innocent*. Trans. M. J. O'Connell. New York: Orbis.

———.*Gustavo Gutiérrez: Essential Writings*. 1996. The Making of Modern Theology series. Ed. J. B. Nickoloff. Minneapolis: Fortress Press.

Halkes, Catharina J. M. 1991. *New Creation: Christian Feminism and the Renewal of the Earth*. Trans. C. Romanik. Louisville: Westminster John Knox.

Hall, Douglas John and Rosemary Radford Ruether. 1995. *God and the Nations*. Minneapolis: Fortress Press.

Hals, Ronald M. 1989. *Ezekiel*. Forms of the Old Testament Literature 19. Grand Rapids: Eerdmans.

Hanson, K. C. 1995. "How Honorable! How Shameful! A Cultural Analysis of Matthew's Makarisms and Reproaches." *Semeia* 68:83-114.

Hanson, Paul D. 1995. *Isaiah 40–66*. Interpretation. Louisville: John Knox.

Harper, William Rainey. 1979. *Amos and Hosea*. International Critical Commentary. Edinburgh: T. & T. Clark.

Hillers, Delbert R. 1972. *Lamentations*. Anchor Bible 7A. Garden City, N.Y.: Doubleday.

———. 1984. *Micah*. Hermeneia. Philadelphia: Fortress Press.

Holladay, William L. 1986. *Jeremiah 1*. Hermeneia. Philadelphia: Fortress Press.

———. 1989. *Jeremiah 2*. Hermeneia. Minneapolis: Fortress Press.

Huey, F. B., Jr. 1993. *Jeremiah–Lamentations*. New American Commentary 16. Nashville: Broadman & Holman.

Jensen, Joseph. 1984. *Isaiah 1–39*. Old Testament Message 8. Wilmington, Del.: Michael Glazier.

Jones, D. R. 1992. *Jeremiah*. New Century Bible Commentary. Grand Rapids: Eerdmans.

Kaiser, Otto. 1974. *Isaiah 13–39*. Trans. R. A. Wilson. Old Testament Library. Philadelphia: Westminster.

———. 1975. *Introduction to the Old Testament*. Trans. J. Sturdy. Minneapolis: Augsburg.

———. 1983. *Isaiah 1–12*. Trans. J. Bowden. Old Testament Library. Philadelphia: Westminster.

Kaminski, Joel S. 1995. *Corporate Responsibility in the Hebrew Bible*. JSOT Supplement Series 196. Sheffield: Sheffield Academic Press.

Klein, Ralph W. 1979. *Israel in Exile: A Theological Interpretation*. Overtures to Biblical Theology. Philadelphia: Fortress Press.

Kleven, Terence. 1996. "The Cows of Bashan: A Single Metaphor at Amos 4:1-3." *Catholic Biblical Quarterly* 58:215–27.

LaCocque, André. 1988. *Daniel and His Time*. Studies in the Personalities of the Old Testament. Columbia: Univ. of South Carolina Press.

Laffey, Alice L. 1988. *An Introduction to the Old Testament: A Feminist Perspective*. Philadelphia: Fortress Press.

Landy, Francis. 1995. *Hosea*. Readings. Sheffield: Sheffield Academic Press.

Lang, Bernhard. 1982. "Peasant Poverty in Biblical Israel." *Journal for the Study of the Old Testament* 24:46–63.

Limburg, James. 1988. *Hosea–Micah*. Interpretation. Atlanta: John Knox.

———. 1993. *Jonah*. Old Testament Library. Louisville: Westminster John Knox.

Lundbom, Jack R. 1997. *Jeremiah: A Study in Ancient Hebrew Rhetoric.* Winona Lake, Ind.: Eisenbrauns.

Mamul. M. 1990. "Adoption of Foundlings in the Bible and Mesopotamian Documents: A Study of Some Legal Metaphors in Ezekiel 16.1-7." *Journal for the Study of the Old Testament* 46:97–126.

Matthews, Victor H. and Don C. Benjamin. 1993. *Social World of Ancient Israel 1250–587 BCE.* Peabody, Mass.: Hendrickson.

Mays, James Luther. 1969. *Amos.* Old Testament Library. Philadelphia: Westminster.

———. 1976. *Micah.* Old Testament Library. Philadelphia: Westminster.

McConville, J. G. 1993. *Judgment and Promise: An Interpretation of the Book of Jeremiah.* Winona Lake, Ind.: Eisenbrauns.

McKeating, Henry. 1971. *The Books of Amos, Hosea and Micah.* Cambridge Bible Commentary. Cambridge: Cambridge Univ. Press.

McKenzie, John L. 1968. *Second Isaiah.* Anchor Bible 20. New York: Doubleday.

Meyers, Carol L. and Eric M. Meyers. 1964. *Zechariah 9–14.* Anchor Bible 25C. New York: Doubleday.

———. 1987. *Haggai, Zechariah 1–8.* Anchor Bible 25B. Garden City, N.Y.: Doubleday.

Miller, Stephen R. 1994. *Daniel.* The New American Commentary 18. Nashville: Broadman & Holman.

Mills, Mary E. 1998. *Images of God in the Old Testament.* Collegeville, Minn.: Liturgical.

Miscall, Peter D. 1993. *Isaiah.* Sheffield: JSOT Press.

Montgomery, James A. 1927. *The Book of Daniel.* International Critical Commentary. Edinburgh: T. & T. Clark.

Moore, Carey A. 1977. *Daniel, Esther and Jeremiah: The Additions.* Anchor Bible 44. Garden City, N.Y.: Doubleday.

Morris, Gerald. 1996. *Prophecy, Poetry and Hosea.* JSOT Supplement Series 219. Sheffield: Sheffield Academic Press.

Motyer, J. Alec. 1993. *The Prophecy of Isaiah.* Downers Grove, Ill.: InterVarsity.

Murray, Robert. 1992. *The Cosmic Covenant: Biblical Themes of Justice and Peace, and the Integrity of Creation.* Heythrop Monographs 7. London: Sheed & Ward.

Neiderhiser, E. A. 1981. "Micah 2:6-11: Considerations on the Nature of the Discourse." *Biblical Theology Bulletin* 11:104–7.

Newsom, Carol A. and Sharon H. Ringe, eds. 1998. *The Women's Bible Commentary: Expanded Edition with Apocrypha.* Louisville: Westminster John Knox.

Niditch, Susan. 1993. *War in the Hebrew Bible: A Study in the Ethics of Violence.* New York: Oxford Univ. Press.

Nielsen, Kirsten. 1989. *There Is Hope for a Tree: The Tree as Metaphor in Isaiah.* Trans. C. Crowley and F. Crowley. JSOT Supplement Series 65. Sheffield: JSOT Press.

North, C. R. 1964. *The Second Isaiah: Introduction, Translation, and Commentary to Chapters XL–LV.* Oxford: Clarendon.

Nowell, Irene. 1992. "Jonah." In *Collegeville Bible Commentary.* Ed. D. Bergant. Collegeville, Minn.: Liturgical.

Olyan, Saul M. 1991. "The Oaths of Amos 8:14." In *Priesthood and Cult in Ancient Israel*. Ed. G. A. Anderson and S. M. Olyan. JSOT Supplement Series 125. Sheffield: Sheffield Academic Press.

Ortlund, Raymond C., Jr. 1996. *Whoredom: God's Unfaithful Wife in Biblical Theology*. New Studies in Biblical Theology. Grand Rapids: Eerdmans.

Oswalt, John N. 1986. *The Book of Isaiah: Chapters 1–39*. New International Commentary on the Old Testament. Grand Rapids: Eerdmans.

———. 1998. *The Book of Isaiah: Chapters 40–66*. New International Commentary on the Old Testament. Grand Rapids: Eerdmans.

Paul, Shalom M. 1991. *Amos*. Hermeneia. Minneapolis: Fortress Press.

Pazdan, Mary Margaret. 1992. "Malachi." In *Collegeville Bible Commentary*. Ed. D. Bergant. Collegeville, Minn.: Liturgical.

Petersen, David L. 1984. *Haggai and Zechariah 1–8*. Old Testament Library. Philadelphia: Westminster.

———. 1995. *Zechariah 9–14 and Malachi*. Old Testament Library. Louisville: Westminster John Knox.

Porteous, Norman W. 1965. *Daniel*. Old Testament Library. Philadelphia: Westminster.

Prinsloo, Willem S. 1985. *The Theology of the Book of Joel*. New York: Walter de Gruyter.

Raabe, Paul R. 1996. *Obadiah*. Anchor Bible 24D. New York: Doubleday.

Reid, Stephen Breck, ed. 1996. *Prophets and Paradigms*. JSOT Supplement Series 229. Sheffield: Sheffield Academic Press.

Ricoeur, Paul. 1976. *Interpretation Theory: Discourse and the Surplus of Meaning*. Fort Worth: Texas Christian Univ. Press.

———. 1981. *Hermeneutics and the Human Sciences*. Ed. and trans. J. B. Thompson. New York: Cambridge Univ. Press.

Roberts, J. J. M. 1991. *Nahum, Habakkuk, and Zephaniah*. Old Testament Library. Louisville: Westminster John Knox.

Robertson, O. Palmer. 1990. *The Books of Nahum, Habakkuk, and Zephaniah*. New International Commentary on the Old Testament. Grand Rapids: Eerdmans.

Russell, David M. 1996. *The "New Heavens and New Earth": Hope for the Creation in Jewish Apocalyptic and the New Testament*. Studies in Biblical Apocalyptic Literature 1. Philadelphia: Visionary.

Sanderson, Judith E., 1998. "Amos." In *The Women's Bible Commentary; Expanded Edition with Apocrypha*. Ed. C. A. Newsom and S. H. Ringe. Louisville: Westminster John Knox.

Schmitt, John J. 1983. "The Gender of Ancient Israel." *Journal for the Study of the Old Testament* 26:115–25.

Schneiders, Sandra M. 1991. *The Revelatory Text*. New York: HarperCollins.

Schubeck, Thomas L. 1993. *Liberation Ethics*. Minneapolis: Fortress Press.

Schüssler Fiorenza, Elisabeth, ed. 1993. *Searching the Scriptures*. Vol. One: *A Feminist Introduction*. New York: Crossroad.

Schwager, Raymund. 1987. *Must There Be Scapegoats? Violence and Redemption in the Bible*. Trans. M. J. Assad. San Francisco: Harper & Row.

Segovia, Fernando F. and Mary Ann Tolbert, eds. 1995. *Reading from This Place*. Volume 1: *Social Location and Biblical Interpretation in the United States*. Minneapolis: Fortress Press.

———. 1995. *Reading from This Place*. Volume 2: *Social Location and Biblical Interpretation in Global Perspective*. Minneapolis: Fortress Press.

Seitz, Christopher R. 1993. *Isaiah 1–39*. Interpretation. Louisville: John Knox.

Simkins, Ronald A. 1991. *Yahweh's Activity in History and Nature in the Book of Joel*. Ancient Near Eastern Texts and Studies 10. Lewiston: Edwin Mellen.

———. 1994. *Creator and Creation*. Peabody, Mass.: Hendrickson.

Smith, John Merlin Powis, et al. 1911. *Micah, Zephaniah, Nahum, Habakkuk, Obadiah and Joel*. International Critical Commentary. Edinburgh: T. & T. Clark.

Smith, Mark S. 1987. *The Early History of God: Yahweh and the Other Deities in Ancient Israel*. San Francisco: Harper & Row.

Smith, Ralph L. 1984. *Micah–Malachi*. Word Biblical Commentary 32. Waco, Tex.: Word.

Stepien, Marek. 1996. *Animal Husbandry in the Ancient Near East*. Bethesda: CDL.

Stuart, Douglas. 1987. *Hosea–Jonah*. Word Biblical Commentary 31. Waco, Tex.: Word.

Talmon, Shemaryahu. 1991. "Prophetic Rhetoric and Agricultural Metaphora." In *Storia E Tradizioni Di Israele*, 267-79. Ed. D. Garrone and F. Israel. Brescia: Paideia.

Towner, W. Sibley. 1984. *Daniel*. Interpretation. Atlanta: John Knox.

Ulrich, Eugene, John W. Wright, Robert P. Carroll, and Philip R. Davies, eds. 1992. *Priests, Prophets and Scribes: Essays on the Formation and Heritage of Second Temple Judaism in Honour of Joseph Blenkinsopp*. JSOT Supplement Series 149. Sheffield: JSOT Press.

Verhoef, Pieter A. 1987. *The Books of Haggai and Malachi*. New International Commentary on the Old Testament. Grand Rapids: Eerdmans.

Walsh, J. P. M. 1987. *The Mighty from Their Thrones: Power in the Biblical Tradition*. Overtures to Biblical Theology. Philadelphia: Fortress Press.

Waltke, Bruce K. et al. 1988. *Obadiah, Jonah, and Micah*. The Tyndale Old Testament Commentaries. Downers Grove, Ill.: InterVarsity.

Watson, Francis. 1994. *Text, Church, and World*. Grand Rapids: Eerdmans.

Watts, John D. W. 1985. *Isaiah 1–33*. Word Biblical Commentary 24. Waco, Tex.: Word.

———. 1987. *Isaiah 34–66*. Word Biblical Commentary 25. Waco, Tex.: Word.

———. 1997. *Vision and Prophecy in Amos*. Expanded Anniversary Edition. Macon, Ga.: Mercer Univ. Press.

Weems, Renita J. 1995. *Battered Love: Marriage, Sex, and Violence in the Hebrew Prophets*. Overtures to Biblical Theology. Minneapolis: Fortress Press.

Wessels, W. J. 1997. "Conflicting Powers: Reflections from the Book of Micah." *Old Testament Essays* 10.3:528–44.

West, Gerald O. 1995. *Biblical Hermeneutics of Liberation: Modes of Reading the Bible in the South African Context*. Maryknoll, N.Y.: Orbis.

Westermann, Claus. 1969. *Isaiah 40–66.* Trans. D. M. Stalker. Old Testament Library. Philadelphia: Westminster.

———. 1991. *Basic Forms of Prophetic Speech.* Trans. H. C. White. Louisville: Westminster John Knox.

———. 1994. *Lamentations: Issues and Interpretation.* Trans. C. Muenchow. Minneapolis: Fortress Press.

Wevers, John W. 1969. *Ezekiel.* New Century Bible. Grand Rapids: Eerdmans.

Wilson, Robert R. 1980. *Prophecy and Society in Ancient Israel.* Philadelphia: Fortress Press.

Wolff, Hans Walter. 1974. *Hosea.* Trans. G. Stansell. Hermeneia. Philadelphia: Fortress Press.

———. 1977. *Joel and Amos.* Trans. W. Janzen, S. Dean McBride Jr., and C. A. Muenchow. Hermeneia. Philadelphia: Fortress Press.

———. 1986. *Obadiah and Jonah.* Trans. M. Kohl. Continental Commentary. Minneapolis: Augsburg.

———. 1988. *Haggai.* Trans. M. Kohl. Continental Commentary. Minneapolis: Augsburg.

———. 1990. *Micah.* Trans. G. Stansell. Continental Commentary. Minneapolis: Augsburg.

Wood, John A. 1998. *Perspectives on War in the Bible.* Macon, Ga.: Mercer Univ. Press.

Woude, A. S. van der. 1960. "Micah in Dispute with the Pseudo-Prophets." *Vetus Testamentum* 19:244–60.

Zimmerli, Walther. 1979. *Ezekiel 1.* Trans. R. E. Clements. Hermeneia. Philadelphia: Fortress Press.

———. 1983. *Ezekiel 2.* Trans. J. D. Martin. Hermeneia. Philadelphia: Fortress Press.